How Come?
In the Come
Neighborhood

How Come?

In the Neighborhood

By Kathy Wollard

Illustrated by Debra Solomon

Workman Publishing, New York

Library of Congress Cataloging-in-Publication Data is available.

ISBN-13: 978-0-7611-4429-8

Workman books are available at special discount when purchased in bulk for premiums and sales promotions as well as for fund-raising or educational use. Special editions or book excerpts also can be created to specification. For details, contact the Special Sales Director at the address below.

Workman Publishing Company, Inc.
225 Varick Street
New York, NY 10014-4381

www.workman.com

Printed in the United States of America

First Printing October 2007
10 9 8 7 6 5 4 3 2 1

To my sisters and brothers,
who lived in my imagination
(and in my heart)
before I found them.

And to Debra Solomon,
whose art has always been a comic
North Star for my writing.
—K.W.

For Kathy Wollard,
whose brilliant writing
has lit so much of my career,
and for my cool Mom, Junebug,
and my wonderful sisters,
Audrey and Barbara
—D.S.

Acknowledgments

Many thanks go to Margot Herrera,
editor extraordinaire; Paul Gamarello,
Orlando Adiao, Irene Demchyshyn,
Brian Belfiglio, Cassie Murdoch,
Alicia Matusheski, Oleg Lyubner,
Peter Workman, and everyone else at
Workman Publishing who contributed toward
making (and getting the word out about)
a third beautiful *How Come?* book.
Thanks also to Marci Kemen, Robin Topping,
Judi Yuen, Jackie Segal, Larry Striegel,
Ted Scala, Peter Bengelsdorf, Steve Wick,
Mary Burke, John Mancini, and everyone
else at *Newsday* who's had a hand in
the *How Come?* column over the years.
And, last but not least, to our wonderful
literary agent, Janis Donnaud.

—Kathy Wollard and Debra Solomon

Contents

Around the House

Me, Myself, I

Out in the Yard

At School

On Vacation

Find Out Even More!
279

Special Thanks
283

Index
285

Everyday Mysteries

Sometimes, the most tantalizing mysteries are right in front of us.

Imagine it's lunchtime, and you've decided to heat up some leftovers in the microwave. While you're waiting, you glance out the window at a row of birds sitting happily on an electrical wire. Suddenly, it occurs to you: Those wires carry thousands of volts of electricity. There's even a canary yellow warning sign on the pole. So how come the birds don't get shocked? Could they have insulated feet?

Taking your lunch into the family room, you flip on the TV, and a movie Western comes on. Some cowboys on horses are frantically chasing a stagecoach. But the coach's wheels are spinning *backward.* How does *that* work?

After lunch, you decide to take a shower before you meet your friends at the mall. You wouldn't dream of singing in front of other people, but alone in the shower you can't resist belting out a few of your favorites—because for some reason, your voice sounds incredibly good in there. How come? (Of course, you'd probably sound even better if the shower curtain wasn't doing that annoying thing of blowing into the shower and clinging to your legs. Why does it always do that?)

Life is so hectic, we often zip right past tons of things in our everyday routine that, when we stop a moment to think, are pretty mysterious. Like *How come the hair on my head grows and grows, but the hair on my arms never gets any longer?*

How Come? In the Neighborhood explores the hows and whys behind these and more than 120 other perplexing puzzles of everyday life. These are the homegrown mysteries right at our fingertips—the backyard biology, kitchen chemistry, and front-porch physics of daily life.

Drawn from the more than 350 *How Come?* columns that have appeared in *Newsday* since the publication of *How Come?* and *How Come? Planet Earth,* all the questions in *How Come? In the Neighborhood* were asked by real kids (and some adults), curious about the world right in front of them.

Is there something you've been wondering about? Send your questions to howcome@how-come.net. We can't wait to use them in a future column or book.

Kathy Wollard

Around the House

Even in the kitchen, that most familiar of all rooms, mysteries abound: Why is water so noisy just before it boils? What makes popcorn kernels explode inside the microwave? Those tiny flies that appear out of nowhere around overripe fruit—where do they come from? And just how does that full-size fly stroll up the kitchen wall and across the ceiling? The mystery tour starts here…

How come water bubbles when it is boiled?

Ever hear the phrase "A watched pot never boils"? Actually, a watched pot isn't really shy; it boils just as easily and quickly as a sadly ignored pot. But waiting for a pan of hot water to start bubbling can be like watching paint dry.

When the long-awaited bubbles finally arrive, where do they come from? When you heat water, its molecules begin bouncing around more energetically. Eventually, when the water gets hot enough, some of the molecules will break the bonds that bind them to their fellow molecules. When that happens, water begins to change from a liquid into a gas. The bubbles you see are little pockets of gas, also known as water vapor.

When the temperature of a liquid reaches the boiling point, the pressure of the vapor in the bubbles is equal to the pressure of the surrounding air. Above the boiling point, the vapor's pressure is greater than the atmosphere's. Bubbles make their great

Evaporating liquids check out...

2

escape, rising to the surface and releasing their vapor into the air with a tiny pop.

When we heat a pan of water, the first crowd of bubbles we see on the walls of the pan are just air that has dissolved in the water, reemerging as a gas as the water heats. But as the bottom of the pan gets very hot, the water begins to turn to steam. The pockets of gas that form on the bottom are the real deal—bubbles of boiling-hot water vapor. However, these steam bubbles soon collapse when they encounter cooler water above.

But as the pan of water heats to the very top, the bubbles are able to rise all the way to the surface. Because they are less dense than the liquid water around them, the bubbles can climb like helium-filled balloons, collecting more water molecules as they float up. Watched or not, your pot has now reached the stage of a rolling boil.

Arriving at the surface, the bubbles burst, releasing their steam into the air. In fact, if you forget about your boiling pot for long enough, the pot will be empty when you return. All the water, now turned to steam, will be hiding in the kitchen air or fogging up the windows.

> **Bubbles form more easily in a pan whose surface is a little scratchy and rough, rather than glass-smooth.**

Water begins forming vapor bubbles at hot spots on the pan bottom. Bubbles form more easily in a pan whose surface is a little scratchy and rough, rather than glass-smooth. A rough surface provides nucleation sites where bubbles can get started and grow.

While water at sea level on Earth boils at 212°F, water's boiling point changes with the air pressure. On a mountain at 10,000 feet up, water must only reach 194°F to start boiling in the thin, lower-pressure air. And in the very lightweight atmosphere of the planet Mars, fresh water can boil at a chilly 34°F. So on Mars, you could dip your hand into a pot of boiling (cold) water. Just don't try using it to cook pasta.

FAST FACT

Water boiled in a glass or ceramic container in a microwave oven can actually superheat past its boiling point, remaining bubble-free. But be careful—when the container is moved, bubbles can form all at once, sending scalding hot water spilling over the sides.

Why do flames point up?

I f you've ever picked up a burning candle—say, from your birthday cake—and tilted it to one side, you may have noticed that while the candle leans sideways, the flame continues to point straight up toward the ceiling. Even if a candle is flipped all the way upside down, the flame will turn skyward, making a mess of hot, dripping wax as it envelops the candle.

Most everyone keeps at least a few candles around the house, whether for special dinners or lights-out emergencies. Of all the everyday objects around us, a candle—a pillar of wax with an embedded string—seems among the simplest and most "homemade."

But Michael Faraday, the brilliant 19th-century English scientist, thought candles were far from simple. "There is no more open door by which you can enter into the study of [science] than by considering the physical phenomena of a candle," he said.

Why Does A Flame Point Up?

Because it's impolite to point at people...

Because it doesn't want to appear sad...

Because that's where the air current's going!

Faraday demonstrated how a burning candle touches on every major aspect of physics and chemistry in a series of lectures titled *The Chemical History of a Candle.*

As a flame burns, it heats the air around itself, creating currents. Heated air near the flame spreads out and rises, since it is lighter than the air around it. Cooler air rushes in to replace it, is also heated, and likewise rises. So there is always an upward-flowing current of air (convection current) around a candle flame. It is this upward current that keeps a flame pointing up. Soot particles sputtering off the end of the burning wick are also carried upward by the current and incinerated, making the flame yellow.

So a flame points upward no matter how we tilt the candle for the same reason that a hot-air balloon pulls up into the sky—even if the passenger basket is lifted up sideways by the ground crew.

> Even if a candle is flipped all the way upside down, the flame will turn skyward, making a mess of hot, dripping wax as it envelops the candle.

Low-Gravity Flames

On your Earth-bound dining-room table, rising hot gases shape a candle flame into a teardrop shape. But a flame looks strikingly different when the candle is lit in a place where gravity is very low (known as microgravity). To keep astronauts safe, scientists have studied how fires ignite in the tiny force of microgravity. In the process, they have discovered some odd things about how a candle flame behaves in conditions of near-weightlessness. Microgravity lets astronauts float and tumble inside the space shuttle. And in microgravity, a candle flame will shrink from an arrowhead or feather shape into a ball or dome shape.

How come? In microgravity, where the idea of lighter and heavier air, and the idea of up and down, are almost meaningless, there are no real air currents around a flame. So a flame tends to stay in a compact sphere. Also, without air currents to quickly replenish oxygen, flame temperature is lower. The flame burns with very little soot and is mostly blue.

How come a glass rings if you run your wet finger around the rim?

Like absentmindedly drumming on a tabletop, idly running a finger around the rim of a glass can make a kind of music—an otherworldly, ghostly music.

Sound waves are the result of vibrations coursing through a material, whether that material is metal, wood, or glass. That's why when we strike a tuning fork, which produces a similar ringing sound, we can actually see and feel the tuning fork shaking. The sound reaches our ears because the tuning fork's vibrations make the air around it vibrate. Waves of air molecules strike our eardrums, causing them to vibrate, too.

Glassware Quartet

When you run your finger around the rim of a wineglass or crystal goblet, it's a lot like tapping the glass repeatedly. You are making the glass vibrate. An object like a wineglass also has its own special resonant frequency, or natural frequency, of vibration measured in cycles per second. When your rubbing finger causes the glass to vibrate near its special frequency, the glass will vibrate more strongly.

Why must your finger be wet? Scientists say that there will be too much friction between a dry finger and glass, causing it to stick too often on its way around the rim. An oily finger (or a greasy rim) will cause a fingertip to slip around too easily, causing little vibration. Like a bow on a violin string, a wet finger creates a good stick:slip ratio, making the glass vibrate strongly. The result is an unearthly ringing sound.

Glasses vibrate at different frequencies, depending on their material (regular glass or crystal), size, shape, and thickness. Their unique sound also depends on how much liquid they contain. So by adding more or less water, you can change the musical note that a glass produces. A set of glasses, filled to different levels, can create a chorus of notes, making a complete musical instrument—a kind of glass harp.

A set of glasses, filled to different levels, can create a chorus of notes, making a complete musical instrument— a kind of glass harp.

Statesman and inventor Benjamin Franklin invented the compact Glass Armonica in 1761. He worked with a glassblower to create varying sizes of bowls, each tuned to a particular note, no water required. The bowls nested on a revolving spindle, making them easy to reach; the operator/musician used a foot pedal to spin the bowls. Franklin's wife was awakened one night by the Armonica's ethereal music drifting down from the attic, and thought she had died and was hearing the music of angels.

FAST FACT

Musical glasses were played in concerts in Europe by the late 1600s, and the "glass harp" remained popular into the 1800s. Three Scottish musicians, for example, played a set of 120 glasses, which ranged in size from a thimble to a 3-gallon jug.

How come we can see through glass?

We can't see through a wood log, a piece of aluminum, or a chunk of cheese. But we can see through plain glass. That's one reason we make windows out of glass, rather than oak, tinfoil, or cheddar cheese.

Visible light zips unhindered through the vacuum of space. But when light strikes solids, it suddenly encounters molecule after molecule set in a rigid structure. Depending on its frequency, light may or may not make it through. Yet some solids, such as glass, look as clear as air; sunlight pours through glass windows, lighting the indoors. How come?

It all comes down to how photons (particles) of light interact with atoms in a material. All matter is made of atoms, tiny particles with a nucleus and a swarm of teensy electrons. Atoms are connected in groups called molecules. In a solid,

Light's Path Through Glass...

Just passin' through!

Sure thing, but first...

... We dance!

Now my turn!

And mine!

AND MINE!

Come back anytime!

Anytime I have energy to spare.

molecules are very attracted to one another—they are bound together, giving a solid (like a wooden block) its definite shape. However, even in a solid, molecules still vibrate and even rotate.

An atom is normally in its "ground state," with its orbiting electrons held close to the nucleus at their lowest possible energy level. There is also a maximum amount of energy electrons can possess and still remain part of their own atom, rather than flying off for parts unknown. Between these ground-state and "ionizing" energy levels, electrons can orbit in intermediate energy states.

But here's the trick: Each kind of atom—oxygen, sodium, etc.—has its own rigidly defined energy levels for its electrons (sort of like the click-through settings on a three-way lamp) with no intermediate settings allowed. So, an electron can orbit, say, at energy level 4 or 5, but not 4.2, or 5.1.

Electrons can both absorb and emit photons of light. Photons are just tiny, measurable packets of electromagnetic energy. So an electron gets a boost to a new energy level by absorbing

Glass molecules reflect some visible light back, which is why you can see the glassy surface. But most visible light makes it through and out the other side.

a photon and drops a level by losing one.

Electrons in the atoms of glass molecules absorb most high-energy ultraviolet photons from sunlight, since the particular energy of UV photons is just right for the electrons to get an allowed boost. (That's why it's hard to get a suntan through a closed car window.) Glass molecules also begin jiggling and bumping as they absorb the infrared radiation in sunlight. (Which is why that same car window gets hot to the touch.)

But visible light doesn't have the right energy to be neatly absorbed by energy-hungry electrons in glass. Glass molecules reflect some visible light back, which is why you can see the glassy surface. But most visible light makes it all the way through and out the other side.

According to Louis Bloomfield, a University of Virginia physicist, electrons in the glass "play" with the photons for an instant and then let them continue on their way. The photons are briefly absorbed and then spat out again, in effect passed from atom to atom in the glass. So even though the glass appears to be transparent, there is actually a lot going on inside.

Why do copper pans turn green?

It happened to your old copper penny. It happened to your copper saucepan stored in the damp basement. It even happened to the Statue of Liberty. What started out bright and shiny and peachy gold became, over time, a metal of a different color: mint green.

While copper may undergo the most shocking color transformation, other metals act like chameleons, too. Shiny silver

> A green patina can actually help to protect copper from further corrosion.

darkens to sooty black. And iron, sooty black to begin with, blooms red-orange. The culprit is corrosion, a chemical transformation of metals that can sometimes riddle them with holes and even reduce them to dust.

What corrodes metals? Many react badly to water (leave an iron frying pan to soak overnight in the sink, and it may have a nice sprinkling of rust by morning). Metals also corrode when

MY CORRODED COMPLEXION

When I first turned green, I was sure I was sick.

I was tired. My torch felt heavy, so did my book.

Say patinAHH!

It's a protective coating—so back to work!

Give me your tired, your poor. It's only verdigris beside the golden door.

they come into contact with acids, salts, and certain gases, especially those containing sulfur. Air is a mixture of gases, such as oxygen and carbon dioxide, along with water vapor, so metals can corrode simply by sitting quietly outdoors.

Since 1982, newly minted pennies contain less than 3 percent copper. But their copper-plated surfaces still obediently change colors, developing a coating called a patina. A new penny starts out bright and shiny. But as the copper chemically reacts with the air, copper oxides form, covering the penny with a dull layer of reddish brown, dark brown, and black.

Most green patina, also known as verdigris, is composed of copper acetate, copper carbonate, or copper sulfates. These "green salts" form when chemicals (for example, acids like vinegar) react with copper or the copper oxides on its surface.

A green patina can actually protect the copper underneath from further corrosion.

Unfortunately, there's good patina and then there's bad patina. Patinas formed by the reaction between copper and chloride ions create powdery green spots that contain hydrochloric acid. That's the same strong acid found in the stomach, which can dissolve not only food but also steel. A copper chloride patina eats away at copper, like rust eats away at the girder of a bridge.

Hundreds of years ago, people used vinegar to corrode copper, then scraped off the green salts to make verdigris paint. Copper jewelry often turns green where it touches the skin, since sweat is wet, acidic, and salty.

The Green Lady

The 151-foot-tall Statue of Liberty is made from some 62,000 pounds of thin copper plates covering a steel scaffolding. After standing in New York Harbor since 1886, the statue has an impressive green patina, which restorers have tried to preserve. While it's interesting to imagine the Statue of Liberty shiny-penny new, we can thank the green coat for keeping most of her copper under wraps, protected from salt water and chemicals in the air.

How can a fly or other bug walk up the kitchen wall?

Have you ever lain on your bed and imagined walking on the ceiling? Sidestepping whirling ceiling fans? High-stepping over the door moldings to get into the next room?

The 1951 movie *Royal Wedding* had dancer Fred Astaire dancing across a hotel room floor, up the wall, across the ceiling and down again. Always supernaturally light on his feet, Astaire was now seemingly freed entirely from the bounds of gravity.

How did Astaire perform the feat? The scene was filmed before the invention of computer-designed special

I've been walking on ceilings since I was a kid.

effects. Movie studio MGM built a room, including a floor, ceiling, and three walls, that actually rotated. As Astaire danced, the whole room turned under his nimble feet. And the movie camera turned with it.

But for many insects and spiders, dancing on the ceiling requires no special effects, and no antigravity boots.

How do they do it? Being tiny certainly helps. Very low-mass animals like wall-

Of course, it takes a lot of training.

walking insects and spiders are affected less by gravity than by the forces on a surface, such as adhesion. (But just try affixing an elephant to the wall with Scotch tape!)

On a rough surface, an insect can use its claws to scale up the surface like a climber on the face of a mountain. But many insects and spiders also rely on special leg or foot pads, often covered with bristly hairs, when they need to climb up surfaces. The pads can flexibly fit into nooks and crannies, helping an insect or spider keep its footing.

Spider legs have seven segments and, in most spiders, the very last segment ends in an array of two or three claws. Surrounding the claws may be a pad of hair, each hair ending in a tiny hair "foot." A spider climbing a wall or scuttling across the ceiling can use the microscopic hair "feet" to grip tiny bumps in the plaster or wallboard. (Spiders also use their sticky silk to navigate walls.)

However, even a ceiling-strolling spider can meet its match in a porcelain sink or bathtub, where it may slide right down a slippery-smooth side, unable to climb out without help.

But some insects have an extra climbing feature built in: They can secrete an oily, sticky substance from claw or leg pads. On a surface, the slimy film allows their feet to adhere just enough to walk, but not enough to get stuck—rather like a Post-it.

The tacky liquid enables many insects to walk up surfaces like glass windows. (Scientists have even seen the tiny, oily footprints.) Outdoors, the thin adhesive film allows insects to scurry across a shiny, waxy leaf without slipping off. Some sticky-footed bugs can even resist a force equal to 100 to 200 times their own body weight. Which explains why many insects aren't easily dislodged from a leaf by big, splashy raindrops, or even the spray of a garden hose.

> On a rough surface, an insect can use its claws, rappelling up the surface like a climber on the face of a mountain. But many insects and spiders also rely on special leg or foot pads, often covered with bristly hairs, when they need to climb up surfaces.

But the secret is in the feet.

How come bananas get brown spots on their peels and then taste different?

Bananas are the mood rings of the produce section. One day, they're a bright spring green. The next, they're tending more toward chartreuse. A day later, they're positively yellow, with green accent splotches at the top and bottom. Then it's on to all-yellow, followed by a few days of fashionable brown leopardy spots. Finally, the spots connect and the banana is draped in brown, which deepens to near black as the once-firm fruit inside disintegrates into mush.

FAST FACT

Bananas are one of the world's favorite fruits—sweet, in an easy-to-peel package, and strangely substantial, the potato of the fruit world. They are one of the first fruits that people grew on purpose in Asia, Africa, and Central and South America.

Why does a banana go through such visible changes, while apples and watermelons look the same day after day? Most other fruits do their best ripening before they're picked. Bananas ripen better off the plant than on it.

Banana plants grow to 25 feet tall, but they're not trees—they're giant herbs, whose stalks produce clusters of fingerlike fruit. There are some 300 different kinds of wild bananas; about 20 kinds are grown as crops. In your supermarket, you may find green plantains, which are eaten as a starchy side dish, but the familiar "dessert" banana is the green-to-yellow Cavendish. (You may also

Bananarama, ode to a banana!

I like you yellow, I like you green.

I don't mind the little brown spots,

find golden "apple" bananas, which turn black when ripe, or red-skinned bananas that turn purple, revealing a coral-colored fruit hidden inside.)

Bananas left on the stem ripen and rot quickly, and taste more mealy than sweet. Picked green, however, their starches can slowly turn to sugar. An unripe banana has almost no sugar. But by the time its green chlorophyll has disintegrated and the banana turns yellow, more than 80 percent of its starch has changed to sweet sugar.

An enzyme called amylase speeds the sugary transformation. Our own saliva also contains amylase, which is why a banana that has been bitten into will ripen quickly around the bite. In a brown-spotted banana, the starch-to-sugar process is nearly 100 percent complete, which is why very ripe bananas taste so much sweeter than green ones.

'cause then you're sweeter than you've ever been!

The Allure of Ripe

Most fruits change from green to another color as they ripen. (Some exceptions: green Granny Smith apples, kiwis, and limes.) Take strawberries. Until the seeds speckling their surface are fully developed, strawberries are white-green, fading shyly into the leaves of the strawberry plant. Unripe berries are rock-hard and taste bitter.

But as its seeds mature, a strawberry turns bright red against its green background, a beacon to animals. An enzyme attacks the pectin fiber, which had held the fruit's cells rigid, making the berry softer and juicier. (The same process goes on in a ripening banana.) Starch and glucose change into fruit sugar and table sugar. A sweet aroma wafts from the fruit. A bird can have a nutritious lunch, and the strawberry seeds can pass through the bird's body undigested, sprouting new strawberry plants where they land.

15

How did the seeds get inside an apple?

A tree laden with apples in September is actually groaning under the weight of hundreds of plant ovaries—their hidden brown seeds are fertilized egg cells.

How did the seeds get inside? It all starts in spring. At the base of each pinkish flower blooming on an apple tree is a tiny ovary containing egg cells (ovules). Nectar-seeking bees and other insects carry the apple-flower pollen from one tree to another, fertilizing the eggs. And while the ovary surrounding them develops into a fruit, the fertilized egg cells grow into hard little seeds.

Each seed contains the embryo of a new apple tree, along with a supply of nutrients to get a seedling off to a good start. Protecting the embryo and its food supply is a hard coat called the testa. Somehow, the seed must free itself from the fruit and end up in the soil. And, of course, it's best

How Did the Seeds Get Inside?...

... shot by a cannon?

...deposited by worms?

... or eaten by the apple?

when the seeds travel some distance, so trees don't get overcrowded. Apples that fall to the ground around the tree and then lie uneaten rot into a vinegary mess, and any seedlings that sprout will be shaded out by the adult tree in the spring.

Wind and water can carry apple seeds into new territory. But apple trees also rely

> Each seed contains the embryo of a new apple tree, along with a supply of nutrients to get a seedling off to a good start.

on animals, including humans, to send their seeds out into the world, creating fledgling apple trees in unexpected places. When a deer is enticed by the smell and sight of a sweet red apple, the seeds eventually pass through its body and into the soil somewhere. And so the yearly cycle is complete.

Poisonous Seeds

Apple trees are part of the rose family, which also includes plum, cherry, apricot, and almond trees. And all of their seeds contain cyanogenic glycosides, compounds that can break down into hydrogen cyanide, a deadly poison.

Because of their tough shells, apple seeds tend to pass through an animal's or person's body intact, the way the apple tree intended. So amygdalin, the seed's cyanide/sugar compound, stays safely trapped inside. But biting into a seed or crushing it in

a juicer frees the amygdalin. Enzymes then release tiny amounts of hydrogen cyanide gas in the body of the apple eater. While the body can safely detoxify small amounts of cyanide, it's a good idea to always remove the seeds from an apple before you eat it.

The pits in plums, cherries, and apricots are easier to avoid. And as for almonds, ordinary "sweet" almonds have been bred to be virtually free of amygdalin and so are healthy (and delicious) to eat.

How do they make seedless fruits?

Seedless grapes mean no gravelly fragments to bite into. Seedless navel oranges mean no white seeds at the center to accidentally swallow. And seedless watermelons mean (sadly, for some) no summer seed-spitting contests. But without seeds, where do new baby grape, orange, and watermelon plants come from?

Fruits found in nature normally develop when egg cells in a plant's flowers are fertilized by sperm cells in pollen that's arrived from another plant of the same species (often carried in by a helpful bee, wasp, or bird). The resulting fruit has genes from both of its parents, just as a human baby has genes from both mother and father.

With fertilization, a fruit develops. And inside the fruit are the seeds for a brand-new (and unique) tree, bush, or vine.

But fertilization isn't always successful—or necessary. Take navel oranges. Without another orange variety to cross-pollinate

with, a navel orange will not set seeds. Still, navel orange fruits will grow even without fertilization.

But with no seeds in the oranges, where do new orange trees come from? An orchard of navel oranges is really a collection of clones, marching off into the sunny distance. Most navel oranges originated from two trees shipped to the United States from Brazil in 1870. New trees are usually created by removing buds from existing navel oranges. A bud, inserted into the bark of a different orange tree known for its disease resistance, grows a new treetop that makes navel oranges.

Ever eaten a seedless watermelon? Rather like a mule is a hybrid of a horse and a donkey, seedless watermelons are the result of crossing two genetically different varieties of watermelon. The hybrid melon has seeds, but when its seeds are planted, the watermelons sprouting from the new plant contain only underdeveloped seeds. The seeds won't grow a new plant. But you can eat a watermelon wedge without having to spit.

When seedless grape varieties are fertilized,

Just as a mule is a hybrid of a horse and a donkey, seedless watermelons are the result of crossing two species of watermelon.

the egg cells form underdeveloped seeds. Grape eaters don't notice them since, unlike functioning seeds, these seeds don't form tough outer coats. When growers need a new grapevine, they just use cuttings from the old vines.

Using techniques like cutting, grafting, and cloning, growers can make endless copies of a desirable plant. That way, the same size, shape, and flavor of a fruit can be reproduced year after year. So those little orange clementines you buy this winter may be nearly identical to the ones you bought last January.

But wild fruit plants benefit from the diverse genes that go into their making. Some seedless fruit plants, like generations of animal clones, may be weakened by their year-after-year genetic sameness.

Some scientists worry, for example, that bananas are an endangered fruit. Bananas, they say, just don't have the variety of genes needed to withstand spreading diseases and foraging insects. Some say that the only way to save the cultivated seedless banana—the world's most popular fruit—is through genetic engineering.

Why do apples turn brown when they're cut?

Slicing and eating an apple can sometimes seem like a race against time. Some apples change color at the drop of a peel, the brown creep beginning within minutes of cutting. Is it something in the air? Something in the apple? Yes, on both counts.

The official name for the blooming beige on a diced apple, a mashed avocado, a pared peach, or a bruised banana is enzymatic browning. Oddly enough, the browning of a cut apple has something in common with both the rusting of iron nails and the bronzing of pale skin during an afternoon in the sun.

How it works: Apples have millions of tiny cells, and hidden within their walls are enzymes and other chemicals. When an apple is cut or damaged (say, dropping and rolling across the kitchen floor, the dog in pursuit), some cells break open.

The brown color that develops after an apple is cut comes from pigments called melanins, which are created by a chemical reaction.

In an intact cell, enzymes are kept separate from plant chemicals called phenols. But when cells are damaged, phenols and enzymes mix. The kind of enzyme that kick-starts the browning reaction is a polyphenol oxidase (PPO). When apple cells are opened to the air, oxygen chemically combines with the phenols. PPO accelerates this reaction to breakneck speed. (Enzymes, specialized proteins, are crucial to the reactions that keep living things alive. Without digestive enzymes, it would take nearly 50 years to digest lunch.)

When iron in an old nail oxidizes, the result is red rust. When oxidation occurs in an apple, the result is brown smudge. The color comes from pigments called melanins, created by the chemical reaction. If melanin sounds familiar, it should: It's also the pigment that turns human skin brown in

OUT, DARN SPOT! OUT

the sun. In fact, another name for polyphenol oxidase is tyrosinase, the enzyme that helps make melanin in skin.

Besides making fruit salads brown and mushy, enzymatic browning helps give raisins, tea, coffee, and cocoa their rich brown color. To really take off, enzymatic browning requires certain conditions, like warmish temperatures and plant material that isn't too acidic.

So refrigerating fruit will slow the browning process, as will cooking. Even better, toss cut fruit like apples or pears in lemon, orange, or pineapple juice. Vitamin C, an antioxidant, will also slow the chemical reaction, keeping sliced fruit fresh. Putting fruit underwater will cut off its oxygen supply. Using a rusty knife or copper bowl will just speed up the browning.

Food scientists are experimenting with silencing the PPO gene in apples, to create fruit that won't brown when cut. But, rather like a tan helps protect us from the sun's ultraviolet radiation, the browning process actually protects fruit from a hostile environment. PPOs are thought to ward off attack by insects and microorganisms. And the melanins produced by PPOs in wounds kill both bacteria and fungi, keeping fruit intact longer. Genetic engineering versus a little lemon juice? Maybe we should give fruit trees a vote.

FAST FACT

Some apple varieties, like green Granny Smiths, are more resistant to browning than others.

How can fruit flies appear if the fruit is wrapped in a bag?

f a black-bellied dew lover lifts into the air when you pick up a squishy banana, don't panic. *Drosophila melanogaster* (Greek for "black-bellied dew lover") is the fruit fly's official scientific name. Long ago, people believed that moldy meat or putrid peaches made their own flies. The theory was called spontaneous generation. Thankfully, it was wrong.

The red-eyed fruit flies that rise in a cloud when you reach for a slimy tomato might have set up house in your kitchen long before your last shopping trip. Or they may have flown in from outdoors that morning,

The Littlest Stowaway

I'm hitchin' a ride inside your house...

Mmm, smells good.

...I'm hidin' once I'm there...

Almost dinner-time.

...I'm havin' babies and eatin' your food...

'Cause I'm a fly and I don't care!

attracted by the yeasty smell of rotting fruit. They may even have snuck in on the fruit itself, unwanted freebies from the produce department.

When fruit flies show up in, say, a bag of bananas, it's because adult fruit flies have already laid eggs on the ripe fruit. Bags usually have air holes, and fruit flies are tiny enough to sail through. Each fruitful female can lay 500 eggs. In just a week, a fruit fly can go from tiny egg to full-grown adult.

Even after you toss your mushy bananas, fruit flies linger. Fruit flies can live happily on bits of fermenting food you may never notice—in the sink trap, under the refrigerator, in floorboards and sponge mops, and in the smelly bottom of the kitchen trash can.

Fruit flies may be pests in the kitchen, but they're stars in the world of science. Conveniently tiny, cheap to maintain, and incredibly prolific, fruit flies create generations of new flies in just weeks. These offspring inherit and quickly pass on their special fly characteristics, making it easy for scientists to study them. Finally, fruit flies have only

> Fruit flies can live happily on bits of fermenting food you may never notice—in the sink trap, under the refrigerator, in floorboards and sponge mops, and in the smelly bottom of the kitchen trash can.

eight chromosomes (we humans have 46). Yet many of their genes are remarkably similar to those found in people. So studying fruit flies is a little like studying human beings—but simplified and speeded up.

Some of the first experiments on fruit flies were done in the early 20th century, when scientists observed how white-eyed fruit flies passed on their strange new eye color to later generations. By the year 2000, scientists had announced they had mapped out nearly the entire genetic code of the teeny flies. Each cell in a fruit fly's body contains more than 13,000 genes. Now, scientists are working to discover what each of those genes does, comparing them to genes in other insects, animals, and human beings.

Besides inheritance, fruit fly research has helped us understand biological clocks, diabetes, Parkinson's disease, taste, smell, and sight (in fruit flies, the optic nerve takes a detour through the wing muscles). And in figuring out how to extend fruit flies' lives (by feeding them less, or keeping them from reproducing), scientists are unlocking secrets of human longevity.

Is a tomato a fruit or a vegetable?

In the supermarket, canned tomatoes are shelved in the vegetable section. Most people think the tomato is a vegetable, because it's used like a vegetable—in sauces for pizza and pasta, in lettuce salads, and as a topping for hamburgers and fries. However, according to the science of plants—botany—tomatoes are indisputably fruits.

The tomato is categorized as a fleshy fruit, of which there are three kinds: drupes, with big pits, like peaches, cherries, and olives; pomes, like apples and pears; and berries, like grapes and raspberries. The tomato is—*ta-da*—a berry!

It's hard to imagine putting cherry tomatoes on your morning cereal, or serving up tomato shortcake, topped with whipped cream. But European ketchup was often made with currants or gooseberries. When tomatoes began to be eaten widely, ketchup makers simply switched berries.

What makes a tomato a fruit? Fruits are a special part of a plant—its ovaries, like the ovaries in a woman's body, where egg cells

Attack of the Killer Tomatoes...

OK, so who called me a Vegetable?

are made. After pollen fertilizes the egg cells, they grow into seeds.

Tomatoes make their first appearance as tiny green balls peeking out of the center of the plant's bell-shaped yellow flowers. As the fruits grow, they continue to be green and hard. But eventually, the tomatoes will soften, sweeten, and change color—usually to red, but sometimes to yellow or orange. The color change signifies that the seeds inside are full-grown and ready to be planted.

Tomato plants seem to have their origins in the Andes mountain region in South America and, by the 1500s, the tomato was being grown in Europe. But people objected to the "bad smell" of the tomato plant, and

> Most people think the tomato is a vegetable, because it's used like a vegetable.

many were wary of the fruit, fearing it was poisonous. (In modern times, evil tomatoes have even starred in their own film, *Attack of the Killer Tomatoes,* in which giant, rolling tomatoes terrorize a city.)

There is a grain of truth to the dark side of tomatoes. Tomato leaves and stems contain the alkaloid tomatine, which can cause vomiting, diarrhea, and depression of the central nervous system. The plant's toxic (and hairy) leaves may account for why people once feared tomatoes. But tomatoes themselves are safe and full of nutrients; in the United States, each person eats between 30 and 80 pounds of the red fruit each year.

Toxic Family

Tomatoes are members of the nightshade family, Solanaceae. Among its 2,000 member species are the very poisonous deadly nightshade and jimsonweed. Also in the family are tasty green peppers and eggplant, innocent petunias, and not-so-innocent tobacco, plus Irish potatoes.

The leaves and stems of nightshade plants contain alkaloids, chemicals that can range from mildly to very toxic. These include deadly nightshade's scopolamine, used to make motion sickness pills, and tobacco leaves' nicotine. Potato plants (but not potatoes, unless they are green) are also poisonous, due to the alkaloid solanine.

Why does bread rise?

When a cake is mixed up, it's put right into a hot oven. But bread is a different story. After bread dough is mixed, it's put in a lukewarm place to rest for a while. Peek in later, and the dough, like magic, has doubled in size. Now take it out and punch the dough back down as if it were a pillow. Set it back in the warm spot, wait a bit, and voilà: The ball of dough is even bigger. It's almost as if there were something alive inside.

Well, actually, there is: yeast. If flour and water could talk during their transformation into bread, they might sound alarmed: "There's a fungus among us!" Because that's what yeast is, a fungus, a relative of the yucky mold that sometimes grows on your shower curtain or on rotting fruit.

Each yeast creature is a tiny, one-celled organism. We can't see the billions of individuals in a packet of yeast, because each one is only .003 inch long. It takes about 560 billion yeast organisms to make up 1 ounce.

The yeast beastie may be wee, but it has a long, daunting scientific name: *Saccharomyces cerevisiae*. Without the tiny *S. cerevisiae* (or another leavening, like baking soda), bread would be flatter than a pancake. Yeast-free breads include tortillas and matzoh. We call such breads unleavened, because their dough wasn't full of big, expanding gas bubbles.

In yeast breads, the bubbles arise because yeast has a terrible sweet tooth. The yeast microbe doesn't like lactose, the sugar in milk. But yeast loves sucrose (table sugar, made from sugar cane or beets), fructose and glucose (found in fruit, honey, and molasses), and maltose

> **Inside its supermarket packet, yeast is resting, lying dormant like a bear in a cave in winter. But sprinkle the yeast with warm water and it wakes up, ready to eat.**

(a sugar made from starches in grains).

Inside its supermarket packet, yeast is resting, lying dormant like a bear in a cave in winter. But sprinkle the yeast with warm water and it wakes up, ready to eat. Mixed into bread dough, yeast immediately begins gobbling up any added sugars. Meanwhile, specialized proteins called enzymes break down some of the flour's starch molecules into sugar molecules—more food for the ravenous yeast.

As the yeast cells digest the sugars, they release two waste products: alcohol and carbon dioxide (the same gas that makes soda pop bubbly). What yeast does to bread dough is called fermentation—just as when the tiny creatures get a crack at a bunch of sugary grapes, leaving wine behind.

When flour is mixed with water, its proteins form an elastic, webby network called gluten. Carbon dioxide collects in the web's air pockets. As the bubbles grow, the dough puffs out like a filling balloon. Like a balloon's rubber skin, gluten is strong enough to hold in gases while expanding in all directions. Kneading the dough helps develop the stretchy structure.

Put in a hot oven, the bread gets even higher, as the yeast continues to feed and the heating gas bubbles expand like bubble gum throughout the dough. Eventually, the heat causes the yeast to die. The alcohol vaporizes, too, leaving just the mouthwatering smell of baking bread.

Why does mold grow on bread and other food?

Ever make a sandwich and notice—just after you've taken your first taste—that the bread is streaked with sickly green? Or start to bite into a ripe strawberry, only to be faced with a fuzzy white coating? In both cases, mold has beaten you to lunch.

Mold and other kinds of fungus are also interested in things we would never put on our plates. Ever open a box of old clothes stored in the basement, only to get a pungent noseful of mildew? To mold, those old shirts are yummy. And then there's that itchy athlete's foot rash between your toes. Yucky toe jam to you, delicious dead skin cells to a fungus.

Fungus isn't a kind of plant, nor a kind of animal. Instead, the fungi—from mold to yeast to mushrooms—form their own official kingdom, composed of up to a million or more species. Astonishingly, about 25 percent of all the biomass (the weight of all living things) on Earth is actually fungus.

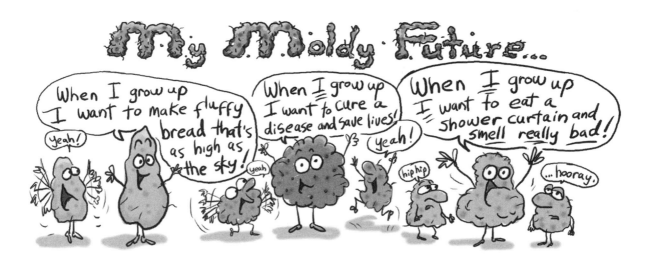

Fungi are nature's champion decomposers, performing the ultimate in recycling. A fungus may attack a fallen tree in the woods, reducing it, over time, to a pile of soil. But fungi will be just as happy dining on leftover spaghetti sauce or a rotting orange in your refrigerator.

We think of mold as slimy and icky (fluffy white tendrils billowing out of a vegetable drawer; slippery black stuff growing under the cap of a forgotten shampoo bottle in the shower). But some fungi are rather appealing, and if mold chows down on your rye, turnabout is fair play: you may eat blue cheese dressing (made with real *Penicillium* mold) on your salad; mushrooms on your pizza; and, if you're British, marmite (a brown yeast spread) on your toast.

One favorite fungus, baker's yeast, makes bread dough rise as it consumes sugar and spits out carbon dioxide (for more on this, see pages 26–27). Molds have also given us important drugs, like penicillin and cyclosporin.

Feasting fungi are after nutrients like sugar. We humans swallow and then begin digesting food in our stomach. Molds digest first, "swallow" later: After secreting digestive enzymes to break food down, fungi absorb the molecules through their cell walls.

Molds are surprisingly complicated. A bread mold with the scientific name *Neurospora crassa*, for example, has about 10,000 genes (humans may have 25,000). Among them are genes that allow this mold to sense red light, even as it lurks on top of your sandwich.

> Fungi are nature's champion decomposers, the ultimate recyclers.

Many-Hued Molds

Molds come in distinctive colors, depending on the pigments they produce. Blue or green molds are often members of the genus *Aspergillus* or *Penicillium*. Red-tinted mold may be *Fusarium*. Black or brown molds include *Alternaria*, *Cladosporium*, *Aspergillus niger*, and *Stachybotrys*, a toxic mold sometimes found in very damp houses.

How does popcorn pop? Why won't regular corn pop?

It's hard to believe that an exploding vegetable is one of the favorite snacks in the United States. But it is, and Americans swallow about 17 billion quarts of supersize corn kernels each year.

Thousands of years before popcorn appeared in multiplexes, people in North and Central America were both eating it and wearing it, as puffy necklaces. Food chemists say that the first wild corn was popcorn, which probably first revealed its inflated goodness when tossed into a fire. Corn poppers, made out of fired clay, came next.

Why does heat make popcorn pop? A Native American folktale explained it this way: Each kernel was home to a spirit, and as the popcorn was roasted, the spirits got madder and madder. They would shake their houses

> **Food chemists say that the first wild corn was popcorn, which probably first revealed its inflated goodness when tossed into a fire.**

and finally burst out in puffs of angry steam.

Of the five basic kinds of corn, only one pops. Popcorn has an especially hard hull, or shell (pericarp). This shell allows a great deal of pressure to build up inside before it breaks. It's also perfect for keeping moisture in the kernel. About 13 to 14 percent of a popcorn kernel is water trapped in the endosperm—the starch inside. And unlike ordinary corn, popcorn has a harder, more translucent endosperm that expands when heated.

When the kernel is heated to 212°F (100°C), some of the water in the kernel turns to steam. The hard hull acts like the lid on a pressure cooker, forcing the steam into the grains of starch. This changes the starch into superhot, gel-like globs.

Popcorn pops the question...

The pressure-cooker effect allows the temperature in the kernel to soar well above the boiling point, to about 347°F. According to chemists, the pressure inside the kernel is about nine times that of Earth's atmosphere when the hull finally explodes, forced outward by steam and superheated water.

Freed to expand in the lower-pressure room air, the steam and hot water carry the inner white starch outside, turning the kernel inside out and swelling it to

40 to 50 times its original size. The peculiar shape of the popped kernel, scientists say, comes from the starch granules, which expand like bubbles when the hull bursts open.

As we all know, not every kernel pops. Why? A cracked hull makes for an unpopped kernel, since steam escapes before it can build up enough pressure. And the water content must be near 13.5 percent—just right—for popcorn to explode. Too dry and there won't be enough steam to break through the hull. Too soggy and the corn will pop into a small, heavy dud.

Scientists who study popcorn have recently discovered what makes some popcorn kernels pop better than others. The poppiest kernels, they say, have an extremely tough hull, with a very orderly arrangement of cellulose molecules. This strong crystalline structure holds moisture in better, so that each kernel explodes with full force.

Why is the cashew the only nut you cannot buy in its shell?

Cashews—the nut that sounds like a sneeze—are the oddballs of the nut world. Think of nuts on a tree, and you might imagine round walnuts hanging on the branches of a walnut tree, thudding to the ground in late summer or early fall. But cashews come in an elaborate disguise. A cashew wearing its shell looks exactly like a fat worm, wriggling out the bottom of a misshapen apple.

Evergreen cashew trees grow only in a tropical or subtropical climate. They can grow to be more than 40 feet tall, their green leaves the backdrop for brightly colored cashew apples, the tree's "false" fruit. Yellow or red cashew "apples" actually look like pears, or oversize hot peppers. The nuts protruding from the apples' undersides are the tree's real fruit. Hidden inside each nut is a single seed—a delicious cashew.

Why not pluck the nut and sell it with shell intact—like a walnut, pecan, or almond? The problem lies in the cashew's family tree. One of the cashew's close relatives is the pistachio, the tasty green (though often dyed red) nut used for snacks and ice cream. Another is the tropical mango. But other relatives—the black sheep of the Anacardiaceae family—include the not-so-nice poison sumac and poison ivy.

All of these plants contain urushiol, an oily chemical that makes a brush with poison ivy such a painfully itchy experience. The cashew's share of urushiols are concentrated in an oily liquid trapped between the two

FAST ⊱🚀 FACT

The cashews we eat come mainly from India, Vietnam, Brazil, and a number of countries in Africa, including Nigeria and Tanzania.

layers of the shell. (It's no wonder that an old name for the cashew was blister nut.)

Because of the lurking urushiols, cashews must be processed very carefully. The process of removing the shells and extracting the liquid includes roasting, burning, boiling, soaking, cracking, and peeling. Instead of being discarded, the cashew nutshell liquid (CNSL) is often sold for industrial uses. CNSL oils are used in waterproof paints, varnishes, and lacquers, while CNSL particles are used to create more friction in brake linings, so cars and trucks can stop on a dime.

Finally, the cashew seeds are cleaned and roasted. This leaves a batch of pristine (and

> Cashews come in an elaborate disguise—the shell looks exactly like a fat worm, wriggling out the bottom of a misshapen apple.

urushiol-free) cashews, ready to eat.

Despite having poison ivy for a ne'er-do-well first cousin, cashews cause fewer allergic reactions than other nuts. But when cashew processing gets careless, there can be problems. In 1982, more than 50 Pennsylvanians who ate cashews sold by their local Little League ended up with poison-ivy-like rashes. The culprit: bits of cashew shells mixed in with the cashew pieces.

Fortunately, such glitches are rare. Cashews make an excellent snack, containing heart-healthy unsaturated oils as well as a good mix of protein and carbs.

Cashews: the Snack that Suffers...

Help!

I'm being roasted to death!

... Then boiled alive...

... Whacked and pulled apart!

I wish I was a peanut.

How does food turn to fat in your body?

Fat is our friend. And like a true friend, it helps us in times of need. When food is scarce—as it often has been for much of human history—fat becomes the shining star. Like the forgotten candy bar you find in your coat pocket when you are ravenously hungry, your body fat will feed you until the next meal.

The average adult body may have 20 to 50 pounds of fat packed under the skin. Eat to excess, and the body can obediently create hundreds of pounds of fat. With memories of famine encoded in its genes, the body doggedly plans for more rainy (foodless) days.

A pound of fat contains about 3,500 calories of energy, enough to get the average person through a day or two of no food;

The SKINNY ON FAT

Fat is our friend...
Until you can't fit in your jeans.

One-half of Americans have way too many fat cells...
But I'll keep you warm!
I'll protect you!
I'll feed you!

Maybe that's why it's so hard to lose weight?
It's hard to say good-bye to friends.
Bye-Bye!

20 pounds can help us survive a month. Fat is also excellent insulation and good safety padding. Fat secretes a long list of hormones and informs the brain about how much of itself there is to use.

Each round fat cell measures between .001 and .008 inch and holds one glistening droplet of fat. Fat cells, caught in a net of fibrous tissue, are the body's own Bubble Wrap. Subcutaneous fat, the Bubble Wrap just under our skin, is usually thickest around the waist and abdomen, thinnest in the eyelids.

There is also visceral fat, deeper fat that's packed around organs like the kidneys. Too much visceral fat in the abdomen is associated with Type 2 diabetes, heart disease, and liver problems.

Our bodies make fat from the food we eat—the fat, protein, and carbohydrates in everything from green apples and green beans to roast chicken and rhubarb. (Not to mention greasy doughnuts and supersweet soft drinks.)

The body wastes the least energy in converting food fat into body fat. Fat droplets in the intestines are broken into smaller drops by bile salts. Enzymes called lipases further

Our bodies make fat from the food we eat—the fat, protein, and carbohydrates in everything from green apples and green beans to roast chicken and rhubarb.

reduce the fat into fatty acids and glycerol. Cells on the intestinal walls absorb the fatty acids, reassemble them, and coat them with protein. By way of the lymph glands, the fats make the jump into the bloodstream.

In the bloodstream, lipoprotein lipase breaks apart the fats again. Some fatty acids are taken in by the liver and muscles. Others travel through tiny blood vessels into fat cells, ushered inside by the hormone insulin. There, three fatty acids are rebound with glycerol, creating stored droplets of fat—triglycerides.

Carbohydrates (sugar or starch) are converted in the intestines to glucose (blood sugar). Glucose is used by every cell in the body for energy. The liver and muscles store some glucose (as glycogen). Leftover glucose can also be converted—mainly by the liver—into fatty acids.

Proteins are reduced to amino acids, building blocks for muscles, organs, and other body parts. Amino acids can also be converted to glucose—and to fatty acids. The end result is the same: more fat stuffed into fat cells, whether the source was butter, banana, or beef.

What are calories, and how do we know how many are in a particular food?

Pick up any package of food in your kitchen and look at the label. Chances are, you'll see the number of calories per serving listed, along with the amount of protein, carbohydrates, and fat. Calories may seem like just another food ingredient. But they're actually a measure of how much energy a bit of food can be transformed into when it's completely burned.

Technically, a calorie is the amount of heat needed to raise the temperature of 1 gram of water 1 degree C (1.8 degrees F). Since the heat needed can vary depending on the temperature of the water, a more precise definition specifies the starting temperature of the water as 14.5° C (58.1°F).

Food scientists determine the exact calories in specific foods using an apparatus

Burning Food for Science...

A jumbo burger

A side of fries

And a Big Gulp soft drink

That was my lunch. All 1400 calories?

called a bomb calorimeter. A sealed steel vessel (the "bomb") is immersed in a measured amount of water. Inside the vessel is a small sample (a few grams) of the food to be analyzed.

Instead of air, the bomb contains pure oxygen. Wires leading into the vessel connect to an igniting device. When electric current is switched on, the food catches fire, completely incinerating in its oxygen atmosphere.

Meanwhile, heat from the burning food passes through the vessels' metal walls and into the surrounding water, raising its temperature. Scientists note the exact degree change and calculate the food's calories.

(To scientists, the calories we're familiar with from food labels and diet programs are actually kilocalories. So one of these calories can raise the temperature of a whole kilogram of water by 1 degree C or 1.8 degrees F.)

For calorie counts on package labels, most manufacturers use a formula rather than an incinerator. Food producers determine the amount of protein, carbohydrates, and fat in a sample of the food made from a given recipe. Carbohydrates and proteins contain about 4 calories per gram, while fat has a whopping 9. So a cookie made from 16 grams of carbohydrates, 8 grams of fat, and 1 gram of protein would contain about 140 calories of energy.

> **Technically, a calorie is the amount of heat needed to raise the temperature of 1 gram of water 1 degree C (1.8 degrees F).**

Of course, our bodies aren't bomb calorimeters, and the food we eat isn't burned and used as efficiently as a sample in a food science lab. We can't digest the fiber in fruits, vegetables, and beans, and so its energy is inaccessible to us. Part of the energy of food is used to fuel digestion itself. And depending on the state of our digestive tract on any given day, we may extract more or less energy from the foods we eat.

Recently, scientists discovered that when we gain weight, bacteria more efficient at extracting energy from food apparently multiply in the gut. When we lose weight, the population shifts to more inefficient microbes. So depending on our percentage of body fat, we may harvest more or less calories from the same candy bar (or chicken breast).

Why does ice cream melt?

Whether premium, low-fat, nonfat, or low-carb, all ice cream melts on a hot summer day, dripping down the cone and onto the front of your shirt.

In melting, ice cream is just behaving like any other bit of frozen, icy matter, suddenly exposed to warm air. Matter changes its state, depending on temperature and pressure. Liquid water boils into a gas (water vapor), freezes into a solid (ice), and melts back into a liquid if ice is left out of the freezer.

But ice cream isn't plain water, and how (and how fast) it melts depends on more than just temperature. The melting qualities of ice cream are actually a favorite focus of some food scientists, since how ice cream melts affects how it tastes.

If you've ever made ice cream at home— or idly read the carton label as you dug in —you know ice cream's basic ingredients: cream and/or milk, sugar, and flavoring, plus egg yolks in the custardy varieties. Some brands add chemical stabilizers and

emulsifiers. Finally, there's the fruit, nuts, chocolate chips, candy, cookie dough, and other extras that create hundreds of flavors.

Scientists call ice cream a frozen foam, since ice cream is partly just thin air. Premium high-fat ice creams contain the least air, while some bargain brands may be more than half air by volume. (Which is why a pint of Häagen-Dazs usually weighs more than a pint of the store brand.)

After the cream, milk, sugar, flavorings (and egg yolks) are combined or cooked together, the mixture is transferred to an icy-cold blending machine. Air is whipped in, and milk proteins and fat droplets surround the air in a honeycomb structure. Ice crystals form throughout the mixture as it freezes. Rotating blades break the crystals into tiny pieces, so that the resulting ice cream has a smooth, non-gritty texture. After final ingredients (from coconut to candy canes) are mixed in, the ice cream is put in the

> Scientists call ice cream a frozen foam, since ice cream is partly just thin air.

deep freeze to harden at about −40°F.

Researchers test the melting rates of different ice creams by putting a scoop on a wire screen in a warm room, measuring the fluid that drips through. Ice cream melts as it absorbs heat from the air, with ice crystals on the outside of the scoop melting first.

Scientists say that the melting rate of ice cream depends mainly on the amount of whipped-in air, the size of its ice crystals, and its framework of fat globules. Airier ice creams (and those containing the additive polysorbate 80) tend to keep their shapes longer in the heat.

But leave the carton out on the counter too long, and your ice cream will suffer the dreaded food-science fate called heat shock. Each time ice cream half-melts and then is shoved back into the freezer, its liquid water refreezes around existing ice crystals instead of forming new ones. Over time, ice crystals get bigger, and your once-creamy treat becomes lumpy, coarse, and crunchy.

How come oil and water (or vinegar) don't mix?

If you've ever taken a bottle of Italian dressing out of the refrigerator, poured bath oil into a bathtub full of water, or watched an oil slick float menacingly toward a beach on television, you know it's true: Oil and water keep to themselves. It takes a lot of shaking to get oil and vinegar (which is mostly water) to mix at all. And even then, you'd better pour fast—the oil is busily migrating up to the surface the second you stop.

Do oil and water have a long-standing feud that started when the universe was young? Not exactly. It's just that oil and water are opposites—polar opposites, in fact.

Oil and water don't mix because of how their molecules are constructed. Molecules are atoms bonded together in a group. Because of the way their atoms are arranged, some molecules have opposite poles, rather like the north and south poles of a magnet. But in a polar molecule, the poles are electrical, not magnetic.

Oil and Water, the Inside Story...

"Oh yuck, here come the olive oils..."
"They're so greasy!"

"Out of our way!..."
"Wet ones!"
"Hey, what's the difference between motor oil and olive oil?"
"The salad!"

"How juvenile!"
"We're outta here!"

Water molecules are polar. A water molecule is shaped like a V, with an oxygen atom at the bottom point of the V and a hydrogen atom on each of the two ends. The bottom of the molecule has a negative electrical charge, while the top carries a positive charge.

In nonpolar molecules, the electrical charges aren't separated, so the molecules don't have opposite positive and negative ends.

Polar molecules are found with other polar molecules, and nonpolar molecules with other nonpolar molecules. Like some kids in a school lunchroom, broken up into cliques and sitting at different tables, they just don't socialize.

Which brings us back to oil and water. Oil and water don't mix because oil is nonpolar and water is polar. But alcohol and water mix seamlessly, since they're both polar. Scientists say that alcohol and water are "miscible," while oil and water are "immiscible."

Since positive charges and negative charges attract, the negative area of a polar molecule attracts the positive area on another polar molecule. So it's natural for polar molecules to be attracted to one another and to mix it up in a solution. And since polar molecules tend to stick together, the ones that are nonpolar, like those in oil, can't easily mix in.

A simple rule to think about what will mix and what won't is "Like dissolves like." So it's easy to mix alcohol and water and fairly easy to mix sugar and water (since sugar molecules are weakly polar). And it's also easy to mix olive oil and corn oil, or safflower oil and motor oil (though you probably wouldn't want to!).

One unexpected result of this rule: If you mix 1 quart of water with 1 quart of alcohol, the mixture will add up to less than 2 quarts. That's because the molecules mix so well that some empty spaces in the two liquids get filled in with molecules, compacting the mixture.

Since some liquids don't mix, toy companies can make those ocean-in-a-bottle toys that use oil, water, and other liquids to make rolling waves full of suspended glitter bits. On the other hand, a toxic chemical could be present in water and be so perfectly mixed in—since it's polar—that we wouldn't know it was there if we didn't run lab tests.

Do oil and water have a long-standing feud that started when the universe was young? Not exactly. It's just that oil and water are opposites—polar opposites, in fact.

41

When I eat eggs, I always wonder: Which came first, the chicken or the egg?

Chicken or egg? Like a hall of mirrors at the carnival, each attempt at an answer just leads to another question. If the chicken came first, then didn't it hatch from an egg? And if the egg came first, wasn't it laid by a chicken? It's one of those questions that seems unanswerable.

Scientists agree on where chickens came from: In a sense, human beings invented them, just like they invented cows and pigs and other domesticated animals.

If chickens were interested in tracing their family trees, they would need to bone up on some DNA research done in Japan. Every chicken that ever lived can trace its ancestors, say researchers, to a particular subspecies of red jungle fowl in Thailand.

The male red jungle fowl looks a lot like

WHICH CAME FIRST...

THE CHICKEN... THE EGG... OR THE DELI?

a storybook rooster. But the jungle fowl isn't identical to a farm chicken. Unlike chickens, female red jungle fowl have no combs. Another jungle fowl peculiarity: After mating season, males replace their bright red-and-orange ruff with a crop of dull, blackish feathers called eclipse plumage.

Scientists think the first domestic chickens were bred from red jungle fowls more than 8,000 years ago in the region now divided into Thailand and Vietnam. People bred chickens first for cockfighting contests, later for eggs and meat.

So the first official chicken pecked its way out of an egg laid by a bird that was not-quite-a-chicken. Depending on how you look at it, the egg—or the wild chicken—came first.

In creating the domestic chicken—and coming up with some 175 varieties—human beings also created a world where chickens rule the roost: There are more chickens on Earth than any other kind of domesticated bird.

And where did birds come from? Scientists think a group of egg-laying feathered dinosaurs were probably the ancestors of today's birds. So if not for dinosaurs, there wouldn't be any jungle fowl *or* chickens.

> If the chicken came first, then didn't it hatch from an egg? And if the egg came first, wasn't it laid by a chicken?

We've solved the riddle of where chickens came from. But what about eggs?

Scientists say eggs—handy miniature incubators of life, nutrients already packed inside—evolved more than 1 billion years ago, in the oceans of Earth. When land animals evolved about 250 million years ago, their eggs had a tough covering to retain moisture on dry land. Egg layers like amphibians, reptiles, and insects flourished. So the first land eggs predated chickens by about 250 million years.

The egg may be one answer to the old riddle, but here's another, if a little longer: The chicken came after the bird, the bird came after the dinosaur, the dinosaur came after the egg. And the egg came long after the first single-celled bacteria, the prokaryotes, evolved in the oceans, some 3.5 billion years ago.

Bad Chicken Jokes

Q. Why did the chicken cross the road?

A: Because the rooster egged her on.

A: Because it was the duck's day off.

A: For her own fowl reasons.

How do chickens lay eggs?

We don't often see a soaring chicken, but chickens may be the most numerous birds in the world. (A good-size chicken farm may house 25,000 cackling hens.) In the United States, the average person eats more than 200 eggs a year; the average chicken produces about the same amount.

> An egg forms in a hen's body in an assembly-line process.

The familiar white or brown chicken egg may be just the right size for breakfast, but birds' eggs come in all sizes. The tiniest—pea-size—are laid by hummingbirds. The largest are laid by ostriches: each about 7 inches long, weighing almost 3 pounds, and as hard as a porcelain sink—you'd need a hammer and a chisel to make an ostrich egg omelette.

But the largest eggs known were those of the now-extinct elephant bird of Madagascar. Measuring more than 12 inches long, each egg held more than 2 gallons of liquid. A single elephant bird egg, over easy, would make a very nice breakfast for 60.

What is an egg? Eggs are the cells in a female body whose job is to make offspring. (Cells are specialized—there are brain cells, heart cells, blood cells, and so on.) An egg cell is usually bigger than the average body cell.

Women's bodies make eggs, but not the hard-shelled kind. A human baby grows inside his/her mother's body, protected from the outside world by her organs and bones and skin. A female bird must spin a shell around her egg, because its destiny is to lie in a nest. The shell is all that separates the vulnerable baby bird developing inside from wind, weather, and predators.

The eggs produced by birds, such as chickens, differ from human eggs in another way: They are chock-full of yolk and albumen. The bright yellow (yolk) and white stuff (albumen) is actually food for the developing chicken embryo, full of protein, fat, carbohydrates, vitamins, minerals, and other nutrients. (In a human egg, there's also a kind of yolk, but a lot less of it.)

An egg forms in a hen's body in an assembly-line process. Hormones signal a yolk to mature in a chicken's ovary; this takes about a week. When the egg is finally released, it is funneled into the egg duct. First, egg white is squirted all over the yolk, which takes several hours. Then, the egg passes into the duct's isthmus, where a shell membrane forms around the egg over an hour's time.

The hard shell is finally added in the uterus, or shell gland, at the end of the egg duct. Calcium is deposited on the shell membrane, strengthening it. The newly minted egg spends about 20 hours in the uterus. Just before it leaves, a thin layer of protein (the cuticle) is added to the outside of the shell.

Finally, the egg passes from the chicken's body to the light of day. If the egg has been fertilized by a rooster—and if it's left alone to incubate—a chick will hatch in about 3 weeks.

EGG ASSEMBLY LINE

Workin' 24/7 to bring you breakfast, lunch, and dinner!

How do cows make milk?

favorite question on school trips to the local dairy farm is: "Do cows have to drink milk to make milk?" The answer is yes—in a way. Like all baby mammals, including baby humans, newborn cows need their mother's milk—the perfect liquid food—to get started in the world. And when a cow grows up, she'll begin making milk herself when her own calf is about to be born.

Each mammal makes milk uniquely suited to its own species. All milk contains protein, fat, milk sugar (lactose), minerals, and vitamins. But each kind of milk—from human to cow to whale to mouse—has a different mix. At a mammal-milk tasting bar, you could tell the difference.

For example, both human and cow's milk are very watery, and each contains less than 4 percent fat by weight. But hooded seal moms make a much heavier milk—less water, more protein, and a whopping 50

MOO FACTORY DELIVERS...

percent fat. Baby hooded seals are born on frigid ice and need to quickly gain a lot of fat to insulate their bodies from the cold. Seal babies drink the super-rich, oily milk for only four days. But in those 96 hours, they can gain more than 40 pounds!

Female cows make milk when they give birth, and their bodies continue to produce milk until their calves stop suckling (or until the farmer stops milking, in about 300 days). Like all mammals, cows make milk from the food they eat. But cows don't just eat dinner. They chew their cud.

Cows are ruminants (as are animals like sheep, deer, camels, and giraffes). All ruminants have special stomachs to digest grasses and leaves. Cows have a four-part stomach. Cows chew their clover or hay just enough to swallow it. Then the first two stomachs get to work softening the food.

After a while, the cow coughs up a ball of partially digested food—cud—and chews it some more. Cud goes up and down, up and

> Female cows make milk when they give birth, and their bodies continue to produce milk until their calves stop suckling.

down. That's ruminating, and the average cow spends up to eight hours a day doing it. Eventually the cud arrives in the second set of stomachs, where it's processed one final time. Moving into the intestines, the cud is officially digested, and its nutrients are passed into the bloodstream.

Milk is made by the cow's four mammary glands, inside the udder. All mammals have mammary glands, which evolved from sweat glands—instead of secreting salty water, they secrete milk.

The mammary glands have alveoli, special cells that filter the raw ingredients for milk from blood that passes through the udder. Some 550 gallons of blood must filter through the udder to make one gallon of milk. A cow makes about 4 to 8 gallons of milk a day—or 64 to 128 glasses.

A full udder sways under the weight of 20 to 50 pounds of milk, so uncomfortable that cows will often walk back to the barn for their twice-a-day milking when the time comes—even without being called.

Why is cow's milk white?

If you've ever gotten a white milk mustache, you might pause to admire it in the mirror before wiping it off. Your upper lip is white, it turns out, for the same reason the sky is an endless blue.

All milk contains protein, fat, milk sugar (lactose), minerals, and vitamins. While the exact composition of milk varies from herd to herd, cow's milk is about 87 percent water, with nearly 4 percent fat by weight. So why is milk white? You may have heard it's because milk's calcium or sugar, protein or fat, are themselves white, and that one and/or all reflect white light. The real answer, food scientists say, is more complicated, but also more interesting.

Think of milk as a liquid that, observed under a powerful microscope, consists mainly of particles of protein and fat suspended in water. Much of the protein in milk is in the form of casein. Casein's long-chain molecules link up to form bumpy,

Why is it white?

Because white is the perfect canvas for chocolate?

Red would spoil cakes and cookies.

And green would make you sick at breakfast.

raspberry-shaped spheres about 90 to 150 nanometers across. (A nanometer is a tiny billionth of a meter.) The protein spheres also contain most of the milk's calcium and half of its phosphate, minerals essential for bone growth in baby cows.

Scientists call these tiny protein balls micelles. The diameter of each micelle is smaller than the wavelength of visible light (400 to 700 nanometers), too small to reflect light. Instead, white light is scattered in every direction when it encounters the micelles on its journey through a glass of milk. Tiny globules of fat add some light-scattering effects of their own. And we see white.

But white light contains a hidden rainbow of colors. And its shortest wavelengths—the blues and violets—are actually scattered more strongly than the longer wavelength reds. We see this in the blue of the sky, caused by the scattering of sunlight from zillions of widely dispersed gas molecules. However, the particles in a glass of milk are so concentrated that the blue tint is drowned out by the scattering of the rest of the colors (as it is near the horizon, where the thicker layer of air makes the sky appear whiter).

To see the skylike scattering of diluted milk, pour a small amount (skim works best) into a glass of water in a dark room, then shine a flashlight through. You should see the liquid turn blue.

> **A milk moustache is white, it turns out, for the same reason the sky is an endless blue.**

Why do Cheerios clump together in the bowl?

Whatever your favorite floaty cereal, you may have noticed the phenomenon: Clumpy bunches of O's, or Lucky Charms, or Cocoa Puffs huddled together in the milk. And, often, a ring of cereal bits cling to the walls of the bowl.

Scientists call it the Cheerio effect, but small, O-shaped rings of oats aren't the only objects that do this. When a man shaves in the morning, the shorn hairs that fall into the sink water will tend to clump together, too. Yuck-O.

What's the attraction? Do small bits feel the need to huddle in the deep middle of a scary pool of liquid? Do the rest cling to the sides, like nonswimmers along the wall of a pool?

Believe it or not, it wasn't until 2005 that science completely explained the Cheerio mystery (even though its namesake cereal had been around since 1941). Scientists say the Cheerio effect is due to surface tension, gravity, buoyancy, and something called the meniscus effect, which involves the attraction between liquids and solids.

Cheerios and other cereals that float are able to resist the force of gravity because of

Together wherever we go-oh! Because...

we're lost...

Where did the box go?

we like each other...

You smell good!

This is fun!

we're afraid!

oh my gosh!

White stuff!

eeeek!

50

the buoyant effect. If an object (like a single Cheerio) is less dense than milk and weighs less than an equal (in this case, Cheerio-size) volume of milk, it will float.

Molecules at the surface of a liquid are strongly attracted to one another and also attracted to the molecules beneath them. But they are much less attracted to the air molecules above. The result is surface tension, a skinlike effect that allows some insects to walk on water.

When a Cheerio floats on milk, it creates a dent in the surface. Each bobbing Cheerio makes its own dimple in the ordinarily smooth surface "skin" of the milk. As the Cheerios drift near one another, they seem to attract like magnets. Actually, researchers say, they consolidate their troughs, creating a bigger and bigger dimple as more Cheerios

drift in. Escaping from the bunch is hard, since it would require a Cheerio to travel up a little hill, against the force of gravity. So Os tend to stay clumped.

So why do Cheerios often cling to the sides of the bowl? Water (or milk) near the side of a glass behaves differently than water (or milk) in the middle. The crescent shape of a liquid where it meets a solid surface is called a meniscus. The liquid can bulge into a convex shape when it is repelled by the solid, or dip down in a concave shape when it's attracted.

Since water molecules are attracted to glass, and milk is mostly water, milk will dip down near the wall of a glass bowl. So Cheerios at the boundaries of the milk will float upward where the dip rises up the wall, forming a ring of cereal.

Snap, Crackle, Pop

Besides Rice Krispies, other puffed cereals can make noise when doused with milk. In the case of puffed rice, cereal makers oven-toast the rice, which has been conditioned with water. As the water turns to steam, rice kernels puff out like popcorn.

Unlike the compact, hard walls of an uncooked rice kernel, the walls of puffed rice are stretched thin, making each kernel fragile. The shock of the cold milk makes the walls crack like a thin glass crystal. As the milk is (unevenly) absorbed by the puffed rice, the crackling sounds come from the fracturing of the walls and the escape of air trapped inside the kernels.

Why does a spinning tunnel appear in hot coffee when you stir in milk?

Pouring cold milk into hot coffee is a lot like watching bathwater swirl down a (hidden) drain. According to physicist Jearl Walker of Cleveland State University, the tiny coffee tornado is most likely to form when you stir coffee first, then pour milk into the swirling center. Since cold milk is denser than hot coffee water, it sinks. Vortex tubes of spinning coffee catch in the descending milk and are stretched out. As they lengthen, their rotational speed increases, forming a tunnel leading down from the surface.

Using powdered creamer, you can do another coffee experiment. As you pour the powder in, try tapping on the inside of the (real, not paper) cup as you stir the coffee with a metal spoon. You should hear the pitch of the tapping sound change from a

IN THAT CUP-A-COFFEE...

I see a whirling net of hexograms!

I see a mini tornado!

I see dandruff.

low clunk to a higher clink and back as the creamer sinks into and mixes with the coffee. (This is also known as the hot-chocolate effect, since it applies equally to chocolate powder mixed into hot water.)

How does it work? Air trapped in the powder is released as the creamer dissolves in the coffee water. Sound travels more slowly in air than in water, and the frequencies at which sound will resonate in a container depend on the speed of sound.

The tiny coffee tornado is most likely to form when you stir coffee first, then pour milk into the swirling center.

So the tapping changes pitch when the sound must pass through a foamy cloud of creamer in the coffee.

To keep take-out coffee hotter longer, scientists say, coffee drinkers should wait to add mix-ins until they're ready to drink it. Even sugar will cool coffee, since it takes energy to dissolve its crystals. Meanwhile, stirring moves hotter coffee from the bottom to the top, where its heat can be radiated away to the air faster.

Patterns in a Coffee Cup

Next time you see a steaming cup of coffee, check the surface for an elaborate six-sided fishnet pattern. For the pattern to appear, the coffee must be hot, and it's best to view it in bright light coming from one side—say, in a shaft of sunlight slanting in through a coffee-shop window.

According to Jearl Walker, it's all a question of fluid dynamics. The pattern appears when the coffee at the bottom of the cup is hotter than the coffee at the top. Currents of hot coffee rise while cooler coffee sinks, forming a regular pattern on the surface. (Imagine hot coffee rising inside the hexagons, cooler coffee sinking along the boundary lines.)

The honeycomb pattern vanishes quickly as the coffee cools and settles down. Walker says you can also make it disappear using a rubber comb, electrically charged by your dry hair. Simply hold the comb just above the surface of the coffee; the static electricity should disrupt the fluid cells.

Why does caffeine in coffee and cola make us feel jittery?

I t's in your iced tea (80 milligrams), your coffee yogurt (45 mg), your cherry cola (30 mg), your chocolate-chip cookie (5 mg). It may be in the pain reliever you take for a headache (65 mg), or the decongestant you take for a cold (30 mg).

Caffeine is naturally found in coffee, tea, and chocolate. More than 100 other plants, including some species of poisonous

GET YOUR MOJO WORKING!

My fingers fly over the keyboard — work is a breeze!

one cup of coffee

holly, also have caffeine molecules hidden in their leaves, seeds, or bark. Extracted, caffeine is a white crystalline powder, with a very bitter taste.

A little tenser — my fists pummel the keys.

three cups of coffee

Caffeine is an alkaloid; other alkaloids found in plants include much more potent nicotine (from tobacco) and opium (from opium poppies). Botanists say plants contain alkaloids as a kind of self-defense. The bitter taste or side effects may keep animals from eating them. Alkaloids may also ward off competing plants: Caffeine leaches into the soil around coffee plants and reduces weed growth.

Alkaloids easily penetrate cell walls in human beings. When enough caffeine enters your bloodstream, there is a cascade of effects. Heart rate and blood pressure temporarily increase; you may gradually feel more wide-awake and alert. Your muscles may feel more tense; you may talk faster. You may have more energy and focus, and both memory and athletic skills may improve.

College students pulling all-nighters before finals, cab drivers working the midnight shift, long-haul truckers, cops on the beat at 2 A.M.—all may use coffee (60 to 150 mg) to stay awake.

Scientists say the fact that caffeine resembles other chemicals circulating in the body allows it to alter brain chemistry. The body's confusion is what makes us feel wide-awake after a grande mocha Frappuccino.

One of these molecular look-alikes is adenosine. Adenosine builds up in cells following a burst of energy, molecules binding to adenosine brain receptors like keys into locks. The receptors then release chemicals that lead to sleepy feelings.

A caffeine molecule looks enough like an adenosine molecule in its three-dimensional shape that it can fit snugly into an adenosine receptor. When the *real* adenosine molecule shows up, it's locked out. But since the caffeine molecule doesn't have the chemical makeup of adenosine, it doesn't trigger sleepiness—allowing us to feel alert longer.

Caffeine also resembles a molecule called cAMP, which helps keep adrenaline flowing. (Adrenaline is the "fight or flight" hormone that makes us hyperalert in an emergency.) And caffeine increases the production of dopamine, a brain chemical that makes people feel excited and happy.

But too much caffeine can make you feel frantic, actually worsening concentration. Caffeine can also make it harder to fall and stay asleep, make the heart beat too rapidly, and make you feel irritable, jumpy, and shaky. What's more, once you get used to daily caffeine, you may get terrible headaches if your intake suddenly drops. You may also feel tired and somewhat depressed.

However, studies have shown that for most people, having a cup or two of a caffeinated beverage every day is probably not harmful to health.

> More than 100 plants have caffeine molecules hidden in their leaves, seeds, or bark.

Massive anxiety... I should've slept last night. I can't remember what I'm doing.

six cups of coffee

How come soda fizzes?

Carbon dioxide is a gas-of-all-trades. Yeast releases it as it feasts on sugars in bread dough, making bread high and springy. Solid carbon dioxide—otherwise known as dry ice—keeps food and medicines icy cold and supplies spooky special effects on Halloween.

Plants adore carbon dioxide—they absorb it from the air, use energy from sunlight to split it into carbon and oxygen, and make

An Ode to Carbon Dioxide...

You're the fizz in my soda...

we're free!

carbohydrates. We get to breathe in the leftover oxygen, without which we couldn't live.

And in a sillier job, carbon dioxide makes soft drinks fizzy, or carbonated. (Now you know why there's a "carbon" in carbonation.) Soft drink makers inject zillions of carbon dioxide molecules into each bottle or can, then seal it up tight.

You're the bubbles on my tongue...

yuck! Liverwurs

Unlike water, which turns to steam at 212°F, carbon dioxide normally boils into a gas at −109°F. Yet an unopened bottle of pop is almost bubble-free. That's because high pressure forces the carbon dioxide into the liquid around it. When you open the bottle, you reduce the pressure. You can see gas bubble up in the soda and rise to the surface, where carbon dioxide invisibly takes flight.

To see how much carbon dioxide, or CO_2, is in your bottle of soda, try this experiment: Pull a small balloon over the lid of an unopened bottle and down onto the neck. Then unscrew the lid through the balloon. You should see the balloon start to inflate.

The first rush of CO_2 will come from the airspace between the surface of the soda and the lid. When the pocket of CO_2 escapes—with a pop and a hiss—dissolved gas in the soda begins to form bubbles, rise, and escape into the air, too. Over the next several hours, the CO_2 will continue to slowly bubble up and rise into the balloon, inflating it.

Soft drink makers add carbon dioxide mainly for taste and "mouthfeel." Carbon dioxide gives soda pop its bright, bubbly "party" taste. Some of the dissolved CO_2

You're the whoosh from the pop top,
You're the burp when I'm done!

FAST FACT

A can of soda at 75°F has an internal pressure of about 55 pounds per square inch (psi). Outside the can, normal air pressure is about 14.7 psi.

reacts with water to form carbonic acid, adding an edge to the drink's sweetness. As a side benefit, carbonation inhibits the growth of bacteria. Without carbon dioxide, soda is just flavored water without the "pop."

And speaking of carbonated water: Scientists had been unable to account for nearly half of the CO_2 released by burning fossil fuels and wood since industry took off about 200 years ago. Now, they think they know where the missing carbon dioxide has been hiding. Like lost treasure, it sank into the planet's oceans. But unlike treasure, carbon dioxide may be reeking havoc, acidifying ocean water and harming sea life. The oceans have absorbed some 118 million metric tons of CO_2, scientists say, and can only hold about 350 million. Carbon dioxide in the atmosphere prevents heat from escaping into space. So when the oceans reach their limit, global warming may accelerate.

Why do ice cubes in trays sometimes grow spikes, like stalagmites in a cave?

Like mirror images, stalactites and stalagmites project down from the ceilings and up from the floors of caves. They grow as mineral-rich water drips down from cracks in a cave ceiling. Hanging icicles of stone, stalactites start out as hollow tubes and grow toward the floor. Meanwhile, minerals dripping down onto the cave floor build up into the solid, spiky formations called stalagmites. When stalactites and stalagmites meet in the middle, they form towering stone columns or pillars.

But while scientists have long known how real stalagmites and stalactites form, thorny ice cubes were a bit more puzzling.

It takes between 3 and 10 minutes for an ice thorn to reach its full height of up to 2 inches.

Researchers at the California Institute of Technology helped solve the mystery of Mohawk-wearing ice by putting a TV camera inside a freezer.

For spiky ice, scientists say, freezer conditions must cause water to undergo supercooling. As the water in an ice-cube tray quickly chills, thin sheets of ice form on the surface. As the ice sheets grow jaggedly in toward the center of each compartment and meet, one or more small holes often remain.

Water is peculiar; instead of shrinking, it expands as it freezes. As a cube continues freezing, water swells upward, pushing through the small holes on the surface of

58

a forming cube. The freezing water piles up around a hole's rim, creating a squat, hollow tube of ice. Frigid water from beneath continues to flow up this tube like an icy geyser, collecting at the top. And so, minute by minute, a spike grows.

Ice cube spikes jut out at all angles, depending on the shape of the tiny funnels they grew through. (A tilted funnel will grow a slanted spike.) It takes between 3 and 10 minutes for an ice thorn to reach its full height of up to 2 inches. The ideal temperature for spike forming, according to the Cal-Tech study, is around 19°F. At too-low temperatures, water that wells up through a surface hole will simply freeze over into an unsightly ice wart.

To make your own ice spikes, it's best to use distilled or highly filtered water. Tap water often contains minerals that slow rapid freezing, just as salt disrupts the freezing of ice on a sidewalk. According to the Cal-Tech researchers, plastic trays work better than metal, since the plastic has a helpful insulating effect. And a frost-free freezer is better than an old-fashioned "defrost me" freezer. The freezer fan's frigid streaming air actually helps spike tips grow.

In the winter, look for larger ice spikes wherever water collects in a contained space, from driveway puddles to plastic bird baths.

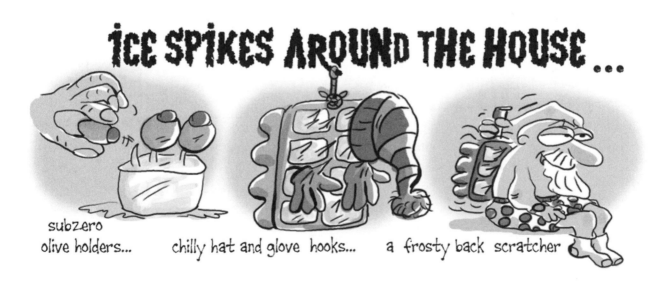

ICE SPIKES AROUND THE HOUSE...

subzero olive holders...   chilly hat and glove hooks...   a frosty back scratcher

Clouds in Your Cubes

Look closely at an average ice cube—a magnifying glass helps—and you'll see cloudy swaths, mini-bubbles, and tiny tunnels, all encased in a clear ice shell. If water starts out clear, why does it develop an opaque center when it freezes into a cube?

When it comes to tap water, what looks like plain water is actually full of invisible gases and lurking minerals. Oxygen diffuses into water from the air or is incorporated when the water is jiggled or sprays through a faucet aerator, rather like air is incorporated into beaten egg whites. Tap water also contains dissolved mineral salts like calcium and magnesium.

Water's invisible elements come out of hiding when an ice cube freezes solid. How come? Each cube freezes from the outside in, water molecules linking up to form what scientists call a crystal lattice. As the cube freezes, trapped gases, mineral salts, and other impurities are gradually pushed into the center by the in-growing crystal shell of pure water. Trapped in an icy cage, air is caught in tiny bubbles and tunnels, while mineral salts have come out of hiding and are suspended in an opaque swath. Adding to the visual mix are tiny cracks separating frozen crystals. The result is a cube with a clear casing and a cloudy heart.

To make the clearest possible cubes at home, minerals and trapped gases must be removed before the tray goes into the freezer. First, start with highly filtered (or even better, distilled) water to minimize dissolved solids. Then, boil the water in a clean pan for 5 minutes, forcing most of the dissolved gases to flee into the air.

Let the water cool a bit and then pour gently into an ice cube tray (shaking the water will reintroduce unwanted air). When you remove your frozen tray hours later, you should have a sparkling array of almost-clear ice.

But no matter how perfect the cube, if ice is left in the open air, cubes will eventually lose their transparency. Each time the ice bin is opened, the cubes are exposed to warm room air. As water molecules from the air bond to the cube's frozen surface, the cube gradually builds up a layer of (translucent) frost. Soon, the once-transparent cube wears a cloudy white coat.

Why do ice cubes swell as they freeze?

Water is peculiar. When most substances change from liquid to solid form, they shrink, becoming denser, their molecules packing more closely together. But when water changes from a sloshy liquid to solid ice, it expands, becoming less dense. Which is why ice bobs to the top of your Coke, rather than sinking like a stone to the bottom.

At normal atmospheric pressure, molecules usually behave in predictable ways as their temperature changes. Molecules fly apart into a gas when heated, condense into a flowing liquid when cooled, and shrink

FAST FACT

When water freezes and expands, it can cause some real headaches. Water pipes freeze and then burst in unheated houses. Water collects in roadway cracks in winter, turns to ice, and enlarges crevices into gaping potholes.

into a frozen solid when chilled still further. The changes in state parallel changes in energy: from high energy to medium energy to barely jiggling.

Boiling water expands into a gas (steam) and wafts off into the kitchen. But we also see water expand when chilled in the freezer. An ice cube tray filled to the rim the night before overflows with big cubes of ice in the morning.

How does it work? Water starts out behaving normally. As its temperature drops, water obediently shrinks together—until it reaches 39°F (4°C). Then, amazingly, water reverses course, its volume slowly increasing as it chills. When water finally freezes, at 32°F (0°C), it expands dramatically.

If Freezing Ice Didn't Expand...

Icebergs would sit safely on the ocean floor.

Scientists say water's quirky behavior is caused by the shape of its molecule and by how the molecules bond to one another. Each water molecule is two hydrogen atoms bonded to one oxygen (H_2O). Because of how the atoms share electrons, a water molecule has a slight positive charge at the end with the hydrogen atoms and a slight negative charge at the end with the oxygen atom. The result? The molecule's

> **Scientists say water's quirky behavior is caused by the shape of its molecule and by how molecules bond.**

charged ends attract the oppositely charged ends of other water molecules (known as hydrogen bonding).

In liquid water, as molecules slip-slide past one another, bonds form, break, and re-form. But by the time water has cooled to 39°F, the molecules' energy has dropped enough that they are very near one another. So each H_2O molecule forms more stable hydrogen bonds with up to four fellow molecules.

By 32°F, the H_2O molecules are snappily lined up in a frozen crystal lattice, an open hexagonal (six-sided) shape. Unlike in liquid water, molecules in ice are held rigidly apart. That means more empty space between molecules—so frozen water occupies more room than liquid.

Presto: Put 10 cups of water in the freezer, take out nearly 11 cups of ice!

ICeD DRINKS WOULDN'T Be MUCH FUN.

You can say that again.

Ice SKaterS WOULD Have tô wear wet SuitS.

What if. . .

If frozen water weren't less dense than liquid, there would be no floating icebergs to sight off the bow of a ship. There would be no skating on ice-covered ponds, while fish and other life shelter in insulated water below. If water froze from the bottom up, much of Earth's water would solidify in winter, and life might be impossible.

Does hot water freeze faster than cold water?

It sounds like one of those questions that must have been answered hundreds of years ago, by a physicist or chemist whose name is in our science textbooks. But this simple-sounding question is actually quite complicated. And there is a lot of disagreement among scientists about the answer.

The commonsense answer: No, of course not. Water freezes because it loses heat. Cold water has already lost more heat than hot water. So since it's already closer to the freezing point, cold water should freeze faster.

But the real answer to the question is: It depends.

Experiments show that hot water will sometimes freeze faster than less-hot water, depending on the starting temperatures, the containers holding the water, and the freezing conditions. (For example, hot water will not freeze faster if the cooler water is, say, $\frac{1}{10}$ degree above freezing temperature already.)

Scientists watch hot and cold water freeze...

Fascinating.

Chilling.

I wish Aristotle could be here.

Imagine two identical buckets, open at the top. Put hot water in one and an equal amount of lukewarm water in the other. Set them outside when the temperature is well below freezing, or in a big freezer. According to one argument—the evaporation theory—the hotter water will evaporate faster. With less water to cool, the water in the "hot" pail may cool to freezing first. Also, evaporation itself makes water lose heat quickly—like sweat evaporating from your skin cools you.

But in the pail of cooler water, a thin layer of ice will quickly form on the surface, insulating the water from further evaporation—and slowing the rate of ice formation below the surface.

There may also be a supercooling effect, in which water remains liquid below its normal freezing point of 32°F, but then freezes faster. How? Normally, ice crystals form at places in water where there is suspended dust or gas bubbles. Hot water that has been boiled has fewer dissolved gas bubbles. With fewer impurities, water can evaporate and cool without forming a layer of insulating ice on top. As it chills to below freezing, ice crystals form spontaneously and spread into an icy slush. Then the water quickly freezes solid.

There's also a simpler reason why hot water may freeze faster than cold. If you put a tray of hot water in your freezer, its heat may raise the refrigerator's thermostat enough to trigger the compressor to start. With the refrigerator pumping heat out of the freezer, your hot tray may enjoy a quicker trip to icehood than the tray of cool water you put in yesterday.

Aristotle noticed the hot water phenomenon back in 300 B.C., but scientific discussion of the mystery had all but ceased by the 20th century. Until, that is, a boy in Africa named Erasto Mpemba, making ice cream, noticed that if he started out with hot milk, his ice-cream mix froze faster. Later, in high school in Tanzania, Mpemba pestered his teachers for an explanation. A professor of physics visiting Mpemba's school was intrigued, and a series of experiments in his lab confirmed the boy's results. In 1969, the professor and Mpemba officially published their findings. Which is why today, the phenomenon of hot water freezing faster than cooler is often called the Mpemba effect.

Hot water may freeze faster than less-hot, depending on starting temperatures, containers holding the water, and freezing conditions.

Why do Wint-O-Green Life Savers emit sparks when chewed in the dark?

It sounds like light those furry little tribbles might have given off in an old *Star Trek* episode. But Wint-O-Green Life Savers sparks are actually a mysterious glow called triboluminescence, produced when sugar and other crystals are crushed or rubbed together.

When you scrape two dry sticks together, the friction can generate enough heat to spark

a small flame. Likewise, friction produced in the right materials, like sugar, can create not a flame, but a burst of static electricity like the sparks that crackle through a dry, clingy blanket on a winter night.

Here's how it works: When you crush Wint-O-Green Life Savers (or any hard candy made of real sugar), the naturally asymmetrical sugar crystals tend to

4th of July- Candy Style

65

break in a lopsided way that separates electric charges in the molecules. So negative electrons are split off from positive protons. Sparks fly when the charges reconnect, like a lightning bolt that reunites positive and negative charges from cloud to ground.

Like regular lightning, minilightning occurs when the electric current excites nitrogen molecules in the air. The nitrogen molecule emits photons of light, mostly in the invisible-to-us ultraviolet range. So by themselves, the sugar sparks are hard to see. (Many UV-sensitive insects, birds, and reptiles, however, might find the sweet lightning very entertaining.) That's where the flavoring in Wint-O-Green Life Savers comes in handy.

Wintergreen oil (methyl salicylate) is key to the electric Life Savers effect. Wintergreen is a fluorescent compound; it absorbs high-energy, short-wavelength light and reemits lower-energy, longer-wavelength light. So wintergreen absorbs the UV light made by the nitrogen molecules in the air of your mouth, emitting a flood of visible bluish light. Voilà: mouth sparks.

Interestingly, much of the mystery behind Life Savers lightning was solved by a scientist named Sweeting. The late Linda Sweeting's experiments showed that impurities in a crystal structure could produce triboluminescence even in symmetrical compounds.

Sparky Experiment

To perform your own electric candy experiment, take some Wint-O-Green Life Savers into a very dark bathroom or other room with a mirror. Let your eyes get accustomed to the dark for about 10 minutes. Then chomp down on the candy while you look in the mirror and watch the (blue) sparks fly. Even better, use a pair of pliers to crush your Wint-O-Green Life Savers in the dark—since it's wet in your mouth, using a tool to smash the candy should make brighter sparks. (It will also preserve your teeth.)

You can try smashing other sugar candies, a sugar cube, or even ripping a piece of adhesive tape off its roll, to see a more muted display of tiny lightning.

Why do some clothes shrink in the dryer?

Ever put a wet wool sweater in the dryer? Tumbling mindlessly in the hot air, the sweater is not only drying out, it's getting smaller and smaller. When you take it out an hour later, the sweater is even cuter than when it went in—because now, it's *doll-size*. Maybe, just maybe, it will fit your Chihuahua.

And hot water can have the same shriveling effect as a hot dryer. Soak a big sweater in hot water, and like the Wicked Witch of the West melting on the castle floor after Dorothy tossed that bucket, the sweater may shrink to Munchkin size.

You might have noticed that the clothing that shrinks is usually made of natural materials, like wool, cotton, or linen, rather than synthetic fibers. If you could pull a

WHAT THE DRYER DID...

Made my skirt a supermicro mini...

Made my shirt a tiny tee ...

Made me very happy!

wad of cotton off a cotton plant, or hold a handful of wool sheared off a sheep, you'd notice that the fibers are bunched up. That's because natural fibers are made of long, crinkly chains of molecules.

In a fabric factory, fibers are carded (untangled) and combed out before they are spun into long skeins of yarn. The yarns are used to make bolts of fabric or knit sweaters and socks. In clothing, the natural fibers are held in an unnatural stretched state. Even so, the fibers require some energy to recrimp themselves.

Which is where doing laundry comes in. Water can make fibers like cotton swell. But as the water evaporates in the hot dryer, the heat gives the chains of molecules in the fiber extra energy. Chains kink as the molecules in line get more energetic, like a swerving conga line of dancers. The result? The weave draws up tighter, like a heated rubber band. And the clothing shrinks—sometimes a little, sometimes a lot. A wool sweater can emerge from the dryer several sizes smaller.

(Rough wool fibers can also tangle and catch on one another in the agitating gyration of a washer, drawing a fabric tighter even before it goes into the dryer.)

Synthetic fabrics, like polyester, have designer molecule chains, shaped as straight as the manufacturer wants. Presto: Little or no shrinking later. But many feel that synthetics can't match the comfortable feel of natural fibers.

What do manufacturers do so that you can continue to wear your clothes after they're washed? They may attach fabric care labels that specify dry-cleaning, washing in cold water, drying on low heat, or drying on a rack or clothesline. They may preshrink fabrics. They also often treat natural fabrics with coatings, like resin, that help fibers resist kinking in water or heat.

> **Clothing that shrinks is usually made of natural rather than synthetic fibers— materials like wool, cotton, or linen.**

FAST FACT

In the 1960s, there was a shrunken-clothes fad. You put on a new pair of jeans, then sat in a bathtub full of hot water, waiting as the jeans shrunk to form-fit. Sadly, preshrunk jeans put an end to the fun of bathing with your clothes on.

Why do things (like blue jeans) get darker when wet?

Rinse off the sidewalk with a hose, and observe the bleached-white cement turning gray. Watch as the incoming tide tints the pale beach brown. And shriek as pelting raindrops turn your plain white shirt into a polka-dotted mess.

Water temporarily darkening many objects it touches is one of those everyday mysteries, something so familiar that we cease wondering about it (if we ever did). And yet, it's genuinely puzzling—especially since the water doing the darkening can be itself crystal-clear.

Many porous objects—paper, fabric, tree

Refraction at Work!

I only look wet because I am wet.

bark, soil, hair—darken as they are doused in water. Why? When light hits an object, some light is absorbed and some is reflected, or scattered, back to our eyes. So when an object looks darker than normal, it must mean that less than the usual amount of light is rebounding back.

When light travels through air—which is mostly empty space, shot through with whizzing gas molecules—it follows a nearly straight path. But when light passes from empty air into, say, water or glass, its journey is slowed. Both glass and water are denser than air, and the light that penetrates their surfaces bends sharply, often causing it to zigzag back out. This bending is called refraction.

Different materials have different refraction indexes, which just means they bend light more or less. Compared to a vacuum, with its bottom-line refraction index of 1, water's is 1.33, glass's about 1.5, and silvery platinum's about 2.3. The greater the difference in the refraction index of two materials, the more the light is forced to change direction as it travels from one into the other.

Take, for example, cotton, a favorite fabric for jeans and shirts. Cotton fabric is a weave of natural fibers (refractive index of about 1.5), the gaps filled with air (refractive index of about 1). So when light enters the fabric, it is refracted sharply at the interface between the cotton fibers and the trapped air. This sharp bending makes much of the light scatter back at us from the surface of the material.

But when the fabric gets wet, water seeps in and fills the air gaps. Water's refraction index of 1.33 is much closer to that of the cotton fibers around it. This means that more light penetrates into the fabric, instead of scattering from the surface. Since less light reaches our eyes, the material appears darker. (And in the case of a colored fabric, the color looks deeper.)

When sand or hair or concrete gets wet, we notice only the darkening. But a wet fabric can also become more transparent. As more light penetrates the material traveling in straighter lines, more exits through the other side. If you happen to be wearing this wet material, the light will bounce off your skin and right back out. Which is why getting soaking wet in the rain can be such an embarrassing situation.

> **Many porous objects—including paper, fabric, tree bark, soil, hair—darken as they are doused in water.**

Why does water dance across a hot frying pan?

It's an old-favorite way to test whether a pan is hot enough—ready, say, to pour in the pancake batter. Heat a frying pan or pancake griddle for a few minutes, then sprinkle in some water. If the drops sizzle and disappear, the pan isn't ready. Wait a minute, then try again. If the drops bead up like water splashed on wax paper and bounce madly around the pan, it's pancake time.

If we'd never seen the skittering water with our own eyes, we might assume just the opposite would happen: At higher temperatures, the water would evaporate faster. Instead, a hotter skillet seems to make water coalesce into tight little beads, which then skip across the surface as if running across hot coals.

This peculiar behavior of water on a heated metal surface even has a name. It's called the Leidenfrost effect, but it has

A Tragic Moment...

First we dance, then we disappear!

nothing to do with frost and everything to do with heat. Johann Gottlob Leidenfrost, a medical doctor in 18th-century Germany, was the first scientist to officially study hot, bouncy water. He observed how water behaved when dropped onto a red-hot iron spoon, measuring how long each drop lasted. Then he wrote up his study in a short work titled *A Tract About Some Qualities of Common Water.*

When a pan's temperature is below 212°F (100°C), water's boiling point, a drop just spreads out and gradually evaporates. As the pan temperature rises above 212°F, a tossed-in drop quickly sizzles away. But keep the pan heating, and presto: rolling balls of water.

So why does water last longer on a surface that is much hotter than its boiling point? It turns out that when water contacts scorching metal, it makes its own insulating layer. How? When water is sprinkled onto a hot frying pan, the bottom of each drop immediately evaporates, forming a layer of vapor. Like a genie on a flying carpet, each drop levitates on its film of steam, flying

> When water is sprinkled onto a hot frying pan, the bottom of each drop immediately evaporates, forming a layer of vapor. Like a genie on a flying carpet, each drop levitates on its film of steam, flying around the surface of the pan.

around the pan's surface for many seconds.

The transition to longlasting drops occurs at or around the Leidenfrost point, or a temperature of about 428°F for water. When drops ride on their steam carpet, they are held about .1 to .2 millimeter above the hot metal surface. This keeps the drop cooler, so it can dart across the pan for up to a minute without disappearing.

The hover effect persists as long as water continues to vaporize from the bottom, until the drop finally vanishes. Heat the pan much past 428°F, and the graceful dance ends, as sprinkled-in water evaporates too quickly.

FAST FACT

The Leidenfrost effect also applies to other liquids. The boiling point of liquid nitrogen at ordinary air pressure is about –320°F. So when liquid nitrogen spills from a tank in a 70°F room, it skitters in drops across the floor, riding a vapor layer like water in a frying pan.

Why does heating water first make a lot of noise, then quiet down as it starts to boil?

Long before the kettle begins to wail, it makes plenty of less-frantic noise. You may hear a buzzing or thrumming sound, along with pops, pings, and growls. While water seems to react harshly to being heated, it mysteriously settles down into a soft, pleasant sound when it finally decides to boil.

Some of the sound may come from the stressed-out walls of the teakettle, which expand a bit when heating and contract when cooling. But most of the noise comes from the

Does Boiling Water Give you a Headache?

Would you believe yes?

heating water itself. The kettle on the burner heats from the bottom up, so the water inside varies wildly in temperature at first. Hotter water at the bottom begins to change from liquid to vapor, forming tiny bubbles that expand like balloons. Like helium balloons in air, the bubbles are less dense than the liquid around them. Breaking free from the hot floor of the kettle, they begin to rise through the cooler water above.

As a bubble rises into water whose temperature is still below the boiling point, the vapor inside it cools and condenses back into liquid. And just like that, the bubble caves in, emitting a mini pop or ping that resonates inside the teakettle. As the kettle heats up, and more and more bubbles form and collapse,

the water begins to get downright noisy.

As the cooler water sinks and warmer water rises, the temperature of the water at the top goes up. Bubble activity gets more and more frenzied, the kettle clamor even harsher. Suddenly, however, the sound mysteriously softens.

Why the downshift? When the water is hot enough, bottom to top, for bubbles to reach the surface without breaking, the teakettle has reached a boil. Once at the surface, bubbles break open with a gentle splash. At a rolling boil, water sounds soft and bubbly, more babbling brook than roaring rapids. Of course, unless you are using an open kettle, the calm will be short-lived, as the whistle swiftly builds up steam.

What Makes a Teakettle Whistle?

While teakettle siren calls can vary from a friendly, high-pitched whistle to a scary air-raid horn, the basic mechanism is the same. Inside the spout of most whistling teakettles are two disks. Each has a hole in the middle. Steam passes through the first hole, into the air-filled space between the disks, and through the second hole. As steam flows across and through the holes, it begins to vibrate and whirl. Escaping through the spout, the turbulent steam causes oscillating pressure in the air, which spreads out into the kitchen and beyond. When the wildly fluctuating sound waves reach our ears (even if we're upstairs), we hear the sound as a whistle.

How come words appear backward in a mirror?

n Lewis Carroll's *Through the Looking Glass,* Alice (of *Alice in Wonderland* fame) discovered that a mirror was a doorway to a parallel universe, where everything is reversed—and anything might happen. While mirrors aren't really an entry to another place, they are very curious objects.

A mirror seems to reverse left and right—making newspaper headlines and T-shirt slogans read backward, and flipping the image of your face and body. But a mirror doesn't flip top and bottom—we don't appear in a full-length mirror with our head at the bottom, feet and floor at the top.

How come? A flat mirror reflects the light bouncing from what we hold up to it—whether a newspaper or our own adorable faces—in straight lines. So the left side of your face appears on the left side of the

Mirror, Mirror on the Wall...

In this mirror I look really fat and small!

In this mirror I look really thin and tall!

In this mirror I can't see myself at all!

mirror, the right side on the right. The top of your head is at the top of the mirror.

A mirror reflects back what we present to it. When we turn a headline around to face the mirror, it reflects it back, letter for letter, left to right: backward. If the headline were on a transparent piece of plastic, and you turned it around to face the mirror, you'd see that it reads backward through the plastic, too.

Likewise, if you hold a piece of photographic film with a picture of you on it up to a mirror, you will see a mirror image of yourself, left and right switched, on the back of the film. In a mirror, you can actually animate that curious image, by moving arms, hands, and head.

(Some say the key to the mirror mystery is that mirrors reverse "in" and "out"—which is why, when you point at a mirror, your reflection points back at you.)

> A mirror reflects back what we present to it. When we turn a headline around to face the mirror, it reflects it back, letter for letter, left to right: backward.

If you really want to, you can see your true image—your face in the world—by using two mirrors. Set the mirrors at a right angle, like two walls meeting in the corner. When you look at your face in the corner—your true face—you may be shocked at what you see.

Despite photos and home videos, few of us have really seen—close up, in real time—what we look like to others. Everyone's face is a little off-kilter in some way—one side of the nose a bit different from the other, eyebrows not exactly matched. Looking in a regular mirror for years, we don't notice these small imbalances.

But looking at your true image makes every quirk evident. Moles and freckles are reversed; your smile is slightly crooked. And perhaps the most unsettling thing: Your hair is parted on the other side. If you can stop looking at your new self, hold up a newspaper—and read the headlines.

Why does the shower curtain blow up and cling to your legs?

Ever find yourself standing in the shower, eyes squeezed shut and covered with soap, when a clammy (and perhaps mildewed) shower curtain suddenly billows in and wraps cozily around your legs? Your shower curtain hasn't gone psycho; it's simply reacting to a dramatic change of pressure in the shower.

Until several years ago, no one had solved the mystery behind the dreaded shower curtain blowback (or blow-in), although there were plenty of ideas. Some suggested that rising shower air, heated by warm water, is replaced by cold room air seeping in from the bottom, causing the curtain to blow in. The problem:

Shower Curtain Alert!

Ya got me!

A bracingly cold shower also causes blow-in.

Other explanations involved Bernoulli's principle. Mathematician Daniel Bernoulli, born in the Netherlands in 1700, is most famous for discovering a fundamental fact of fluids: The pressure of a fluid varies inversely with its speed. So as water flows through a pipe, its pressure drops as it speeds up. Bernoulli's principle applies to everything from the fluid air streaming over a jet's wings to the blood pulsing through our veins.

While Bernoulli was silent on the subject of shower curtains, many thought that his principle could explain the Cling Wrap phenomenon. The air inside a shower, driven by the water, flows faster along the curtain. The resulting low pressure causes the curtain to sink inward.

Well, not exactly. A holiday trip to the in-laws was one scientist's catalyst for finally solving the mystery. University of Massachusetts engineering professor David Schmidt took a shower at his mother-in-law's house and was plagued by an especially clingy curtain. Back home, he modeled a typical shower on his computer, dividing the splashing shower into 50,000 tiny cells. The model accounted for the spray of droplets, including the way drops change shape and break up as they fall. The simulation ran for weeks, doing more than a trillion calculations as it created a 30-second snapshot of shower time.

Schmidt found the Bernoulli effect operating near the showerhead, with air moving faster and pressure dropping on the inside of the shower curtain. However, the spray of water droplets created an even stronger effect. As they accelerate toward the shower floor due to gravity, drops are slowed by friction with the air (aerodynamic drag).

The shower air reacts by beginning to move in a circle, like a dust devil. But the shower devil is horizontal, its very low-pressure vortex aimed at the curtain. The vortex is only strong enough to pull in a lightweight shower curtain. Schmidt says the vortex becomes visible if smoke is blown into a shower.

A heavy shower curtain, or one with magnets, can resist the pull. Low-flow showers create a weaker vortex than big-bruiser showerheads. Curving shower rods, popular in hotels, hold the threatening curtain farther away from the splashing water (and you). Or do away with fickle fabric entirely, and install a shower door.

> **Shower air whirls, like a dust devil tipped on its side.**

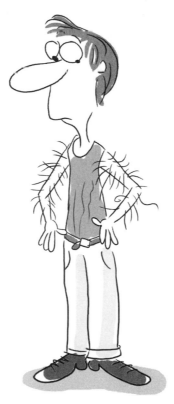

Me, Myself, I

No one knows your body better than you do, but it's still pretty mysterious. Just how do arm hairs know to grow only so far and then stop? And what's the deal with the funny bone (which actually isn't so funny)? Why do we shiver when our bodies are burning up with a fever? And how come we sound so much better singing in the shower than we do outside it? Look into the bathroom mirror—this section's all about you.

Why does my hair get tangled?

The culprit in tangling is the cuticle, the hair strand's outer coating of cells. Scientists compare the cuticle to a shingled roof. Run your fingers down a hair strand; it should feel smooth. But rub against the grain—lifting up the "shingles" of the hair shaft—and the hair will feel rough and ruffled.

Curly or straight, a sheltered hair—untouched by brushing, combing, tugging, heat, and humidity—is like a smooth, shiny cylinder. Real hair, however, is rarely like the perfectly glistening hair of shampoo ads.

A hair strand that has spent months or years growing slowly out of a head has endured its fair share of abuse. Near the root, the just-minted section is covered in flat, neatly arrayed shingles, like a brand-new roof. But traveling farther along the strand, the shingles begin to look worn and scratched.

> The more damaged a hair's cuticle, the more friction between hair strands, and the more tangle-prone the hair.

Still farther from the scalp, the hair's shingles sport jagged edges. Some have loosened and drifted, leaving gaps where the bare hair shaft is exposed. At the very tip of the strand, the shingles may actually have worn off, the hair shaft frayed like an old rope. You guessed it—split ends.

Now, the flatter and more intact the cuticle, the smoother and shinier the hair. The more ruffled-up and damaged the cuticle, the duller and more strawlike the hair—and the more prone to tangle. That's one reason why, after a shower and shampoo, hair near the scalp may be sleek and reflective, while the ends are a dull mass of tangles.

Why does cuticle damage cause tangling? Hair becomes tangled, experts say, when the ruffled-up "shingles" of one strand catch on the equally damaged shingles of nearby strands. The hairs tangle together into loose knots, and the knots may tighten down during a try at combing or brushing. (Ever get a brush caught in your hair?)

The more damaged the cuticle, the more friction between hair strands, and the more tangle-prone the hair. Water raises the scales on hairs, making them even more tangly. Left alone, a bunch of wet tangles can dry into a matted nightmare. Which, as a last resort, may even have to be cut out of the hair.

What ruffles the cuticle? Blow-drying, perms, straightening and dyeing sessions, brushing hair too often and too roughly.

Conditioners help prevent tangling by temporarily smoothing out the cuticle's rough edges. The slick coating helps strands slip apart instead of snarl. Hair products that are more acidic than alkaline will also help the cuticle lie flat, keeping hair tangle-free and shiny. Such products are called acidifiers or citrifiers. They are actually updates of an old homemade cuticle tonic: rinsing hair in lemon juice.

A Tangled Tale...

Oh, What bad luck. My brush is stuck...

Trapped in my 'do for a week or two...

Guess I'll need lemon juice to pull it through.

How does the hair on our arms know to stop growing?

Whether a hair is rooted on your head and looking forward to grazing the middle of your back someday, or rooted on your arm and destined for getting caught in your watchband, each hair starts out the same.

The cells fill with keratin, a tough protein that also makes fingernails. When the slender cells reach their maximum length, they die, piling up in a tube. New cells joining at the bottom push this tube up through the skin. Presto: a hair.

Head hair grows from ½ to 1 inch a month. Each follicle has a set growth

Disgusting, but fun!

phase—the length of time it will steadily churn out new hair cells. For an average head-hair follicle, the growth phase lasts three years or more. Then the follicle stops making new cells down below, and the hair shaft breaks off at the scalp. After a few months' rest, the follicle revs up and jumps back into the hair business.

The growth phase of head hair varies from person to person and also changes as we age. If your follicles have a long growth phase, plus your hair grows quickly during the phase, you can grow your hair very long (long enough to sit on, if you wish). It all depends on the genes you inherited from your parents.

Hair growth in eyebrows, nose, on arms and legs, and on other body parts like chest and back is also controlled by genes. Why do these hairs stop short? The cells that make arm, eyebrow, and other short hairs are programmed to have very brief growth cycles—measured in a few months. The hairs grow slowly, too. So hair on these body parts remains short—from less than an inch (as in eyebrow hair), to a bit more than an inch (as in body hair).

> **Each hair follicle has a set growth phase—the length of time it will steadily churn out new hair cells. For an average head-hair follicle, the growth phase lasts three years or more.**

Why? Take the eyebrows. Eyebrows keep sweat from running freely into the eyes, and also help us convey emotions through facial expressions like surprise, or anger. Short eyebrows—rather than twin eyebrow ponytails—suit this purpose. And hair on arms, legs, and chest are remnants of the coat of hair that kept our primate ancestors warm and protected from the elements.

Of course, there's always that rogue hair that has its instructions scrambled (although no one knows exactly why or how). The late scientist Edward Teller was famous for his scarily long eyebrows. And you may have noticed a weird hair sprouting from your body that seems bent on being long enough to braid.

Many men find that as they age, nose and ear hair go a little crazy, even as scalp hair is thinning. Scientists say that it's a result of male hormones called androgens. Which is why women, whose bodies make fewer androgens, don't usually open their birthday presents and find electric nose-hair clippers.

Why do we have eyebrows?

Two slim patches of hair, one above each eye, like twin caterpillars: Eyebrows are one of evolution's more clever uses of body hair. The brow bone juts out above eyes, protecting them. And the multitasking brow hairs act as handy-dandy filters and as conveyers of emotion.

Spend any time in the sun, and you'll realize your forehead is rich in sweat glands. A sweating forehead helps keep the head (and brain) from overheating as sweat evaporates into the air. And as sweat rolls down the forehead, the eyebrows help trap this salty, stinging liquid before it can drip into our eyes.

Likewise, eyebrows help keep rain out of our eyes when we are caught in a downpour. Like the gutters on a house, angled eyebrow hairs direct liquids away from the eyes and down the temples.

Eyebrows may also warn of an insect approaching the eye, since a crawling bug causes hairs to move to and fro like grass. These little hair strips also catch dust and dirt, like two doormats positioned above the eyes.

> Eyebrows can warn of an insect approaching the eye, since a crawling bug causes hairs to move to and fro like grass.

Eyebrows, like head hair, are also a kind of adornment. Like dirt-catching eyelashes, eyebrows accentuate the eyes and make us more attractive to other people. Which is why there's a market not just for mascara, but for eyebrow pencils, gels, and tweezers to create just the right thickness, shape, and arch.

Fashions in eyebrows come and go, from the pencil-thin flapper look of the 1930s to the bushy brows of the 1980s. But shaving off the eyebrows has rarely caught on, since it deprives us of a key element of

facial expression. One of the main functions of eyebrows, scientists say, is to convey emotion.

Other animals have eyebrows, but human eyebrows stand out on otherwise almost hairless skin. Think of eyebrows knit in concentration . . . raised in surprise . . . or set in a stern frown. Even from some distance away, we check out other people's facial expressions—and especially their eyebrows—to figure out their mood. This has obvious survival value, whether you are being approached by an angry member of another tribe or an angry teacher from across the room.

FAST FACT

Scientists say the 100-millisecond "eyebrow flash" is a particularly important means of communication. This brief brow raise signals welcome, agreement, approval, or appreciation.

BROW TALK

How come we can't sleep with our eyes open?

Scientists aren't entirely sure why human beings sleep with their eyes closed. But they say it makes sense for several reasons. The lids covering our vulnerable eyes protect them from dirt, drying out, and from what we might do while we're asleep (like turning over and pressing an open eye into a pillow—or a cave floor).

But more important, having our eyes closed helps our bodies produce the hormones that cause us to sleep. The hormone melatonin regulates the body's circadian rhythms, including the sleep/wake cycle. Melatonin is synthesized in the brain's pineal gland. But it's also manufactured by the eyes themselves, in the retina. Darkness triggers its production; bright light stops it.

Seeing While ZZZing

You're asleep and your blink switch is off. "Ok..."

Your eyes stay open... "Ugh!"

and dry out like potato chips. "Ick"

According to recent studies with birds, the eyes function as a biological clock for the entire body. So sleeping with closed eyes is part of resetting our internal clock, keeping our body in sync with the light and dark cycle of each day on Earth.

Even though closed-eye sleeping in humans is the norm, we can be asleep with our eyes half- or fully open (especially during a long, boring lecture). And eyes are open during sleepwalking. (Which is why you can safely walk downstairs, get a glass of water, and climb back into bed, never waking up.)

Other animals have different sleeping styles. Fish sleep with their eyes completely open. And some animals will sleep with one eye open when necessary. If a sleeping bird feels vulnerable, half of its brain will actually remain awake, reflected in one open eye.

In a study of sleepy ducks lined up in a row, ducks in the protected center slept with both eyes closed. But the ducks on either end tended to sleep with one eye open. Web-footed sentries, they kept the eye facing away from their fellow ducks open, half their brain alert and attuned to danger.

Scientists call this monocular sleeping,

Having our eyes closed helps our bodies produce the hormones that cause us to sleep.

in contrast to the binocular sleeping we humans are fond of. Monocular sleeping apparently works best when animals aren't too tired. In studies, sleep-deprived chickens closed both eyes, indicating an overwhelming need to put their whole brain to sleep.

Whales, dolphins, and some reptiles seem to engage in half-brain sleeping, too. And sea lions, seals, and some manatees also apparently keep half their brain awake when they need to.

But even when we wake up in the morning, bright light streaming into wide-open eyes, our human brains may not have totally escaped the clutches of sleep. Scientists call it sleep inertia—you're officially awake, but your brain hasn't yet ramped up to full power. In one study, volunteers shown simple math problems three minutes after awakening from a full night's sleep did only 65 percent as well as usual. In fact, it took more than two hours for their brains to completely wake up to the task. It turns out thinking ability is diminished more by morning grogginess than by sleep deprivation—an argument against sleeping until the last possible minute before that big exam.

How do the kidneys make urine?

Picture a kidney bean, the kind you often find in chili or three-bean salad. Now imagine that kidney bean swelled almost to the size of your fist. That's what a kidney looks like. (The bean is nearly the right color, too—kidneys are purple-brown.)

Kidneys are just as essential as our pumping hearts: They filter out waste from

> **Kidneys filter out waste products that would otherwise poison us.**

the blood and then manufacture urine to get rid of those toxins, which would otherwise poison us. The kidneys also make sure that sodium, potassium, calcium, and other minerals stay at correct levels in the blood. They maintain the body's water at a normal level, they help regulate blood pressure, and they prompt bone marrow to make more

INSIDE REPORT: NEPHRONS AT WORK

red blood cells if the supply is low—all by sending messenger hormones into the bloodstream. The kidneys are in effect analyzing your blood as they process it.

Nephron sounds like the dying planet the alien invaders abandoned in favor of conquering Earth. But a nephron is the kidney's tiny filtering unit. A human kidney is only about 4.5 inches long, yet a million nephrons are packed inside.

Each nephron consists of a thin tube surrounded by a ball of tiny blood vessels. Like coffee filters, nephrons filter blood's watery part, reabsorbing some substances (like sugar) and getting rid of waste. What's in the waste? A main ingredient is urea, left after you digest the protein in your chicken sandwich, or from the small amounts of muscle that broke down during gym class. The waste may also include toxic chemicals, and remnants of drugs such as antibiotics and aspirin. The kidneys secrete these wastes into the urine they make from excess water.

Living much of life upside down? You're in luck. Urine doesn't flow from the kidneys down to the bladder because of gravity—it's squeezed from the kidneys by muscles in the tubes connecting them to the bladder. So even if you're hanging from a tree, standing on your head, or floating in zero gravity in space, your bladder will still fill with urine.

Kidneys 101

- Your kidneys are situated on either side of your spine, under the last rib, surrounded by a thick layer of protective fat. Your right kidney is a bit lower than your left, shoved down by the bulky liver above it.
- Your kidneys process about 45 gallons of blood a day—720 cups—to remove about 6 to 8 cups of excess water and waste.
- By the end of each hour, all your blood has flowed through the kidneys for cleaning.

How come urine is yellow? Does it ever reflect the color of the food we've eaten?

Urine's normal color is pale yellow. But the color of urine can actually change, taking on a rainbow of hues, depending on what we drink or eat, what medicines we're taking, and what illnesses we're unlucky enough to have.

As blood flows through the kidneys, it is processed by tiny filtering units, called nephrons. Some water and other substances (sugar, vitamins, amino acids from proteins) are reabsorbed and sent back into the bloodstream for reuse. What's remains behind is urine: 95 percent water, plus urea (left over after your body digests protein),

Reasons for Rainbow Urine...

salts, minerals, creatinine (from muscle breakdown), uric acid, hormone remnants, and toxins.

Why is urine yellow? Urine has a lemon tint because red blood cells don't last forever. The lifespan of a red blood cell is about 120 days; worn-out cells are processed by the liver. When the liver breaks down the hemoglobin in a red blood cell, a yellow pigment called urochrome is left over. Urochrome passes into the bloodstream and is filtered out as a waste product by the kidneys. Presto: yellow urine.

But urine may be almost colorless if you drink a lot of water. On the other hand, if you are sweating heavily and drinking little water, urine becomes concentrated, turning the color of dark amber.

A red tint to urine may indicate a small amount of blood, perhaps from a bladder infection, kidney or bladder stones, or even from running with a full bladder. Any hint of blood in the urine warrants a trip to the doctor. But some people get reddish-purple urine whenever they eat beets. If urine is acidic, eating blackberries can turn it red. If

The color of urine depends on how hydrated you are. It may be almost colorless if you drink a lot of water. But if you are sweating heavily and drinking little water, urine becomes concentrated, turning the color of dark amber.

urine is alkaline, eating rhubarb can give it that rosy glow. Lead and mercury poisoning can also cause red urine.

Greenish urine can be caused by a urinary tract infection, bile pigment, or certain drugs. Spring-green urine can be caused by taking an excess of B vitamins.

Urine with a Windex-blue tint (in babies, blue diaper syndrome) can mean you inherited a tendency to have high levels of calcium. But it can also mean an infection with *Pseudomonas* bacteria.

Dark yellow urine may be a sign of a liver disorder called jaundice. Too many carrots or too much vitamin C can turn urine Halloween orange. Dyes in foods like candy and soft drinks or in pill coatings can also color urine red, green, or blue.

Brown, smoky, or black urine can be caused by the liver disease hepatitis, the presence of blood, antimalaria drugs, copper poisoning, the cancer melanoma, certain laxatives—even eating too many fava beans.

If your urine is an unusual color, talk to your doctor.

How come we throw up?

Nearly all of us have vomited at least once in our lives, especially as kids. You may throw up during an illness, lose your cookies after a churning amusement park ride, or barf after running all-out in the school track meet. You may even throw up before giving a speech in front of a big group.

Vomiting is swallowing's opposite: Food is ejected, sometimes violently, from the stomach through the mouth. Puking is the body's valiant attempt to rid itself of irritants or toxins and also to steer us away from potential harm. A very foul odor—say, of putrid meat—may make us instantly nauseated; we may even throw up. This unpleasant experience ensures that we won't actually take a bite of something rotten.

Think *vomit*, and we automatically think *stomach*. But next time you feel the urge to download dinner, blame your brain. Scientists say the brain has its very own Vomit Central.

This bilateral "vomitation" center in the brain's medulla, or lower brain stem, is where an upset stomach gets its marching orders.

Vomit consists of half-digested food, perhaps with some recognizable chunks of your last meal (stray green bean, anyone?), mixed with mucus, corrosive stomach acid, saliva, and other digestive chemicals, like bile. (It's the bile that gives vomit its lovely greenish tinge and long-lasting flavor.)

Vomiting involves a symphony of activity, which science has yet to completely figure out. Signals from our upset stomach and intestines travel up the vagus nerve to the brain. Meanwhile, near the vomit center, the chemoreception trigger center monitors the body for chemical imbalances and toxins, also passing the information along to Vomit Central. Signals from other places, from the common bile duct to the inner ear, can also play a part.

Vomiting's stage 1 is nausea, that queasy, sickening feeling that makes us lose our appetite. The stomach's digestive activity may become sluggish, while the upper intestine may become positively hyperactive.

Stage 2 is retching. In these "dry heaves,"

Puking is the body's attempt to rid itself of irritants or toxins and to steer us away from potential harm.

the chest and abdominal muscles contract, lifting the top of the stomach into the esophagus. Retching primes the pump for puking.

Stage 3 is show time. Vomit Central signals the small intestine to send some of its nearly digested (but possibly spoiled) food back into the stomach. The diaphragm contracts downward, allowing the esophagus and its doorway to the stomach to relax open. Intestinal wall muscles squeeze the stomach and its contents. Meanwhile, the stomach's lower exit door snaps shut. So there's no way out but up.

What makes us vomit? Distending the stomach by eating too much, anxiety, migraine headaches, the hormones of early pregnancy, some drugs and chemotherapy, food poisoning, head injuries, motion sickness, drinking too much alcohol. And, especially, getting a gastrointestinal bug (like winter vomiting disease and the infamous Norwalk virus). Rarer causes include intestinal blockage and kidney failure.

The silver lining? Physicians say that no matter how awful you feel just before you vomit, you will probably feel amazingly better afterward.

Why is blood blue in our veins, but red when it comes out of a cut?

Look at the inside of your wrist, and you might see them: blue veins, criss-crossing like tiny tree branches. It's natural to assume that blood running through our veins tints them blue, and that blue blood turns red when it hits (oxygen-rich) air.

As it turns out, the color of blood does change. But the change happens inside the body, and it's not a shift from blue to red.

Blood's natural color is red. The red

FAST FACT

In our faces, tiny blood vessels called capillaries lie just .001 inch beneath the surface of the skin. Which is why your nose turns Rudolph-red when you eat hot food, and a red blush spreads across your face when you're embarrassed. If our capillaries contained blue blood, we'd all blush blue.

comes from the erythrocytes, or red blood cells, which make up about 40 percent of blood volume. It's the job of red blood cells to ferry oxygen all around the body, where it's soaked up by hardworking cells in the brain, kidneys, skin, and other organs.

Red blood cells pick up oxygen in the lungs, where it ends up after we inhale it from the air. The erythrocytes travel through arteries with their oxygen cargo, like train cars on branching tracks.

Inside each erythrocyte are some 250 million hemoglobin molecules composed of proteins and iron. Hemoglobin is dark red in color. Oxygen, it turns out, happily gloms onto iron. And when it does, hemoglobin brightens to fire-engine red. That's the color of the oxygen-laden blood coursing through our arteries.

Once the oxygen is delivered, hemoglobin still has work to do. The cells receiving oxygen give up carbon dioxide (CO_2), the waste product of their energetic activity. Hemoglobin obligingly carts the CO_2 to the lungs by the back roads of the veins. From the lungs, we exhale the carbon dioxide into the air.

Having given up its oxygen, blood traveling through the veins is dark red, a wine-colored maroon. (However, when blood from a vein spills out of a cut, it may absorb enough oxygen from the air to brighten up a bit.)

So why do veins look blue, rather than burgundy? Scientists at a laser research center in Toronto set up an experiment using blood-filled glass tubes in place of

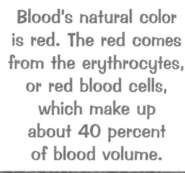

Blood's natural color is red. The red comes from the erythrocytes, or red blood cells, which make up about 40 percent of blood volume.

veins and a fatty, milky fluid in place of fair skin. The homemade "veins" appeared red before they were immersed in the fluid. But submerged to a certain depth, the blood-carrying tubes turned blue.

How come? The researchers found that when ordinary light falls on our skin, longer-wavelength red light travels further into the skin than shorter-wavelength blue light before being reflected back out. So when a vein is at least .02 inch below the skin's surface, blue light reflects out before it can be absorbed by the vein, and the vein will look blue. Veins closer to the surface look red.

BLOOD CLOT CENTRAL

PAPER CUT ALERT!!

Send in the fibrin, she's opening the junk mail!

Why do wisdom teeth come in so late, and why must they be pulled?

Wisdom teeth are one of nature's little mysteries: teeth that finally push through our gums when we are teenagers, only to be yanked out by the dentist as soon as they're discovered. Wisdom teeth are the appendixes of the tooth world.

Actually, wisdom teeth are the final set of molars to sprout in the mouth, back in the far corners. Molars are flat-top teeth (unlike the pointy, vampirish canines).

The molar specialty is grinding food down into fine particles, like a mortar and pestle.

While wisdom teeth seem to come in very late, they are actually right on schedule according to the tooth timetable. The first set of four molars appears around the age of 6 or 7, the second set at age 12 or 13. The third set—the wisdom teeth—begin showing up around ages 16 to 21.

According to the *Oxford English Dictionary*, the term *wisdom teeth* has been around since at least the 1600s. Why *wisdom* teeth? The third molars usually appear just about the time we are becoming grown-ups and have supposedly achieved adult wisdom.

But unlike other teeth, which seem to

FAST FACT

In 1974, scientists discovered a skull of the early human species Australopithecus afarensis. *The skull belonged to a long-dead girl that scientists named Lucy. Noting that her wisdom teeth had erupted but hadn't yet worn down, they guessed that Lucy was about 20 when she died—some 3 million years ago.*

arrive and get straight to work chewing without any trouble, the third molars are the mouth's problem children. Wisdom teeth may grow in at odd angles, peek only partially out of the gum, or even get stuck underneath the gum and bone. A wisdom tooth can even aim straight at the molar next to it.

> A wisdom tooth may grow in at an odd angle or even aim straight at the molar next to it.

A partially erupted wisdom tooth may trap food and bacteria below the gum line, or between itself and the healthy tooth next door, leading to infection. Growing out at all angles, wisdom teeth can injure second molars. Which is why dentists often recommend pulling the teeth before they can do much damage.

If wisdom teeth are such a pain in the mouth, why do we even have them? It's a primate tradition. For example, apes have wisdom teeth, but the teeth appear around age 11. (Non-human primates, which don't have as big brains and as much to learn as we do, have shorter childhoods.)

Our ancestors made good use of their wisdom teeth. A rough, natural diet required a lot of grinding down. Early humans had larger, heavier jaws, with plenty of room for 32 full-size teeth.

But as we humans evolved bigger brains requiring more skull room, jaw size tended to diminish. And so today, the last teeth to grow in—the wisdom teeth—often find the space that remains too cramped for comfort.

Call 'em the Rowdy, Club-going Teeth

They arrive late...

They don't care if there's enough room...

And they get thrown out a lot.

Chew on this...

The big BAAAD molars are here!

BAM!

Stop pushing!

DENTIST

And don't come back!

Why do we sound so much better when we sing in the shower?

Even if your family groans when you sing along to the car radio, even if you didn't make the cut for the choir, and even if you got asked to be the drummer rather than the lead vocalist in your friends' garage band, you sound exactly like your favorite pop (or opera) star in the shower.

How come? And why do we enjoy singing in the shower to begin with?

First, there's the psychology and brain chemistry of shower crooning. In the shower, we are behind closed doors (bathroom and shower), water blasting. Under the comforting blanket of hot water and steam,

Best Place to Record a Song...
(don't try this at home !)

Tra-La-La!

we feel relaxed and unselfconscious. The splashing water also produces negative ions, which are thought to make us happier. And so we are inclined to burst into song, confident that no one can really hear us, anyway.

But we probably wouldn't keep on singing if we didn't sound so mysteriously good. We can thank shower acoustics for putting us in the running to be the next Bathroom Idol.

Scientists say that a shower stall acts a bit like an electronic sound mixer, naturally improving the quality of your singing voice. How it works: The hard tile or glass in most showers absorbs very little sound, bouncing most sound waves right back. (Ordinary ceramic tile reflects about 98 percent of the sound striking it.) As the sound ricochets back and forth between walls in the confined space, your voice is effectively amplified. Presto: instant vocal power.

Meanwhile, the shower also acts like a bass booster. A cavelike space such as a shower stall has its own special resonant frequencies: Sounds that happen to match those frequencies will resonate. In an ordinary, smallish shower, the resonating frequencies fall in the lower range of the human voice. So when you sing low notes, the shower obligingly amplifies those sounds, like turning up the bass on a stereo.

Finally, there's a touch of reverberation. As sound waves bounce around the shower stall, some travel longer paths before entering your ears. This stretches out the sound, like an electric organ played in reverb mode. And the prolonged, echoing notes make your voice sound richer to you.

Reverberation also makes you sound like you're in tune, even when you're really not. As your voice bounces between the walls (and through the spray of water, where sound waves temporarily accelerate), the sound gets a bit blurry. The fuzziness smoothes out variations in singing pitch, rather like a karaoke machine.

Shower karaoke is an illusion, of course; you're not really hearing your true singing voice. But to feel like a pop star for 15 minutes in the morning, shower in a smooth-tiled stall with a glass door (instead of a curtain) for the best reflections. And for the most impressive bass boost, make sure your shower is on the small side. Scientists say that bigger-size spaces have their strongest resonant frequencies below the range of human hearing.

> A shower stall acts a bit like an electronic sound mixer, naturally improving the quality of your singing voice.

Why does it hurt so much when you bump your funny bone?

If you've ever hit your elbow—especially the underside—against something hard, you know the feeling. It's a vibrating, tingling pain, extending down to your pinky finger. It's the kind of feeling that makes you jump around holding your elbow, unable to do more than yelp for a few seconds.

Congratulations. You've struck your funny bone. Now wasn't that hilarious?

Actually, not so much. The funny bone sensation, it turns out, is funny only in the peculiar, not the "ha-ha," sense of funny. And to make matters really peculiar, it's not, in fact, a bone that makes your arm feel funny.

Bend your elbow—go ahead, we'll wait—and feel around for bumps. There's the pointy outside bump, the one you use when elbowing someone in the ribs to get their attention. Then there's that bony knob on the inside of the joint.

Running through a passageway between the bumps is the source of all the funniness—a big, fat nerve. It's called the ulnar nerve, after the ulna bone in the lower arm. The ulnar nerve runs from the neck into the hand. It sends nerve impulses back and forth from the spine to the ring and pinky fingers, and controls the small muscles of the hand, helping us pick things up.

So far, sounds like a typical nerve. But what makes the ulnar different is its pathway to the hand. Most nerves lie under a padding of fat, protected from the bumps of everyday life. The ulnar nerve runs in a bony groove (the cubital tunnel) through the elbow, where all that stands between tabletop and nerve is a thin layer of fat and skin.

So when you bump your elbow in just the right spot, the ulnar nerve is slammed between a rock (your bone) and a hard place (the table or wall or chair arm). Hitting raw nerve is no fun (ever had the Novocaine wear off while getting a deep cavity filled?).

The exquisitely sensitive nerve fires off an electrical impulse, and you feel a tingling, electric pain that travels from your elbow, down your arm, and into the fourth and fifth fingers of your hand. Ouch.

Some say the funny bone is "humorous" because the ulnar nerve runs along the humerus bone in the upper arm. But the only thing funny about hitting the ulnar nerve is that the pain doesn't feel like a cut or a burn or a bruise. It's an odd sort of pain—kind of excruciating, actually. (So just say no to anything advertised as tickling your funny bone.)

> HA HA Ouchie!

Running through a passageway between the bumps in your elbow is the source of all the funniness—a big, fat nerve, known as the ulnar nerve.

FAST FACT

Have you ever spent a long time with your elbow bent, weight resting on the joint, and had the side of your hand go numb? Stretching out your arm restores the feeling.

How come I shiver and feel so cold when I have a high fever?

Lie in the sun on a summer day and as your skin heats, you feel warmer and warmer. But come down with a fever, and even as your skin feels burning-hot, you feel icy cold. Your temperature rises, but you have the shivering chills, even as you pile on the blankets.

Our normal body temperature ranges between about 97 and 100°F. If our temperature is too high, we get the signal to sweat and feel like changing into lightweight clothing. Hidden in the center of the brain,

FAST FACT

Our body temperature is usually lowest in the morning, higher in the late afternoon and evening. But the temperature doesn't vary much, since the body has its own thermostat.

the hypothalamus gland keeps our body temperature in a narrow range by comparing the temperature of the blood to its thermostat set point. If our temperature drops too low, our bodies may shiver to make heat, and we'll feel like putting on a sweatshirt or diving under the covers.

When we get sick, however, our inner thermostat can be reset, the heat turned up to fight the infection. Immune system cells become activated during an infection and float through the blood, targeting bacteria and viruses. Some of these immune cells produce proteins called cytokines. These particular cytokines are pyrogenic— they cause fever. Floating through the bloodstream, the pyrogens come in contact with nerve cells around the outside of the brain, which send messages to the hypothalamus and brain stem.

In a fever, messenger hormones cause blood to flow away from the skin to deeper

layers in the body, minimizing heat loss. Sweating dwindles to a minimum, and the body's temperature may rise 2 to 7 degrees. The extra heat seems to make immune cells better at killing bacteria, as well as making it harder for invading microorganisms to reproduce.

So why do we feel so cold, when we are actually heating up like a slice of toast? Once its set point has been raised—say, to 102°F—the hypothalamus sends a message to the 98.6°F (37°C) body that it's too cold. Shivering and chills ensue. And until your temperature rises to the new set point, you feel teeth-chatteringly cold and dive

> When we get sick, our body's inner thermostat can be reset—the heat gets turned up to fight the infection.

under the nearest blanket. Once your body's temperature has reached it new set point, you will no longer feel so chilly.

Just as you paradoxically felt cold as you heated up, so will you feel hot as you cool down. When your body has decided it doesn't need to be baking at 102°F anymore, your set point may be reset to, say, 99°F. Now the hypothalamus is telling the body that it's too hot—by about 3 degrees. So as your fever breaks and your body begins to cool, you suddenly feel too warm. You begin sweating and throw off the covers. Once your temperature matches your set point again, you'll feel just right.

Hypothalamic Hokey-Pokey!

Pull your right leg in!

Push your left leg out!

Pull your left leg in and shake it all about. You curl your body up...

Then you moan and shake...That's what it's all about!

Why can't we tickle ourselves?

Are you ticklish? Do you giggle uncontrollably, squirm away, run screaming? The sound of two kids in a tickling war, laughing so hard they can't stand up, can make anyone within earshot start laughing, too. In fact, even the verbal threat of being tickled ("Coochie-coo!") can provoke a giggling fit. And the sight of wiggling fingers coming your way, scientists say, can produce the same reactions in your brain as actually being tickled.

What is it that makes tickling so frantically funny? Scientists say the tickling effect depends crucially on the element of surprise. Even if you expect to be tickled—even if your sister is approaching menacingly from the other side of the couch—you don't know the exact instant it will happen. It's a lot like someone jumping out from behind a door in a dark room—or a spider suddenly dropping from the ceiling onto your shoulder. Despite the fact that it drives us crazy, studies show that most people like being tickled, seeing tickling as a playful way to express affection.

If tickling is so entertaining, then why—during the commercials—can't we just tickle ourselves, provoking gales of giggles?

FAST FACT

According to one study, the most ticklish parts of the body are the underarms, followed by the waist, ribs, soles of the feet, behind the knees, throat, neck, and palms. Another study found that the right foot is more ticklish than the left.

THE NO-GIGGLE TICKLE

No tee-hees, Nothing at all.

Me, Myself, I

Researchers say it's because the brain is so good at screening out sensations of what it knows we ourselves are doing. If it weren't, we'd have a hard time just getting through an afternoon.

Why? All day long, our senses are besieged by incoming sensations from the world at large. There is also the constant drumbeat of sensations arising from our own actions: the pressure of the floor on our walking feet; of our own arms resting against our sides as we sit; the movement of our tongue as we speak or chew. The brain mostly ignores these and many other expected sensations.

But if, during lunch, someone sneaks up behind you and lightly touches your shoulder, you may literally jump out of your chair. Your brain is programmed to react on full alert to such unexpected, not-coming-from-you sensations. Reacting to surprises helps keep us safe, since a surprising touch or encounter (think poisonous spider or purse snatcher) can mean danger.

The sight of wiggling fingers can produce the same reactions in your brain as actually being tickled.

So when you try to tickle yourself, it's a ho-hum situation for the brain. Scientists doing tickle research (publishing papers with titles like "Central Cancellation of Self-Produced Tickle Sensation") have looked at the brains of people being tickled. On an MRI, scientists say, a self-tickle causes very little activity in the brain's somatosensory cortex, which lights up when the tickling is being done by someone (or something) else.

Studies show it's the cerebellum, located at the rear of the brain, that predicts the consequences of a self-tickling movement, sending out the signal to cancel a ticklish response when it's "only you." Researchers have also found that the response to outside tickling was more intense when an expected tickle was delayed by a split second, producing a surprise similar to real-life tickling. The more unpredictable the tickle, the more delicious the panic we feel.

105

What are our tonsils for?

Once upon a time, getting your tonsils out was almost a rite of passage in childhood. Around age seven or eight or so, usually after a string of strep throat infections, you went into the hospital for an operation and woke up without your tonsils. Afterward, you got to eat lots of ice cream to soothe your painful throat. Like another frequently removed organ, the appendix, tonsils were seen as almost disposable body parts—not very important; won't be missed.

Today, however, opinions about these two little clumps of tissue are changing. Doctors aren't so quick to remove them. And researchers are discovering that the tonsils are actually front-line guards in the defense against bacteria, viruses, and other pathogens making their way into the body.

In fact, there are four different kinds of tonsils ringing the back of the throat,

including tonsils at the root of the tongue and tonsils behind the nose (the adenoids). The tonsil collection is part of the body's immune system, the defensive network that includes the lymph nodes, spleen, and all the varieties of disease-fighting white blood cells.

But it's the twin palatine tonsils, situated on either side of the dangly uvula above the back of the tongue, that we know as *the* tonsils. These tonsils are fleshy, olive-shaped pink masses. If you look in a mirror, open your mouth wide, stick your tongue out, and say "aaaahhh," you should be able to see the two spongy-looking tonsils.

The tonsils are made of lymphoid tissue, like the lymph nodes that stud the body in spots like the neck and underarms. Even though tonsils are small, their surface area is large. Cleverly, each tonsil has 10 to 30 deep crypts, or closed caves. So germs from food, air, saliva, or other sources easily come into contact with part of the tonsils' surface as they pass through the back of the throat. Meanwhile, the tonsils are teeming with lymphocytes, white blood cells whose

For a long time, tonsils were seen as almost disposable body parts and were often removed. Today, however, opinions about these two little clumps of tissue are changing.

business is to identify incoming bacteria and viruses and direct the immune system's fight against the invaders.

Recent studies show that tonsils may play an important role in stopping lung infections—like flu—before they get a foothold. Besides their local, back-of-the-throat activities, the tonsils also seem to influence how the rest of the immune system targets an infection. The tonsils sit in a strategic position in the body—a key entry point for pathogens, an open doorway. By "sampling" bacteria, viruses, and other intruders that stream their way from mouth and nose, tonsils help the body mount a concerted defense.

Tonsils are most sensitive, researchers say, when we are three to ten years old. During those years, it's common for tonsils to become swollen and inflamed when they get overwhelmed by, say, strep bacteria. Antibiotics give the immune system a fighting chance to douse the infection. But if recurring infections cause abscesses in the tonsils, or if tonsil size interferes with breathing during sleep, the doctor often will still recommend removal.

Why are our five fingers different lengths?

Hands and fingers aren't unique to human beings; other primates have them, too. Take a look at a gorilla's or chimp's hands and you'll see a set of four fingers, varying in length from index to pinky, along with a real thumb. (While other animals, such as raccoons, have paws that resemble hands, official "hands" belong only to primates.)

Hands are useful for grasping—hanging on to a tree limb (or hanging on to a ladder), picking berries (or picking up groceries), throwing a clod of dirt (or throwing a baseball). If our fingers were the same length, our hands wouldn't be such flexible tools.

When we hold a spherical object like an orange in the palm of our hand, the fingers actually curve around evenly, giving us a firm grip. Tapering fingers (and strong thumbs) allowed early humans to use

specially shaped stones to smash, scrape, and cut other objects. (A long pinky finger would be more likely to get caught and squashed.) Besides precision grips, our different-length fingers also provide a balanced support for crawling or leaning on our hands.

Among different species of primates—from baboons to monkeys—fingers and thumbs vary in shape and length. Long, thin fingers are best for tree swinging. Chimpanzees, who themselves make and use simple tools like termite catchers, have hands that most resemble ours.

Most primates, from chimpanzees, gorillas, and orangutans to Old World monkeys, have opposable thumbs that can bend outward at up to a 90-degree angle from the other fingers. The most developed opposable thumbs are handy for holding small objects between the thumb and index finger.

Thumbs have only one middle joint, rather than the two joints found on the four regular fingers. The four longer fingers can curl further around an object, while powerful muscles allow the thumb to lock in the grip, viselike. Human opposable thumbs are, compared to those of other primates, bigger and stronger. A chimp can pick up a peanut from the ground but can't open a tightened lid on a jar of peanut butter. Our own powerful thumbs seem to have evolved in tandem with our toolmaking skills.

Among individuals in each primate species, fingers and thumbs vary, too. Compare your hands to those of your friends, and you'll see subtle and not-so-subtle differences. Boys and men often have longer ring than index fingers. Girls and women tend to have similar-length ring and index fingers, or shorter ring fingers. Scientists say the differences are due to the influence of the hormones estrogen and testosterone in the womb.

> Besides giving us a more precise grip, our different-length fingers provide a balanced support for crawling or leaning on our hands.

FAST FACT

One study found that male physicists, chemists, and mathematicians had ring and index fingers about equal in length, while male economists and social scientists had longer ring fingers. Another study found that men with substantially shorter index than ring fingers tended to be more physically aggressive than others.

Spotty Fingernails

At some point, you've probably noticed a white spot or two on your fingernails. What are they? Some cultures see them as a good luck sign and even call them fortune or gift spots. There's also the old idea that someone with a white spot is in love, or that the number of white spots equals the number of sweethearts a girl has.

But falling in love or winning the lottery actually have nothing to do with white spots, unless you happen to hit one of your fingers in all the excitement. Dermatologists (skin doctors) say that white spots and smeary streaks happen to all of us, and are usually nothing to worry about.

The official name for white nail spots is the somewhat scary-sounding punctate leukonychia. (In total leukonychia, the entire nail turns white.) Dermatologists say the spots appear because of repeated dings to the nail bed at the base of a fingernail (say, by a striking ball when playing sports). Much rarer causes include infections, systemic illnesses, and dietary deficiencies.

White spots are a mix of keratin (a tough protein) and air. The spots are places where, due to a minor injury to the nail bed, new nail cells were incompletely formed or keratinized. The white spots move toward the tip as the nail is pushed up by new growth from the nail bed. Since a nail grows about .04 inch in ten days, it can take months for the spotted part to reach the tip for trimming off. Meanwhile, you can look at your nail spots and relive memories of all the injuries to your fingers in the past year.

Why do we have wax in our ears?

Suffering from a little waxy build-up? While not so good for polished wooden furniture, it may actually be a positive thing when it comes to ears.

The basic ingredient of earwax is made by thousands of tiny glands studding the outer walls of the ear canal. These glands produce an oily substance called cerumen, which picks up dead skin cells as it wells out. The end result is what we call earwax.

Earwax starts out pale yellow. But by the time it's ready to fall out, debris-encrusted wax is a dark, crumbling mass.

Since sound waves travel through the ear canal on their way to the eardrum, what's the point of clogging the tunnel? Skin lining the canal is very thin and dries out easily. Earwax coats the skin, holding moisture in. But earwax also acts as a water repellent. When shower and pool water run out the way they came, we can avoid the painful infection known as swimmer's ear.

Earwax also acts as a sticky trap for anything that blows (or crawls) into the ear. A plug of earwax may contain tiny hairs, teensy bugs, soot, dust, soil, and bits of plants. Earwax is the body's fly paper.

Ear glands are constantly making fresh new wax underneath the old. Older, dirt-laden wax slowly migrates to the entrance of the ear, helped along by jaw movements as we talk or chew. The old wax, along with dead skin cells, dries up and drops out of the ear, adding to the dust in the world.

Although our ears are self-cleaning, too much wax can occasionally build up. Some clues: Sounds seem more muffled; the ear feels stuffed up; the canal itches or aches. As wax presses on nerves, the throat feels tickly,

> **Earwax starts out pale yellow. But by the time it's ready to fall out, debris-encrusted wax is a dark, crumbling mass.**

and you may develop a slight cough. The affected ear may also buzz or ring (a condition called tinnitus), and you may feel dizzy.

While putting a few drops of mineral oil into the ear may help the plug slip out, other home remedies range from useless to dangerous. Cotton swabs can push wax further into the ear; hairpins can puncture the eardrum. Your family doctor can use ear drops and special tools to remove the wax safely.

Earwax is your friend; squeaky-clean ears actually invite infections. Studies show that fresh cerumen is a natural germicide that can kill staph, strep, and *E. coli* bacteria. So earwax protects the body from intruders trying to enter through a side door.

Continental Earwax Divide

Why do some people have more waxy buildup than others? Part of the answer lies in genes. Some people are born with narrower, clog-prone ear canals, some ear canals are especially hairy, and some just make more wax. Intriguingly, humans from different parts of the world have different earwax. People whose ancestors came from Europe or Africa tend to have "wet" earwax, about half fat by weight. People whose ancestors came from Asia, including Native Americans, tend to have low-fat "dry" earwax.

Why do I see wiggly white shapes when I look into the bright blue sky?

Have you ever looked up into the blue sky on a sunny summer day and then noticed that the sky was covered with a moving field of bright paisley shapes? You may have wondered if there was something wrong with your eyes.

But when you see the blue-sky motion, you are actually watching something moving in your own body. This something is part of the defense system our bodies use to protect us from infection: the white blood cells.

The blue-sky effect was first officially described by a German scientist in 1924 and is sometimes called Scheerer's phenomenon. It is also known as the blue field entoptic phenomenon (*entoptic* means "originating

LEUKOCYTE: THE MUSICAL

113

in the eyeball"). But it wasn't until 1989 that scientists figured out exactly how it worked.

Crisscrossing the eye's retina are many small blood vessels, the capillaries, ferrying the oxygen-rich red blood cells that feed our eyes. But we don't see dark red lines crisscrossing our vision. That's because the brain helpfully edits out the image of the blood-filled capillaries when it processes the images we see.

Most of what moves through the capillaries are red blood cells. But there is also the occasional leukocyte, or white blood cell. When we look up at a bright blue sky, the red blood cells strongly absorb the blue light. But the red blood cells are so close together that they don't show up as individual dark spots. And our visual processing system edits the darkened capillaries out, as usual.

But the occasional white blood cells that pass through *don't* absorb much blue light. They are also much bigger than the red cells. So as they pass by, they act like moving holes in the capillaries. And we see bright, moving white shapes in the sky.

Why do the shapes seem to wriggle and dart? Many of the retina's capillaries are S-shaped. So with each beat of the heart, the white cells move jerkily through the blood vessels, causing us to see bright shapes moving along a snaky path in the sky.

The wiggly spots are paisley- or fish-shaped, with what appear to be little tails. Leukocytes are, in fact, naturally knobby. But some researchers say that the tail is just an afterimage, the glowing image we see after we stare at something very bright, like a lightbulb.

Seeing the white squiggly shapes can actually be a sign that your eyes are healthy. In fact, the blue-field effect is sometimes used to see whether blood flow to the eyes is impaired. Ophthalmologists create the paisley effect using blue light, and then ask the patient to match the shapes they see (and their speed) to a computer-generated screen of moving dots.

FAST FACT

Noticing blue-sky squiggles is different than seeing "floaters." Floaters are debris in the eye's vitreous humor, often appearing as dark shreds that move slowly or not at all. These spots call for a visit to the eye doctor.

How come minty toothpaste makes your mouth feel so cool?

Are you a fan of curiously strong mints, toothpaste that tingles, menthol cough drops that open your stuffed-up nose? How about double-cold mint ice cream? Or mint-infused hair conditioners that deep-freeze your scalp, like being outside in icy weather without a hat?

Even when our minty toothpaste or chewing gum is at room temperature, the brain interprets the sensation we're feeling as "cold." How come?

The main compound that can make mouth or skin feel chilly in a warm room is menthol, a main ingredient of peppermint oil. (Menthol is a kind of plant chemical called

Is it the menthol or...

...is there an AC unit in my mouth?

...is there an ice storm in my mouth?

...is a snowman asleep in my mouth?

115

a terpene. Terpenes also give pine, lemons, camphor, and turpentine their familiar scents.) Until about 2001, scientists weren't sure how menthol created its frigid side effects. They knew that the sensation of heat depends on certain channels in nerve cells (neurons) in places like the mouth and skin. These ion channels open to allow electrically charged sodium and calcium atoms to enter the nerve cell. Signals then travel from neuron to neuron to the spinal cord and brain, which decodes the signal as heat. Interestingly, both warm temperatures and chili peppers trigger the channels to open, leading to the sensation of "hot hot hot."

The equivalent "cool" receptors were discovered when researchers found an ion channel on neurons that opens at temperatures of 46 to 82°F. (While that might not seem cold, to our nearly 99°F

bodies, a temperature of, say, 58°F feels downright chilly.)

And just as the capsaicin in chili peppers opens the hot channels, so menthol opens the cool channels. So like low temperatures, menthol causes neurons to send a "chilly" signal to the brain. When that happens, as the candy commercial goes, we "get the sensation."

Channels that respond to even colder temperatures are yet to be found, but menthol may open those, too. And some scientists argue that our perception of a chill is even more complicated, involving channels that shut down as well as open up in reaction to cold or menthol. Recently, scientists have discovered that menthol also opens up at least one heat channel, perhaps explaining why eating a strong mint is a bit like biting into a burning-hot chili pepper.

Cool Mint Alternatives

How about attaching mint's icy sensation to other favorite flavors and scents? In 2001, food scientists in Germany announced that they had identified four cool-triggering compounds in the dark malt used to make certain beers. Starting with the malt chemicals, researchers have created synthetic compounds that produce extreme cooling effects in the mouth and skin, 35 to 250 times as intense as those triggered by menthol. The idea is to give products, from soft drinks to shower gels, a minty-cool sensation . . . minus the mint.

Out in the Yard

Even the smallest, tidiest yard is a jungle, with deafening cicadas, kamikaze bees, raccoon eyes glowing in the dark. Strange things happen there, too. Why do flying geese draw the letter V in the sky? Why does the wind whistle and moan outside your bedroom window? And why does the moon, rising above the horizon, look so impossibly huge? Step outside and see for yourself.

Do bugs sleep?

At a summer picnic, with flies soft-landing in the potato salad, ants swarming the coconut layer cake, and mosquitoes dive-bombing Uncle Harry, it's easy to assume bugs never nap.

And until recently, most scientists thought bugs rested but never really slept. But new research indicates that at least some insects may have periods of sleep remarkably like ours.

In humans (or our dogs), an EEG (electroencephalogram) can trace the distinctive electrical waves of a sleeping brain. But scientists still don't know exactly what sleep is for. They do know that sleep is essential for life in mammals and birds, all of which sleep and apparently dream. Reptiles sleep, too, although scientists aren't sure they dream. Sleep is so important that an animal deprived of it for long enough will eventually die. In fact, animals will also die when deprived of just the dreaming part of sleep, also known as REM (rapid eye movement) sleep.

Sleep clearly recharges the body, but it may exist mainly for the benefit of the brain and nervous system. Scientists say that while we sleep, the brain does its daily cleaning and organizing, erasing nonessential memories and consolidating and storing others. After a good night's sleep, we wake up with a relatively clean slate.

Some of the most intriguing sleeping-insect research has been done on the tiny fruit fly, already the source of much of what science first learned about how genes work. Studies found that fruit flies are still for a total of about 6 to 12 hours a night. Tired flies find a resting spot and then slump face down. The flies remain motionless, except for occasional twitches of legs and proboscis. And the longer they "sleep," the harder it is to wake them up by tapping on their cage.

Most intriguingly, flies deprived of their nightly naps rested longer over the next few days, just like sleep-deprived humans. And jittery, caffeine-fed flies rested less that night, just like someone who's spent the day slurping Starbucks lattes. On the other hand, flies given adenosine, a chemical that causes sleepiness in mammals, rested more.

The scientists' conclusion: certainly looks like sleep. Scientists are hopeful that research on fruit fly genes (mutant flies need less sleep) will help decipher the biological clock in human beings. Research on insects is also helping scientists trace the evolution of sleep and answer questions like "When did sleep first appear?" and "What's the simplest creature to do it?"

Observations and experiments have so far shown that besides fruit flies, cockroaches, paper wasps, scorpions, and honeybees all seem to snooze. Honeybees may sleep about 8 hours a day. Inside the hive, they may crawl into empty cells or simply crash on the hive floor, lying on their sides. And as in a dreaming dog—or person—a bee's legs (and antennae) may jerk in its sleep. The idea of a slumbering, dreaming bee makes the world seem like an even richer place. It might even be time for a new adage: "Let sleeping bees lie."

> **Observations and experiments have so far shown that fruit flies, cockroaches, paper wasps, scorpions, and honeybees all seem to snooze.**

How can birds sit on electrical wires and not get electrocuted?

High above the ground, electrical and telephone poles and their connecting wires must seem made for birds, like artificial trees with limbs that stretch on forever. Sometimes a hundred birds will be stretched out along a wire, in a kind of high-tension convention.

How come a bird on a wire doesn't get shocked? When the bird perches on a live wire, its body becomes charged—for the moment, it's at the same voltage as the wire. But no current flows into its body. A body is a poor conductor compared to copper wire, so there's no reason for electrons to take a detour through the bird. More important, electrons flow from a region of high voltage

Birds on the wire...

TURN BACK!

STOP

Scram!

I think they're trying to tell us something.

to one of low voltage. The drifting current, in effect, ignores the bird.

But if a bird (or a power-line worker) accidentally touches an electrical ground while in contact with the high-voltage wire, it completes an electrical circuit. A ground is a region of approximately zero voltage. Earth, and anything touching it that can conduct current, is the ground. Like water flowing over a dam into a river, current surges through the bird's (or person's) body on its way into the ground. Severe injury or death by electrocution is the result.

That's why a squirrel can run safely across an electrical line, only to sadly die when its foot makes contact with the (grounded) transformer on the pole at wire's end.

It's also why drivers and passengers are warned to stay inside the car if it runs into a downed power line. Touching the ground with your foot would complete the circuit: Electrons would flow from the wire, into the car, and through you on their way into the soil. (Inside the car you are usually protected by the car's four rubber tires, which act as insulators between car and ground.)

A bird's body is a poor conductor compared to copper wire, so there's no reason for electrons to take a detour through the bird.

Likewise, birds can get in trouble with power lines if wing or wrist bones—or wet feathers—connect bare wires and a ground, such as the pole.

Raptors (birds of prey) are especially likely to be killed by power lines, particularly in the western United States. In wide-open plains and deserts, power poles are often the only high perches available for hunters like bald and golden eagles and great horned owls, which survey the landscape for prey and take off into rising wind currents.

Because of their large wingspan, such big birds can easily come into contact with two wires at once or a wire and a transformer. And raptors will sometimes brush against a live wire while settling onto a (grounded) pole top. Thousands are killed by power lines each year.

How to protect big birds? Power lines can be made less dangerous by widening the gap between conducting and ground wires, by insulating wires and metal parts, and by moving wires farther away from pole tops. And guards can be built around favorite raptor perches.

Why do bats hang upside down?

Hanging upside down on the monkey bars is fun for a few minutes, but it would be real torture if you had to do it for hours on end. But the average bat can spend most of a day hanging by its feet, dead asleep. Bats—unlike people—have bodies that are uniquely designed for an inverted lifestyle.

Some fast bat facts: Bats are mammals, like us, that nurse their young with milk from their own bodies. Among the nearly 5,000 species of mammals of Earth—from cats to whales to gorillas—only bats can fly. And bats use a sophisticated system of echolocation, like a submarine's sonar, to avoid obstacles or pluck insects out of the air—even in total darkness.

FAST FACT

Some bats give birth upside down, catching bat pups in their wings as they drop.

Even though they're mammals, bats know some flying tricks that would put the average bird to shame. Bats have four large flying muscles to a bird's two, making a bat a furry little acrobat that can come in for a landing upside down.

Bat legs are specially designed, too— very light and slender, great for flight, but tiresome to perch on. Their oddest feature: Bat knees—in fact, bat hind legs—are attached backward. This rotation of the joint helps bats navigate in flight and easily land and hang upside down.

Besides its rear-facing knees, a bat has strong feet tipped by long, curved claws. Bat feet have tendons designed to clamp a bat to its roost. How? As soon as a bat hangs itself from a branch or rafter, the weight of its body, tugged by gravity, makes its feet go into auto-lock. Since the feet lock by themselves, a bat does not have to hold on and can drift off to dreamland, with no worries of falling. (In fact, the tendon "locks" are so strong that a bat will often remain hanging even after it's dead.)

And while a bat is hanging from its roost, it can use its rubbery neck to check out what's going on around it. Eerily, a bat can look straight down or even 180 degrees behind itself while dangling by its feet.

But why sleep upside down to begin with? Hanging around in high, sheltered places—near barn ceilings, in caves, in tree holes—keeps bats safer from predators, like cats, coyotes, hawks, and people. And when a bat is ready to prowl the night for a tasty bug dinner, it can flex its muscles, unlock

Bats' oddest feature is that their knees—in fact, their whole hind legs—are attached backward. This helps them navigate in flight and easily land and hang upside down.

from its roost, and drop straight into flight. Unlike in birds, there is no energy-wasting takeoff required, and a bat effortlessly gains momentum as it falls. Hanging bats spend up to 20 hours a day asleep.

But not all bats sleep hanging by their toes. Disk-winged bats snooze upright, in hiding places like curled-up banana leaves. But they have their own unusual feature—suction cups on feet and wrists, to allow them to attach to surfaces as securely as their upside-down relatives.

AUTO-LOCK FEET...WHO NEEDS THEM?

Why do smaller animals (like cats) have faster heart rates?

Press two fingers on the inside of your wrist. Feel the beat, once every second or faster? The pace of our own hearts seems normal to us, but other creatures skip to a different rhythm. It's a world of differently beating hearts—from the impossibly fast pitter-patter of a bunny heart to the ponderous thump . . . thump . . . thump of a blue whale heart.

Hearts beat to push blood throughout the body, from head to far-off toes. With each squeeze of your heart, about 3 to 4 ounces of freshly oxygenated blood is pushed through the arteries.

Among mammals (animals that make milk to feed babies), heart rate varies according to size: The bigger the mammal, the slower its heart beats. An elephant's big heart thumps about 30 times a minute; a bat's heart races along at nearly 700 beats a minute.

This might seem backward, since a larger

My beatin' heart...

It beats for you!

Thud Thud

Mine beats faster, my love is true!

Boing Boing Boing Boing

Their pulses pound as slow as goo! So let them go or I'll be blue.

Tick Tick Tick Tick Tick Tick Tick Tick Tick Tick

body requires more blood. (And since a single beat seems to cover a lot of ground in pushing blood around a tiny body.) But it actually makes a lot of sense.

A larger animal is crammed into a proportionately smaller body "suit" than a little animal. In other words, a small animal has more surface area compared to its mass than a bigger one. And since animals lose heat through their skin, the body of a smaller animal must work harder to maintain its temperature.

So small animals burn calories very quickly; their bodies "burn out" quickly, too, like a fast-burning candle. But big animals have slower, thriftier metabolisms; like a slow-burning candle, they last longer. The average 12,000-pound elephant weighs

> A cat's heart beats about 140 times a minute. But the tiny heart of a mouse races at about 400 beats a minute (seven times a second).

almost 200,000 times as much as the average 1-ounce mouse. But an elephant needs only 10,000 times the calories of a mouse, because of its slower metabolism. Live fast, die young: mice live, on average, for only 3 years. But elephants can live to the ripe old age of 70.

The faster metabolism of smaller animals requires that their hearts supply oxygen at a higher rate. So they must beat fast to keep up with the demand. A cat's heart beats about 140 times a minute. But the tiny heart of the mouse it's searching for in the house is racing at about 400 beats a minute (seven times a second). A shrew's heart pit-pats 800 times a minute, and a camel's beats once every 2 seconds.

The Extremes of Heart Rate

The slowest heartbeat of all belongs to the blue whale, whose heart is the size of a Volkswagen Beetle. When the whale is swimming near the water's surface, its heart is beating about six times a minute—once every 10 seconds. But if the whale dives, its heart, conserving oxygen, slows to three beats a minute. Compare that to the fluttering heart of a hummingbird, racing at 1,200 beats a minute as the bird executes such aerial acrobatics as flying backward and upside down.

How come flowers have a scent?

Ever bury your nose in a rose and take a deep breath? Walk past a fence dripping with honeysuckle just to inhale the heavy perfume? Or breathe in the spicy scent of apple blossoms, bees buzzing all around?

If the scent of flowers attracts *you*, imagine what it does to insects, which can crawl right into the bloom's perfumed room. And that's the main idea behind flower fragrance: Entice those pollinators, keep 'em coming back for more.

Bugs that feel the urge to climb inside a just-bloomed flower and scramble around inside are doing the flower's bidding— whether they know it or not. Their bodies become covered in pollen; when they move on to the next flower, some of the pollen falls off inside. When the pollen works its way into a flower's ovaries, the plant has been fertilized.

Flowering plants have an arsenal of attraction to keep insects (and birds) interested, from enticing colors to alluring

Carrion fly florist shop....

Smells like death and decay— my mom will love it!

shapes to hidden Cracker Jack prizes, like sweet and nutritious nectar. Until recently, scent was considered inferior to color and form in attracting insects, perhaps because we humans have a bias toward the visual.

But botanists (people who study plants) now have sophisticated new equipment and methods to uncover the molecular secrets of flower scents, and how, exactly, they are designed to attract some insects and not others. Experiments have shown that given the alternative of a brightly colored flower under glass to a flower they can't see (but can smell), insects tend to fly to the scent.

And plants are exquisitely tuned to the habits and preferences of the insects they require to reproduce. Sneaky snapdragons release their perfume between 9 A.M. and 4 P.M., timed to match the local beehive's work shift. Some of the sweetest-smelling flowers release their fragrance mostly after dark to attract moths that fly at night. (Slip around the garden at night and sniff for yourself.)

Besides coordinating the timing of their fragrance release, plants tailor their scents. Orchids are especially crafty, producing scents that, to a male wasp or bee, smell exactly like an attractive female. After trying to mate with a flower, wasps and bees soon learn the error of their ways and leave covered in pollen. Which was the idea all along.

Each flower's scent is a unique recipe that includes anywhere from fewer than ten to hundreds of chemical compounds, such as aldehydes and alkanes, acetates and esters, alcohols, ketones, sulfur and nitrogen compounds, and fatty acids. But not all of the compounds have a pleasant fragrance.

If you were a plant interested in attracting, say, a carrion fly or a dung beetle, what would you smell like? That's right, some flowers smell like road kill or feces, rotten eggs or rotting fish. Among them are the corpse flower, the skunk cabbage, and the dead-horse arum. Repulsive to us, but quite the lure to many flies, which like nothing better than to lay their eggs in a decaying animal carcass.

If the scent of flowers attracts you, imagine what it does to insects, which can crawl right into the bloom's perfumed room. That's the idea behind flower fragrance: Entice those pollinators, keep 'em coming back for more.

Why do skunks spray, and what's in the spray?

Skunks, nature's master perfumers, make their own eau-de-swamp scent. It comes only in spray form, and it's *unforgettable*.

Skunks store their potent perfume—a thick, yellow, oily liquid—in grape-size glands under their bushy tails. But contrary to cartoons, skunks don't smell skunky. The oil is kept safely inside until needed, like water in a fire hydrant. And even when spraying, a skunk takes pains to ensure that none gets on its own clean fur.

It's a myth that skunks go around spraying willy-nilly. Surprise a skunk? You won't necessarily get doused, and you'll probably have time to get out of its spraying range. Scared or annoyed skunks usually give predators and others plenty of warning before the first blast.

Before resorting to spraying, a skunk may growl, hiss, and spit like a threatened cat, fur standing on end. The skunk may also chatter its teeth and stamp its feet. Finally, it'll raise its tail and may even do a handstand. What all this body language amounts to is a big neon sign: STOP, OR I'LL SHOOT!

But if a clueless creature doesn't turn back and just keeps coming? Then, a skunk will reluctantly bring out the big guns.

Another name for skunk spray is musk, and the organs that store it are called musk glands. Each of the two glands has a small opening into the skunk's anus, where the

> Before resorting to spraying, a skunk may growl, hiss, spit, chatter its teeth, and stamp its feet. It may also raise its tail and even do a handstand.

FAST FACT

A skunk can shoot its noxious musk about 15 feet, and up to 10 feet with great precision, aiming right for a predator's face.

L'Eau de Ick!

Easy-to-use spray container...

Avoid eye contact.

oil emerges in a stream like water from a water pistol, and can hold about a tablespoon of oil. Every spray contains up to a teaspoon of the smelly stuff. So there's enough for about six good sprays, if necessary, to get the message across.

Skunk spray is a lot like tear gas, and an animal hit in the face will find its eyes burning. While the effect is blinding, as eyes blink and squeeze out stinging tears, it's only temporary. But it lasts plenty long enough for Ms. (or Mr.) Skunk to make a quick escape.

Then, of course, there are the noxious fumes. Skunk spray has a lot in common with rotten eggs, or natural gas with added

Get noticed at parties...

I think I'm going to throw up.

sulfur fragrance, or intestinal gas. The culprit: odorous compounds called thiols. Bonded sulfur and hydrogen atoms in thiols attach to the same nose receptors that sniff out hydrogen sulfide (swamp gas). Human noses, exquisitely sensitive to thiols, can detect just ten of the pungent molecules wafting through a billion air molecules.

Skunk musk also contains compounds called thioacetates, which slowly break down into thiols. So even after the original thiols are gone, new ones replace them, helping the skunk smell to lovingly linger on fur or clothing.

Be Unforgettable! And stay that way...

See you later!

We hope not!

Why is grass green?

Human beings evolved in verdant nature, not in beige cubicles, so we have a natural fondness for green. Green is calming; studies have shown that looking at an expanse of green actually lowers blood pressure.

Green is near the middle of the spectrum of light we call visible. Hidden in ordinary white light is a rainbow of brilliant colors— red, orange, yellow, green, blue, indigo, violet. Pass a beam of sunlight through a prism—or a raindrop—and the colors spread out like a peacock's tail.

Light travels in waves so tiny that they must be measured in billionths of a meter (nanometers). Different colors of light are simply different wavelengths of light. Waves of violet light, the most energetic kind of visible light, measure about 400

Rejected Lawn Colors...
Red Grass, really scary!
Keep OFF!
Will Do!

nanometers from crest to crest. Less energetic red light has waves about 700 nanometers long. Green is the happy medium: medium energy, with waves about 510 nanometers long.

Green light shimmers all around us outdoors. Grass is green for the same reason most tree leaves are green in summer: Each blade is shot through with chlorophyll, the ultimate green chemical.

How come? Plants whip up their own sugar diet, and chlorophyll is the key to plant luncheons. Chlorophyll uses energy from sunlight, carbon dioxide from air, and water

FAST FACT

There is more green chlorophyll on Earth than any other pigment, which is why we see green just about everywhere we look.

from the earth and sky to manufacture carbohydrates for plants to consume and store. The process is called photosynthesis, which means "putting together with light."

During photosynthesis, a plant gives off molecules of oxygen, just as we exhale carbon dioxide. Which makes all the chlorophyll around us responsible for the oxygen in our atmosphere. Without oxygen to breathe, we wouldn't be here. No wonder seeing green lowers our blood pressure.

And interestingly, chlorophyll is nearly identical in structure to oxygen-carrying heme in the hemoglobin in our blood. In a chlorophyll molecule, the central atom is magnesium; in heme, the starring atom is iron. One tints plants green, the other colors blood red. (Chlorophyll is also a relative of vitamin

Grass is green for the same reason most tree leaves are green in summer: Each blade is shot through with chlorophyll.

B_{12}, which has cobalt in place of magnesium.)

There are actually two forms of chlorophyll, named (not so inventively) chlorophyll A and chlorophyll B. The two differ only in one side chain of atoms. But that slight difference means the chlorophylls complement each other in the wavelengths of light that each absorbs.

The two chlorophylls absorb mainly the blue, violet, and red wavelengths of light. However, both turn up their nose at light with wavelengths around 500 nanometers, the green region of the spectrum. Using the rest of the visible light rainbow while rejecting green means that green is reflected or transmitted rather than absorbed. So green light streams out at us from every chlorophyll-rich object in the world—including blades of grass.

White Grass, too sterile ...

And soils easily, so take your shoes off!

Brown Grass, looks dead...

At least then you don't have to mow it.

Why does grass only smell strongly when it's cut?

Like running barefoot through fresh-cut grass? Like the smell even better? According to "favorite smell" surveys, along with scents like baking bread, laundry dried on a clothesline in the sun, just-ground coffee, and summer rain, cut grass is near the top of most people's lists.

It's a good thing most of us are so fond of the fragrance, because so-called turf grass is everywhere in the United States. All the lawns, golf courses, parks, playing fields, and other green expanses add up to an astonishing 30 million–plus acres of grass, just waiting to be mowed.

Left to its own devices, grass will grow only so tall and then go to seed, developing a spray of seedpods at the end of each long seed-bearing blade. But most people never let their lawns reach the gone-to-seed phase, instead mowing them once a week and creating a neatly trimmed outdoor green carpet.

It's the mowing, of course, that creates the cut-grass scent. An untouched blade of

Whose Favorite Smell?

Ahhh, the perfume of cut grass!

What's that stench?

That horrible odor!

That frightening reek!

grass smells earthy and green up close. But it takes cutting (or tearing) to release the heady fragrance we associate with high summer.

According to botanists (plant scientists), the smell of cut grass is caused by gases emitted from each injured blade. Chopped grass releases a long list of volatile organic compounds (VOCs). The VOCs include, among others, methane (swamp gas), acetone (as in nail-polish remover), ethanol (grain alcohol), and acetaldehyde, a chemical similar to the toxic preservative formaldehyde.

Plants produce the VOCs within seconds of cutting. Some also produce the chemicals when they are damaged by frost. Botanists are still studying why wounded plants give off a burst of VOCs. One reason, they suspect, is that the chemicals have an antimicrobial action, protecting the cut part from invasion by microbes already on the leaf's surface.

> An untouched blade of grass smells earthy and green up close. But it takes cutting (or tearing) to release the heady fragrance we associate with high summer.

Gassy Grassy Pollution

Some scientists suggest thinking of cut grass as a kind of chemical polluter. Volatile organic compounds from wounded grass react with nitrogen oxides in the air, helping to form more ozone near the ground (where we don't want it). And grass sheared off and left drying on the lawn releases even more VOCs—up to ten times as much as the cut grass still rooted in the ground. So mowing the nation's lawns may be a significant source of air pollution, scientists say—even trumping the pollution belched out by gas-powered mowers.

Still, most scientists say there's no reason not to go ahead and enjoy the green-grass smell on a summer's day. When we bite and chew raw vegetables, they point out, the veggies release their own small burst of VOCs—just as grass, clover, and other plants do when a hungry horse tears off a tasty mouthful.

Why is water so slippery?

You see the sign on rain-slicked curves and bridges, in lobbies where melting snow is tramped in by boots, and in the lunchroom after the janitor mops up a spill. CAUTION: SLIPPERY WHEN WET. Suddenly, an ordinary asphalt road or linoleum floor has been transformed into a horizontal slide, to be approached gingerly. The culprit? Plain old water.

What a layer of water does to a road or floor is the same thing it does to a twisty plastic slide at a water park: It reduces friction. When one surface rubs against another, the nooks and crannies catch, producing a dragging effect. Scientists say friction is a force that acts in the opposite direction to the motion of an object. So friction slows the progress of your feet across a linoleum floor. But add water and your shoes glide on a liquid film, reducing your soles' contact with the floor's snaggy imperfections.

Far-Flung Friction Fun...

Stationary skating ... on rubber blades.
Leaves you free to work on arm movements.

Lounge-around Luging ...on a Velcro track.
Helps keep the insurance premiums down.

Still-life skiing ...with sandpaper skis.
It's easier on the knees!

On the road, rainwater also stirs up oily residues, increasing the slip factor. Greases and oils are the champion friction reducers, which is why they're used to lubricate moving parts in cars, bikes, and other machinery. But not many people would plunk down an all-day admission to a Grease Park, donning a bathing suit to careen down the Giant Butter Slide or speed through the Corn Oil Chute. Water, however, provides just the right amount of lubrication to keep your body zipping along a plastic or fiberglass slide.

What a layer of water does to road or floor is the same thing it does to a twisty plastic slide at a water park: It reduces friction.

So water gets much of its slippery reputation from its friction-dampening effects. But liquid water is also slippery all by itself. By its very nature, a liquid is a collection of molecules slip-sliding past one another. Which is why you can dive into a swimming pool of water, neatly slicing through the surface, and glide on across the pool. (Just try that on your solid mattress. Actually, don't!)

Finally, there's the surface slipperiness of water in its solid form—ice. Water freezes into a solid when (at ordinary pressures) its temperature drops to 32°F and below. Then, the slippery fun begins. Drop an ice cube and watch it go slip-sliding away across the kitchen floor. Or go skidding yourself down an ice-topped sidewalk.

Until recently, scientists thought ice's slickness was due to pressure or friction creating a thin layer of liquid on top. So the weight of an ice skater on a frozen pond would create pressure, forcing the top layer of swollen ice to condense and melt into liquid. And the friction between the skate blades and the ice would heat the layer, adding to the melting effect.

What scientists have discovered, however, is that ice just sitting there minding its own business is already incredibly slippery. Studies show that molecules on the surface of ice constantly vibrate up and down, rather than stay frozen in their crystal lattice. The vertical vibration creates a liquidlike layer atop the ice, reducing friction to a minimum—and making for winter thrills and spills.

How are shadows formed? How can you make them bigger or smaller?

In *Peter Pan*, by J. M. Barrie, Peter loses his shadow when Nana the dog grabs it as Peter escapes out a window. Finding the shadow, Nana's owner, Mrs. Darling, rolls it up and puts it in a drawer for safekeeping.

Real shadows are more ephemeral. Try to grab a shadow, and your hand will simply pass into its shade. Try to jump on your own shadow, and it jumps with you, ever connected to your feet.

A shadow appears when an object stands in the way of light. The less light that can pass through an object, the more solid its shadow. So a translucent beach ball casts a faint shadow, while

ME AND MY LIGHT SOURCE...

Hey, there you are!

Where ya going?

Bye-bye!

your body casts a solid dark shadow.

On a sunny day, a shadow is a patch of night. Any light source can make a shadow—the Sun, a lamp, a flashlight, the silvery Moon. Try making your own shadows using an unshaded lamp, your hand, and a plain white wall. You'll discover that if you move your hand closer to the wall, the shadow becomes more sharply defined. Or if you move the lamp close to your hand, your shadow becomes fuzzier. Move the lamp away, and the shadow becomes sharper again.

Finally, the larger the light, the fuzzier the shadow. When a lightbulb wears a lampshade, the shade creates, in effect, a bigger, more diffuse light source. Which is why a lampshade makes for a blurrier shadow than a bare lightbulb.

The Sun is enormous (a million Earths could fit inside it), but it is also enormously distant (93 million miles away). So the Sun appears as a rather small light source in the sky. Which is why the combination of the Sun, you, and the sidewalk make such great shadows. The Sun is very bright but very far away, you are very solid, and the sidewalk is very near.

Even the sharpest shadow is a bit blurry around the edges. Outdoors, this out-of-focus quality is a result of the Sun being larger than a point in the sky. Light streams from countless points on the Sun's disk, each ray traveling on its own course and creating a shadow of its own. The rays of light diffract around your body's edges, creating an interference pattern of darkness and light, and a shadow with fuzzy edges. If light were to come from one shrunk-down perfect point, there would be one sharp, clean shadow.

On an overcast day, with the Sun hidden behind clouds, the whole sky acts as a diffuse light source—like an enormous lampshade. Your body still casts a shadow, but it is so hugely spread out and fuzzy that you can't see it at all.

Shadow Play

To make your Sun-made shadow bigger or smaller, simply venture outdoors several times from early morning until noon. Your shadow will be longer when the Sun is low in the sky, shorter when the sun is higher. With the Sun directly overhead, shadows dwindle to nothing. You'll cast the longest, skinniest shadow near sunrise or sunset.

How do cicadas make their loud and varied sounds?

It wouldn't be midsummer without the dog-day cicadas, their plaintive chorus rising and then dying away. Then there are the waves of 13- and 17-year cicadas, which make their deafening appearance in late spring. Cicadas can be as noisy as kitchen blenders, and almost as annoying.

Cicadas are the loudest insects known. Why all the racket? Most cicada sounds are all about the mating. Cicadas have only a brief time to find a partner and create a new generation of nymphs before their life above ground is over. So when you hear a cicada chorus so loud you're prompted to shut your window, think "speed-dating."

How can something so small (the average North American cicada measures less than 2 inches) make a sound so earsplitting? It's

> In the cicada world, it's the guys who are the singers. Male 17-year cicadas make at least five different sounds.

not that cicadas have big mouths. In fact, it's all about the abs. Male cicadas are the singers, and they make the noise using tymbals, a pair of ridged membranes in their lower abdomens.

A cicada pulls in his ab muscles around the tymbals, causing them to cave in like a struck drum. The sound resonates in the cicada's mostly empty abdominal cavity, like a resounding note in a concert hall. The cicada's angled wings form a natural megaphone, enhancing the sound further as it exits. And we hear a noise that can reach 80 to 90 decibels, as loud as a vacuum cleaner or lawnmower.

There are more than 2,500 cicada species around the world, each with its distinctive calls and songs. In North America, male 17-year cicadas make at least five categories of sounds.

Ever hear a cicada make a short, harsh buzz as you approach? Entomologists call that an alarm call; males make it when they feel threatened. Then there's the calling song, which attracts other cicadas to a group chorus (often in the highest tree branches). The calling song often consists of one to three calls separated by several seconds of silence.

Many years ago, a man leaving for a date with flowers and candy was said to be "going courting." It's not flowers, candy, or a high salary that attracts female cicadas. It's the sound of his court call that will win a male cicada a mate.

A court 1 call is similar to a calling song, with shorter gaps between calls. A male makes this sound when he has settled down from his flying and branch-pacing and is trying to woo a nearby female cicada. Court 2 calls are continuous; a male makes this sound as he strolls up to a friendly female. Court 3 calls are a series of quick buzzes that a male makes just before he and his lady friend mate. And while a flirting female cicada doesn't have hair to flip, she does flick her wings, making a come-hither rustle or pop in response to a male's noisy overtures.

Each cicada species makes its own unique sounds. The cassini cicada's calling song is a series of *tick-tick-tick*s followed by a loud shrill *buzz*. But the septendecim cicada's song sounds like the word *pharaoh*, chanted over and over.

139

Why does the sky inside a rainbow look brighter than the sky outside it?

Most people are so pleasantly distracted by the unearthly, glowing colors of a rainbow—violet, blue, green, yellow, orange, and red—that they don't notice what the sky around it is doing. But the next time you see a rainbow, compare the sky under the arch to the sky above it. Under the arch, the sky seems lit up by the rainbow itself. If you're lucky enough to see a double rainbow, you'll notice that the sky *between* the two arches appears darkened.

The light or dark bands are rainbow side effects. Here's how it works.

A rainbow is a trick of light. For you to see a rainbow, sunlight must come from behind you and shoot into raindrops in front of you.

somewhere UNDER the rainbow...

Not so high... the sky is lit up quite brightly... And there's a second rainbow in the sky.

Look, Toto, rainbow shine!

All the better to see you with, my pretty!

It makes me afraid!

We know.

When light enters a raindrop, it begins to bend. That's because it's passing into water, which is much more dense (closely packed) than air.

White sunlight is really made of colors, and a raindrop bends (refracts) each color, or wavelength, of light a little more or less as the light beam enters. (For example, blue light is bent more than red.) So the white beam splits into its true colors, each going its own way.

Inside the raindrop, the colored rays collide with the mirrorlike raindrop wall, bend again, and shoot back out of the raindrop. As they exit, they bend a third time as they move from dense water into open air. This happens in millions of raindrops—and you see a rainbow of colors curve across the sky.

Because you are standing on the ground, you see only certain colors coming from certain raindrops. Red and orange bend most, so the highest drops send these colors down to your eyes. Blue and violet are less sharply bent, so you get them from lower drops. Yellow and green are all you can see from drops in the middle of the sky.

Why is the sky under the rainbow especially luminous? In addition to the

For you to see a rainbow, sunlight must come from behind you and shoot into raindrops in front of you.

"rainbow waves," there are lots of light rays emerging from the raindrops at sharper angles (but no rays at wider angles). What this means is that extra light floods out just under the rainbow arch, brightening the sky.

A secondary rainbow sometimes appears when colors reflect from the wall inside the raindrop *twice* instead of once before exiting. When these twice-reflected rays emerge from many different raindrops, we see a second rainbow in a different position.

Between the two bows, the sky appears dimmed. Why? Since there is extra light below the primary bow (and extra light above the mirror-image secondary bow, too), the sky between the two bows appears dark by comparison.

FAST FACT

The piece of sky sandwiched between two rainbows is called Alexander's Dark Band. It was named after Alexander of Aphrodisias, a Greek scientist who wrote about the puzzling band some 1,800 years ago.

Why do bees die after they sting someone?

Boxer Muhammad Ali once said that in the ring he would "float like a butterfly and sting like a bee." Actually, Ali stung more like a wasp than a bee. After delivering its own version of a sharp punch, a honeybee is out for the count.

The world is full of bees; up to 30,000 different species buzz around the flowers of Earth. Bees belong to the Hymenoptera order, which also includes wasps, hornets, and even ants.

Surprisingly, most bee species are solitary, with female bees laying eggs in individual nests. Honeybees and bumblebees, on the other hand, are wildly social, living in a complex tribe. A single queen does all the egg laying. A community of thousands of female workers clean, tend to the larvae (baby bees), and make nectar runs. Meanwhile, hundreds of male drones lounge about, their only job being to mate with the queen. Up to 50,000 individuals live in a hive, a small humming city of bees.

Most bees are "live-and-let-live" creatures. It takes a lot to provoke the average bee—like stepping on a worker sipping water from a blade of grass, or, especially, threatening its hive home. After all, the hive is full of everything a bee holds dear—bee queen, bee children, bee friends, and a pantry full of food.

> Most bees are "live-and-let-live" creatures. It takes a lot to provoke the average bee enough to sting someone.

The only weapon the average bee has to defend itself and its tribe is its stinger. Only female bees have stingers. Workers, which don't usually lay eggs, have an egg duct modified into a stinger and connected to a venom sac. The stinger's end is barbed like a fishhook. So when a female bee projects her tiny harpoon, it embeds in the skin. Once hooked in flesh, muscles around the venom sac continue to pulse out poison for up to a minute.

To Bee or...(pending loss of Stinger), Not to Bee...

Whether 'tis Nobler to suffer...a bunch of bad luck...

or to take arms against a sea of troubles...

and by opposing, end them. Bummer...

A female bee uses her stinger only as a last resort, since in trying to pull away, she rips the organ from her abdomen. Sacrificing herself for her fellow bees, the bee soon dies of her injury.

Not all bees sting, however. A minority of species are stingless, defending themselves by biting. (Interestingly, stingless bees produce a tiny fraction of the honey of their lancet-equipped cousins.)

Then there are the members of the Hymenoptera order that can sting again and again, living to tell the tale. Wasps and hornets have smooth stingers that deliver a shot of venom and then neatly retract. These pollinators seem to be on a hair trigger, stinging with less provocation than the average bee.

Bumblebees also have non-barbed stingers and can sting more than once, but they are the gentle giants of the bee world. And all queen bees are likewise exempt from the suicide stinger. Since the queen is so important to the future of her clan, she carries a smooth stinger, the better to kill off rival queens and reign another day.

FAST FACT

Without bees, human beings would have trouble finding enough to eat. According to bee researchers, honeybees alone pollinate about one-third of the crops that make up the human diet.

Do earthworms eat dirt?

We're most likely to see them after a long, soaking rain in the spring: earthworms, curled motionless on the sidewalk, or wriggling slowly and aimlessly along, seemingly dazed by the air and light. Having emerged, temporarily, from their dark existence, they seem ill-at-ease aboveground, like fish flopping on a beach.

But if you think of a small red earthworm as simply something to step over on a rainy day, or a long, wriggly nightcrawler as nothing more than fish bait, think again. In 1881, biologist Charles Darwin had this to say about earthworms: "It may be doubted whether there are many other animals which have played so important a part in the history of the world."

Why? Earthworms quietly toil beneath our feet, squiggly underground farmers. They literally create the fertile soil in which all the plants around us are rooted, from

CHEZ WORMS

"I love this place!"

"All you can eat, all of the time!"

"The guidebook gave their rotting leaves and crumbled manure five stars!"

"Oh, the topsoil we're gonna make tonight!"

mighty oak trees to rustling fields of corn to rambling raspberry bushes.

What's in dirt for the worms? Mixed in with soil are all the yummy bits that earthworms live to eat: decaying roots, rotting leaves, crumbled manure from passing animals. Then there are tiny, tasty living creatures—fungi, bacteria, nematodes, protozoa. Finally, there are the remains of once-living animals, from insects to birds to bigger animals, decomposing in the ground.

Earthworms don't have hands, and they don't have teeth. But they do have strongly muscled mouths. As an earthworm tunnels through the soil, open-mouthed, it is also having supper. An earthworm may swallow its own weight in dirt each day. But it's the food trapped in the dirt that a hungry worm is after. Like turkeys and chickens, earthworms have gizzards, which contain sandy grit, to help them grind and digest their food.

When an earthworm has finished digesting its dinner, it leaves behind waste called castings. Castings contain raw dirt the earthworm swallowed, plus well-digested, broken-down leftovers of organic material. Worm castings are the best fertilizer around, full of nitrogen, phosphorus, and potassium,

Earthworms literally create the fertile soil in which all the plants around us are rooted.

a rich black compost in which plants thrive.

As earthworms tunnel, they mix and aerate the soil like thousands of tiny rototillers. Loosened soil gives roots room to stretch luxuriously out and down. Meanwhile, earthworm-built channels funnel rain to the deepest roots. Less runoff and erosion help fertile soil stay put.

It can take 500 years for 1 inch of topsoil to build up from the breakdown of rocks and organic material. Yet topsoil can be bulldozed to parking-lot oblivion or washed away by flooding in minutes. A healthy population of determined earthworms, however, can engineer 1 inch of rich soil in about five years—less than the time we spend in elementary school.

FAST FACT

There are nearly 3,000 separate kinds, or species, of earthworms tunneling through the thin layer of topsoil on our planet. They range in size from less than an inch to an African worm that can stretch more than 13 feet long.

How come birds like geese fly in a V formation?

Have you ever watched a flock of geese take off from a pond? With head nods all around, one goose flaps off, followed by the whole honking crowd. Rising into the sky, they may spread out into a V, with some geese flying frantically to close gaps and neaten lines.

But geese aren't the only birds that provide free air shows. Several other large birds that fly long distances also like to travel in Vs—swans, ducks, and even cranes.

No one knows for sure why these birds fly in a V (ever try to interrogate a goose?), but scientists have good theories. Some have even modeled flying V formations on computers, noting air flows through a flock.

Birds like Canada geese may not bother to get their V together for a hop to the next pond. But when they embark on a real trip—especially migration—geese form the tightest, most perfect Vs.

One theory is that the V shows social dominance in a group of geese—the most experienced "head" geese take the lead.

But the main reason for the V, scientists think, is aerodynamics.

> **The main reason for flying in a V, scientists think, is aerodynamics. Each flapping bird creates air turbulence behind itself, and flying directly behind another bird would be like trying to swim behind a motorboat.**

Scientists say that the V formation makes flying long distances easier. Each flapping bird creates air turbulence behind itself, and flying directly behind another bird, they note, would be like trying to swim behind a motorboat.

However, flying behind and to one side, a bird gets a lift from the resulting slipstream: Each bird's wingtip rests on the rising air streaming from the wing of the bird in front of it. One study showed that a goose flying as part of a V—conserving energy—may be able to fly 70 percent farther than if it were flying solo.

Geese may also like the V for the same reason bomber planes flew in V formations in World War II. The V shape, with each bird slightly higher than the one in front of it, lets each goose keep track of the whole bunch, allowing the best view and quickest head count. Plus, the open V allows geese to see what else might be approaching through the air, a feat that would be more difficult if the birds were bunched up in a mass.

But geese don't always form perfect Vs. Sometimes, one arm of the V is much shorter than the other, making a check mark instead of an alphabet letter. Scientists say

FAST FACT

Ornithologists (people who study birds) note that no matter which goose flies at the apex of the V, one thing is certain— it's always a female.

that birds may favor this formation when a crosswind is blowing.

And while it looks as though one goose is in charge, people who've studied geese flights say that the leader trades off with other birds. It's exhausting leading the way, buffeted by the wind. So after a while, the lead bird drops to the rear, where wind drag is lowest, for a much-needed breather.

Geese Yappin' on Formation Flappin'

How do birds sleep on their feet without falling?

Ever see a parakeet dozing in its cage, head tucked into its wing? Birds certainly sleep. But they have a few tricks that help them stay safe from predators (like cats) while keeping them securely fastened to the branch they've picked to snooze on.

Unlike us humans, some birds can enter a state of half-sleep. However, a bird's half-sleep is very different from feeling "drowsy." In unihemispheric sleep, half of the brain's cerebrum is actually awake and half is asleep. Likewise, during half-sleep, one eye will often be open and one eye closed. Unihemispheric sleep allows many birds to keep an eye (and half a brain) peeled for predators. In fact, some kinds of swifts may even half-sleep as they fly. Besides birds like bobwhites and chickens, whales and dolphins also do the half-sleep, as may some reptiles.

However, birds also spend time with their whole brains asleep. And when they do, they indulge in brief periods of dreaming. Scientists say that half-sleep and shortened

MULTITASKING, BIRD STYLE...

Sleeping while Grocery shopping...

Must get CORN FlAAAAKES!

Sleeping while Flying...

The wrong side of his brain is awake!

148

periods of REM (dreaming) sleep help protect vulnerable birds from predators. In nature, it's usually predators that have the luxury of enjoying lots of deep, dream-filled sleep, with both eyes firmly shut.

> The only birds that sleep in nests are baby birds and the adults taking care of them.

Most birds sleep during the night, just like us. The only birds that sleep in nests are baby birds and the adults taking care of them. When not nesting, most birds sleep perched on branches, or in handy tree trunk holes.

So how does a bird sleep on a branch without falling? Is it just that birds have expert balance, like little flying trapeze artists? Actually, birds don't even have to think about holding on. Once they come in for a landing, a perch locks in, automatically.

Here's how it works. When a bird alights on a branch, bending its legs and settling its weight down, its leg muscles naturally shorten. When the muscles contract, the attached tendons pull on the toe bones, which curl into a tight grip. So as a bird bends its ankle, its toes (claws) curl more tightly. Tendons at the toes also have a rough underside that adheres to the rest of the tendon stretching down from the ankle. The end result is a secure inner latch that allows a bird to drift off to sleep, with no worries about falling.

Sleeping while Studying...

Half a brain is better than none!

Shelter from the Cold

Ever wonder how birds sleep in winter without freezing to death? Many birds congregate in big flocks in dense bushes or evergreen trees, huddling near the trunk, sheltered from the elements and sharing body heat.

Bobwhites, on the other hand, gather into a tight circle on the ground, tails in, beaks out, like wagon trains stopping for the night. The bobwhites keep one another warm while keeping an eye out for danger from all directions.

How come animal eyes glow in the dark?

Shine a flashlight into your yard after dark, and you may see a pair of eyes glow green or yellow against black—before they seemingly float away. Was it the neighbor's cat? A marauding raccoon? Or perhaps an owl, perched on a fallen log?

While human beings often feel superior to other animals, when it comes to night vision, it's no contest. Many animals, from insects to mammals, have a special eye accessory called a tapetum lucidum,

designed to squeeze every spare photon of light out of the darkness. We don't.

The idea is simple but elegant: Light passes into the eye's retina. Any light that isn't absorbed travels on to the tapetum, where it is reflected back to the retina for another chance at absorption. When the resulting image is processed by the brain, it's much brighter than it would have been had those stray photons simply been lost. The tapetum lucidum is a light amplifier,

HIGH BEAMS PREFERRED

the reason your cat may see a 600 percent brighter backyard than you do after dark.

Tapetum-equipped animal eyes glow when some reflected light exits through the pupil without being absorbed by the retina. And so we see our flashlight (or headlights) reflected back at us, as if from a mirror.

Who has glow-in-the-dark eyes? A surprisingly long list of animals, many (but not all) fond of hunting or foraging at night. Besides cats and raccoons and owls, proud tapetum owners include deer, crocodiles, harbor seals, dragonflies, zebras, ferrets, moths, sharks, elephants, spiders, whales, and even moo-cows.

Glowing eyes come in a rainbow of colors. Some dogs' eyes shine yellow or green, others' blue. Owls usually have red eyeshine; some possum eyes glow pink.

Different animal groups have differently constructed tapeta. The tapetum's reflective material may include everything from guanine, a building block of DNA, to

Glowing eyes come in a rainbow of colors. Some dogs' eyes shine yellow or green, others' blue. Owls usually have red eyeshine; some possum eyes glow pink.

cholesterol, zinc, Vitamin B_2, and collagen.

Scientists say the tapetum is usually designed to reflect the wavelength of light an animal is most likely to encounter. So some deep-water fish, for example, have tapeta that selectively reflect the blue-green light of their murky underwater home.

Biologists think that the differences in animal tapeta show that these handy light boosters evolved independently in many different species, starting some 350 million years ago. We humans, however, must make do with flashlights, headlamps, and night-vision binoculars.

FAST FACT

Tapetum lucidum comes from Latin, meaning "bright carpet"—a bright carpet of cells inside the eye.

What's the difference between a rabbit and a hare?

Both rabbits and hares, along with little animals called pikas, are lagomorphs (like human beings, chimpanzees, and monkeys are primates). Within the Lagomorpha order, rabbits and hares make up their own family, Leporidae.

What's the difference between rabbits and hares? Hares are usually bigger, weigh more, and have more powerful hind legs and feet. A hare can outjump and outrun a rabbit—which, in a race from a coyote, is a big advantage. Hares also have longer ears. While rabbit babies are born hairless, blind, and helpless, hare babies are born furry, eyes open, and are hopping within hours. Hares also always live above ground.

(Bugs Bunny lived underground, poking his head out to chomp calmly on a carrot behind some clueless enemy like Elmer Fudd. But judging from his size and ears,

CRAZY WABBIT AND DR. HARE

Hares are bigger, faster, and stronger than rabbits...

...This makes me feel incredibly puny and inferior...

And it makes me feel great!

Bugs was more of a "hare" brain than a cwazy wabbit. In fact, his first film was called *A Wild Hare*.)

Many animals called rabbits are really hares. Jackrabbits? Hares. Snowshoe rabbits? Also hares. On the other hand, the Belgian hare is actually a rabbit. The bottom line: If you see an extra-big rabbit with extra-long ears, jumping like a miniature kangaroo, that's no rabbit.

The 55 species (kinds) of rabbits and hares include the cottontail rabbit hopping in suburban yards, the Arctic hare, the

Compared to rabbits, hares are usually bigger and have more powerful hind legs and feet.

swamp rabbit, the Alpine hare, the Manchurian hare, the pygmy rabbit, the wooly hare, and the tiny volcano rabbit, which lives on the slopes of volcanoes in Mexico.

The snowshoe "rabbit" is also called the varying hare. In summer, this hare's hair is brown; in winter, it turns snowy white, helping the hare blend in with the wintry landscape and avoid hungry animals like coyotes. It also grows big tufts of fur on its hind feet, making it look as if it strapped on snowshoes.

Do Rabbits Really Live Underground?

Contrary to storybooks and cartoons, rabbits don't always live underground. Many hide (and sleep) in shallow bowls or burrows in the grass. But in winter, underground homes are warmer—and a good place to hide out. So rabbits like cottontails may take over deep burrows left behind by other wild animals, tunneling out rabbit runs tailored for their own use.

But European rabbits (which live all over the world) create complex tunnels underground for use year-round. These tunnel hotels are called warrens. Warrens may be used by group after group of rabbits for many years; new rabbits add on to the tunnels like new homeowners add on rooms to the old houses they buy. A warren has many entrances and exits, bedrooms for sleeping, and nurseries where baby rabbits doze, nurse, and practice taking their first unsteady steps. All this bustling bunny activity may be taking place under your feet, as deep as 10 feet beneath the grass in your own yard.

How does a moving bicycle stay balanced?

When you first learn to ride a bike, it seems almost impossible. How do you keep it upright and moving at the same time—when your dad has taken off the training wheels?

But after the first few scary (and probably short) rides, you realized that you don't have to concentrate on balancing yourself or the bike. It seems to happen naturally.

An amazing fact: While bikes have been around for more than 100 years—and there's a sketch of a bikelike invention from the 1490s—scientists *still* disagree about what, exactly, keeps bicycles balanced as they move.

A briskly moving bicycle, rider in the seat, doesn't easily tip over. At the slowest speeds, however, a bicycle becomes more unstable—which is why you wobble severely when you slow down to match the pace of a strolling friend. And a stopping or stopped bike is unstable—you must be ready with a dangling foot to keep it from falling over sideways.

Some say that the key to the balance in a moving bicycle is the gyroscopic effect of its wheels. A spinning gyroscope naturally resists changing the tilt of its spin, and so gyroscopes are used in the automatic steering systems of airplanes and rockets. The gyroscopic forces of a bike's spinning wheels likewise make them resist toppling over. And the faster the wheels spin, the more stable they are.

Curious about this theory, British scientist David E. H. Jones tried to invent

Why Bikes stay up...

Very strong brain waves...

The bike Genie...

an unrideable bicycle, one that wouldn't stay upright, providing clues to how a rideable bicycle works. The report of his experiments was published in *Physics Today* in April 1970. Jones found that many odd bike configurations *were* rideable—even one that deliberately canceled out gyroscopic effects. This seemed to prove that such effects aren't the key to bike balance.

However, in an experiment with a riderless bike, Jones found that gyroscopic action did help stabilize the moving bike. So while the higher center of gravity of a bike with a rider would seem to make it more unstable, Jones's experiments indicated the opposite. Finally, when Jones tried out a bike

A briskly moving bicycle, rider in the seat, doesn't easily tip over. At the slowest speeds, however, a bicycle becomes more unstable.

that was steered by using the rear wheel instead of the front, the moving bike would invariably topple over.

While Jones's experiments cast doubts on existing theories of bike balance, he wasn't able to propose an alternative. So the debate rages on.

Some say that a bike automatically balances under its center of gravity, like a penny rolling across the floor. Some argue that a bike stays balanced mainly because riders make unconscious adjustments in their own tilt and steering to keep the bike upright and on course, relying on muscles, eyes, and the inner-ear balance system. (If you ride a bike with wet, dirty tires down a long sheet of paper, you should see a track of wobbles and corrections.)

Despite the lack of a good theory, bikes go on balancing, even if it seems impossible: "Look, Ma—no hands!"

Smart tires.

What happens to helium party balloons set free in the air?

A balloon inflated with air from your own lungs will bounce lazily from sofa to lampshade to piano. But it will stop where gravity has tugged it, because a rubber balloon full of air is (no surprise) heavier than the air around it.

A balloon newly filled with helium will keep going, right up to the ceiling—and stay there. Until its helium slowly leaks out—right through the walls of the balloon—and the deflated balloon sinks into a crumpled heap on the carpet. Party's over!

Helium's secret is that it weighs next to nothing. It's the second lightest element in the universe (only hydrogen is wispier). Each atom of ordinary helium has just two protons and two neutrons at its center, orbited by two measly electrons.

Oxygen, on the other hand, has eight protons, eight neutrons, and eight electrons.

FORMULA FOR BUOYANCY AND TEARS

Other elements are even heavier. For instance, an iron atom has 26 protons. Which is why iron frying pans stay put on the stove rather than carrying their load of grease up to the ceiling.

Besides the traces in the air, there's helium underground. When radioactive rock decays, it releases (nontoxic) helium. In the United States, companies drill for helium in Texas and Oklahoma, where helium gas hides in natural gas pockets.

When a balloon is filled with helium, the weight of the balloon plus the helium inside is less than that of the air it displaces, so a balloon floats up. But while a colorful helium balloon rising into the sky on a sunny day may be a beautiful sight, the aftermath isn't usually so pretty. Some balloons continue rising high into the upper atmosphere. The higher a balloon floats, the thinner the air around it. This allows the helium inside to expand, making the balloon bigger and bigger. Eventually, about 28,000 to 30,000 feet up, the outside air pressure is so low that the bloated balloon bursts.

Many balloons never reach such heights. As helium gas escapes through the pores and neck of the balloon, it rises only so high before it begins to sink again.

> **Helium is the second-lightest element in the universe (only hydrogen is wispier).**

Whether a balloon explodes into pieces or gradually deflates, it eventually ends up back on Earth—often landing in the ocean, since so much of our planet is covered with water. Clusters of party balloons float on ocean currents, and shredded or deflated balloons are often swallowed by whales, sea turtles, and other sea animals. Volunteers at one beach cleanup in 1999 collected over 32,000 balloons and balloon pieces that had washed up on shore. And oceanographers have reported seeing balloons bobbing hundreds of miles out at sea.

In the fall of 1993, a starving pygmy sperm whale was rescued on the New Jersey coastline. Doctors found a garbage bag, cellophane, and a Mylar balloon lodged in her digestive tract. To such whales, balloons may resemble (edible) jellyfish. That whale survived, but many animals aren't so lucky.

Meanwhile, many released balloons simply catch in trees and power lines, especially if they have an attached string. (Metallic balloons can actually short out the power, in a shower of sparks.) Releasing party balloons into the air turns out to be, in the end, no different than tossing something out a car window or into the ocean.

Why do we sometimes see the Moon in the daytime?

The Moon in the daytime, bleached white against the blue sky, is beautiful but seems strangely out of place. Actually, however, you're nearly as likely to see the Moon in the daytime as you are at night—as long as you're paying close attention.

Moons and planets shine by reflected light. In our solar system, light from the Sun bounces off all eight planets (nine, counting Pluto) and their dozens of moons. During the daytime, the skies of Earth are full of stars and planets, just as they are at night. However, the Sun's glare, reflecting off the

DAYTIME MOONSHINE...

"I'm out there workin' 24-7..."

"...Shining, Reflecting Shining, Reflecting!"

"Yeah, for a big gray rock you do OK!"

gas molecules in Earth's atmosphere, drowns the whole panorama in light.

But if you took off in a rocket ship from your backyard one sunny afternoon, and kept rising and rising, above the clouds and through the thinning air, you'd soon see stars. Surrounding the blanket of Earth's atmosphere is the nearly limitless dark emptiness of space. It's always there, just beyond the glare.

How can we see the Moon in the daytime? The Moon is made of grayish rock, and reflects only about 7 percent of the light striking its surface. So sunlight reflecting off the Moon is a lot like light reflecting off an asphalt parking lot at the mall. The Moon looks so brilliantly bright at night only in comparison to the pitch-blackness of the sky around it.

But the Moon is so close to us (about 240,000 miles) that the light it mirrors back to us is still much brighter than that of the nearest bright stars. For example, the Moon is 33,000 times as bright as Sirius, the star that shines brightest in the night sky.

For part of each month, the Moon rises in the morning or afternoon. So we sometimes see a crescent or half-moon in the daytime sky. As the month wears on, the Moon rises later and later, until it is rising while or after the Sun sets. (In all locations except near the North and South Poles, the full moon sets as the Sun rises—which is why we see full moons only at night.)

So the Moon is as much a daytime object as it is a nighttime sentinel. Even if, in the afternoon, it looks like a pale, ghostly version of its vibrant after-dark self.

And although they don't shine as brightly as the Moon, you can often see the brightest planets and stars around sunset and sunrise, when the sky is still light. You may even see the planet Venus—resembling a dazzlingly bright star—in broad daylight, if you happen to be looking in just the right spot.

During the daytime, the skies of Earth are full of stars and planets, just as they are at night.

Why does the Moon look gigantic rising on the horizon but small overhead?

Have you ever been riding in a car in the evening and noticed something huge and yellow behind the trees and buildings in the east—and then realized it was the Moon? Especially in the fall, the pumpkin-colored harvest Moon, looming up over the horizon, looks enormous and even spooky. It's not hard to imagine a broomstick-riding witch flying across.

But picture this Halloween scene when the Moon is high in the sky, small and white, and it's just not the same.

Scientists say that to most of us the horizon Moon appears to be twice as big as the overhead Moon. People have been arguing over why for more than a thousand years. Astronomers, psychologists, and nonscientists all have their theories. In 1989,

> Scientists say that to most of us the horizon Moon appears to be twice as big as the overhead Moon.

researchers even published a book of such explanations, titled *The Moon Illusion.*

You can prove to yourself that the Moon is actually the same size no matter where it is in the sky, using a key or a ruler. Note the Moon's width at the horizon, and later, compare it to the Moon's width overhead.

You may even make the size illusion vanish. Some people suggest bending over and looking at the horizon Moon upside down, in a kind of lunar yoga. Others recommend looking at the Moon through a cardboard tube that blocks out landscape features.

What causes the illusion? In the past, some textbooks stated that the Moon appears larger at the horizon because dense air near the ground refracts (bends)

160

moonlight, causing a magnifying-glass effect. This theory, scientists now say, is not really a contender: While there is refraction, it doesn't magnify the Moon's image and would actually tend to make the Moon appear squashed.

Most agree that the illusion is a matter of perception—a trick of the brain. Some argue that the horizon Moon looks bigger because it is framed by smaller objects like trees, houses, and hills, making it huge by comparison. However, that doesn't explain why the Moon looks so big rising over the flat expanse of the ocean. (And it also doesn't explain why the pretend Moon in a planetarium appears to be the same size at the horizon *and* overhead.)

Several complicated theories involving the brain's visual system also try to explain the Moon paradox. Here's a simplified version of one popular explanation: The brain perceives the sky (and Moon) above us as closer than the sky (and Moon) at the horizon. When an object is perceived to be nearer, the brain may compensate by making it look smaller to us. Likewise, an object thought to be farther away will be seen as larger.

For now, the Moon illusion remains one of nature's loveliest unsolved mysteries.

How come we only see one side of the Moon?

Standing on Earth and observing the Moon night after night, it would be easy to decide that our Moon doesn't rotate at all. Whether it's full-on bright or coyly lit in slices, the Moon always shows us the same man in the Moon, with the Mona Lisa smile. The other side is mysteriously and forever turned away.

However, the Moon didn't always just stare at us. Billions of years ago, an Earth-bound observer (had there been one) could have seen all sides of our newborn satellite. Why does the opposite side no longer spin into view? The Moon's slow-poke rotation means Moon days are now about 656 hours, or 27.3 Earth-days, long. Which exactly matches how long the rocky satellite takes to journey around our planet.

To see why synchronous rotation means the Moon never turns its back on us, put a

The Man in the Moon on Synchronous Rotation...

656-hour days can be really BORING!

Would you rather stare into a black void 24/7?

...Or gravitate toward the action on Earth?

chair in the middle of the room, and have a friend sit in it. The chair is the Earth; you are the Moon. Walk slowly around the chair, facing it at all times. Your friend will see only your smiling face. But you'll find, when you've gone once around, that you've faced all sides of the room. Congratulations: You've rotated on your axis, even though the chair observer has never seen your backside.

But it's no coincidence that the Moon behaves this way. In fact, it's a typically Moony thing to do. Just as the Moon's gravity creates tides in the oceans of Earth, so has Earth's greater gravity raised tides in the first-molten, now-stony body of the Moon. In the distant past, the Moon was spinning faster and orbiting closer. But the Earth's pull, offset by the tendency of a moving body to fly off on its own, deformed the Moon, making it slightly egg-shaped. And the Moon's rotation gradually slowed as it lost energy to the internal upheaval.

As its spinning braked, the Moon bulged more on one side than the other, the man-in-the-Moon side jutting out some 2 miles

Over time, the Earth's gravitational pull has deformed the Moon, making it slightly egg-shaped, and the Moon's rotation gradually slowed as it lost energy to the internal upheaval.

more (and feeling more of the Earth's gravitational force). This is the side that ended up facing us when the Moon reached a comfortable equilibrium, becoming tidally locked by the Earth.

Scientists say that many moons became tidally locked after they formed, and now show only one face to their home planets. Among the dozens in synchronous rotation in our solar system are Mars's Phobos and Deimos; Jupiter's Io, Europa, Ganymede, and Callisto; at least 17 of Saturn's moons, including Enceladus and Titan; Uranus's Miranda and Ariel; Neptune's Triton; and dwarf planet Pluto's companion Charon.

FAST FACT

Since the Moon's orbit is also pulled this way and that by the Sun and other planets, we actually get glimpses of about 9 percent of the Moon's backside. Which, by the way, experiences both day and night, just like the facing side.

Why does a pool of oil on the wet driveway develop rainbow colors?

Have you ever noticed the shimmering rainbow on the side of a soap bubble? Or the rainbow effect on a butterfly wing (or an abalone shell)? All these—and the swirling colors in an oil slick—are examples of iridescence.

How do a clear, clean bubble and a black spill of oil both come to display a floating rainbow? The answer has to do with light, and how it interferes with itself.

Like people, waves of light can get in one another's way. Two light waves that exactly coincide with each other, crest matching crest, make for brightened light. But if a cresting wave matches up with a falling wave, the two cancel each other out—making that spot dim or dark.

Interfering light waves create the colors we see in oil slicks and soap bubbles. White light from the Sun contains a rainbow of colors; each color has a different wavelength. You can see this rainbow when you hold a prism in sunlight and the colors spill out the other side.

A thin film of oil or soap floating on water has two surfaces—top and bottom. Sunlight reflects back from both surfaces, causing light waves to interfere with one another inside the film. Bursts of color can appear in places where the waves of one color—such as green or red—match up and reinforce each other.

That's why an assortment of brilliant colors swirls in an oil slick. The exact colors you see depend on the angle from which you are viewing a thin film and on the film's thickness.

But interference occurs in more than oil slicks and soap bubbles. It's also why you

> **Interfering light waves create the colors we see in oil slicks and soap bubbles.**

see a gleaming rainbow in the surface of a compact disc. Shimmery, iridescent colors appear in everything from peacocks to pearls, beetles to butterflies—on any object that has a thin film to redirect light.

Ordinary color, such as the red of a robin's chest, or the orange of a monarch butterfly's wings, comes from pigments. The pigment melanin, for example, gives our skin, hair, and eyes their color. And in autumn, anthocyanin pigments color leaves red and purple.

But it's the structure of an object that produces a rainbow effect. A can of motor oil is black; a thin film of the same oil floating on water plays with light, making brilliant phantom colors.

Take butterfly wings. Their standard colors come from pigments. Their iridescent colors appear because of wing structure.

How? Butterfly wings contain very thin layers of chitin—the hard material that makes shells for insects and shellfish—separated by air. So each thin layer is like the thin film in an oil slick, and each layer makes light iridesce. Multiple layers produce spectacular effects (morpho wings look bright blue from above, deep violet from the side), making butterfly wings shine far more brilliantly than a roadside pool of oil.

When we spin a bucket of water around, why doesn't the water spill out?

Swing a bucket of water around with enough energy, and not one drop falls out. Why does the water stay inside? For clues, think about clothes clinging to the sides of the washer drum in the spin cycle, or even Earth speeding around the Sun at 67,000 miles per hour.

When you swing a bucket of water around your body on a vertical, up-and-down path, you are exerting a centripetal (toward the center) force on the bucket. You are forcing an object in motion to take a circular path. Meanwhile, the force of gravity is tugging the pail and its contents down, toward the Earth.

Swing the bucket fast, and the water,

When the Centripetal Bathtub Stops...

It's a mega-mess time!

It's no-more-fun time!

It's scrape-the-kid-off-the-wall time.

trying to fly out, presses against the bottom of the pail. As the bucket swings through the top of the circle, the water's motion up and out more than balances the force of gravity "down," so none spills.

What if you don't swing the pail fast enough, or stop halfway through? Instant watery disaster. Think about that load of laundry. Before the clothes begin to spin, they lie limply on the bottom of the washer, overcome by the downward force of gravity. But click on the spin cycle, and the clothes are picked up and thrown to the sides. Slow or stop the spin, and the clothes come tumbling down.

Likewise, swing the pail too slowly, and the water will begin to tumble down and out. Stop the pail abruptly, and you're soaked. Gravity wins again.

Then there's Plan C: The Letting Go. Remove the centripetal force, and a moving object's own inertia is revealed.

The bucket is restrained by your grip on the handle or rope. And the water is

When you swing a bucket of water around your body on a vertical, up-and-down path, you are exerting a centripetal (toward the center) force on the bucket.

stopped by the bottom of the pail. So if you let go of your bucket mid-swing, it will take off on a straight path into the wild blue yonder. Freed from the centripetal force you supplied, the bucket and its contents will continue on their merry way (well, at least for a short freedom-filled distance).

Now think about Earth. If our orbiting planet were to slow down, or suddenly careen to a stop, it would be pulled by gravity into the Sun—just as the water fell from the bucket when it slowed or stopped.

On the other hand, what if an annoyed Sun were to disappear in a huff, taking its gravity with it? The speeding Earth would be freed from the centripetal force that keeps it running around the big star like a faithful puppy. Our planet would slingshot off in a straight line. Zooming off into the wild black yonder of space, Earth would continue on its merry way until it was captured by the gravity of another star, slammed into a fellow planet, or was sucked into a black hole.

Why do raccoons wash their food?

Raccoons sometimes dunk food in water before eating it, leading people to wonder. Washing? Moistening? But raccoons have also been known to dip their dinner in dirt, like dredging a piece of fish in flour. So scientists think the dunking—observed mainly in captive raccoons—is a hardwired echo of other hands-on behavior, like catching crawfish.

Raccoons, after all, are able to identify food by touch alone. Repeated object-dunking may be a compulsive reaction to captivity. Or perhaps raccoons, with their ever-curious hands and minds, just like to play with their food.

Raccoons, like bears, are omnivorous—they take what food they can get, depending on the season and the local pickings. So

besides its favorite freshwater menu, a raccoon might settle for a raw egg, a handful of blackberries, an ear of sweet corn, or a few acorns.

A raccoon's favorite home is a hollow tree near a pond or stream or river. But raccoons can also camp out in an abandoned groundhog burrow, an old shed, or the crawl space under a porch. So it's not surprising to catch a raccoon in the beam of your flashlight, looking like a masked robber picking through your trash can. Leftover pizza rind? A soggy potato chip? A bite of salad with

> The key to a raccoon's success is its remarkably human "hands," front paws with five slender fingers.

ranch dressing? It's all good.

The fact that raccoons can make do with many kinds of food has helped them adapt to life around people. But the key to a raccoon's success in adapting to a world of tract houses, gas stations, and blacktop driveways are its remarkably human "hands," front paws with five slender fingers. Raccoons have very nimble fingers and love to use them, examining shiny objects, unlatching hated cages, or turning doorknobs to creep into well-stocked kitchens.

Why Do Raccoons Have Masks?

With their Zorro masks and convict-striped tails, raccoons are always ready for a costume party. Newborn baby raccoons don't have black masks or dark tail rings. But by two weeks of age, little markings have filled in.

Why the masks? Raccoons use their faces (as we do) to communicate. Scientists say that the mask, rings, and other markings help raccoons identify one another. But the markings may also help raccoons blend into a forest background of brown bark and dappled shadows.

Raccoons like to spend lots of time at the water's edge, searching for tasty crabs, crawfish, frogs, turtles, and water insects. Like the black smeared under the eyes of a football player to reduce the sun's glare, a raccoon's mask may cut the glare of sunlight (or moonlight) off water.

Why do moles dig holes?

Moles are miniature mammals that live underground in the dark. Moles dig holes for the same reason human beings build houses and restaurants. Like us, moles want a roof over their heads (even if the roof is made of mud) and a bite to eat (even if the bite is a bit of earthworm).

The biggest moles measure about 9 inches long, while the smallest are a mere 4 inches, including tail. Moles wear a soft coat of velvety fur in a variety of colors, from black to silver.

FAST FACT

Moles are among Earth's older mammals, part of an order called Insectivora (all of whom really, really like to eat bugs). Insectivores have been around for at least 130 million years. Shrews and hedgehogs are among the other insect-eating mammals still thriving today.

A clue to the mole lifestyle is provided by a mole's teeny-tiny eyes, which are only good for telling light from dark. When you live in a very dark place, other senses—hearing, smell, and touch—are the most important.

Moles like loamy or sandy soil the best, since it's easy to tunnel through. While tunnels in the ground may look alike to us, moles have their own system. Feeding tubes leading from the ground down are actually handy insect traps, collecting bugs that drop in for an unplanned visit.

Deeper tunnels—sometimes 3 feet below the surface—are used to hide from predators (like snakes, foxes, owls, hawks, and dogs) and to take shelter from the rain, snow, and cold. Branching off the tunnels, dugout rooms, lined with leaves and grass, are used by nesting mother moles and for sleeping. In fact, tucked away in their basement bedrooms, moles can spend up to ten hours a day snoozing.

Moles love earthworms, beetles, ants, and underground bees and hornets. But moles also eat plants, and some dine on mice, frogs, and fish. (Some moles are excellent swimmers.) To find a tasty earthworm, a mole relies mainly on snout sensors (tiny bumps and whiskers), and sensitive hairs on feet and tail.

Moles may dig up to 100 feet of tunnel a day, but some feeding and deep tunnels stay in use for years. A mole's front paws are shaped like side-facing shovels tipped with five long, heavy claws each, perfect for enginelike tunneling in the dark.

One of the most otherworldly and alien-appearing animals on Earth is the star-nosed mole. At the end of its snout, this mole wears a spray of 22 fleshy pink spines that resemble tiny fingers. Packed with more than 25,000 sensors, the snout's "star" is exquisitely sensitive to the lightest touch. The star-nosed mole uses its half-inch star to detect insects in soil. In a fraction of a second, a worm or other tasty tidbit is located and swallowed.

> A mole's front paws are shaped like side-facing shovels tipped with five long, heavy claws each, perfect for enginelike tunneling in the dark.

MOLE TALK...

Making me a salad?

How come trees have rings?

What if there were a record of what had happened to our planet before human beings wrote down what they were seeing? What if there were a way to know when a volcano erupted a continent away, a comet crashed into an open plain, or a rash of sunspots erupted on the Sun's fiery face?

There is such a silent diary being kept; it is locked in the heart of trees.

The hidden rings revealed when a tree trunk is cut horizontally or sampled with a corer are like natural hieroglyphs, from which scientists can read some of the history of Earth. There is even a branch of science dedicated to translating the riddle of the rings: dendrochronology.

Deciduous (trees that drop their leaves) and coniferous (cone-bearing) trees in temperate climates usually have distinct

A Coniferous Diary Written in the Rings . . .

growth rings. Trees expand outward by growing a new layer of wood cells just under the bark. In the spring, the growth layer makes large, thin-walled cells called early wood. As the season becomes drier, the cells produced become smaller and thicker-walled late wood. By fall, the tree has stopped making new cells. You can tell one yearly ring from the next because the darker, late-wood cells from one year lie beside the next year's lighter, early-wood cells. By counting rings, we can get a good idea of the tree's age in years.

Rings are thinner when rainfall is scant or temperatures plunge too low during the growth season. Sunlight, soil fertility, and diseases and pests all affect rings, too.

Because rings vary, sometimes dramatically, from year to year, they provide clues as to what happened in the past—droughts, floods, erupting volcanoes, forest fires, global cooling and warming. By counting the rings backward in time, we can often figure out when such events occurred.

To read the record hidden in the wood, scientists can drill into trees and pull out slim cores. By matching up rings from living trees, dead trees, and ancient wood, scientists can cross-date rings and make a timeline extending far into the past.

One of the best ring histories hides in bristlecone pines, slow-growers that take 3,000 years to reach their full height (40 to 60 feet). By matching up the overlapping rings of living and long-dead bristlecone wood, scientists have dated events back to about 7000 B.C.

Tree rings help scientists track climate changes. When volcanoes erupt, spewing soot and sulfur droplets, the atmosphere darkens, making for frosty summers and thin rings. The widespread thinning of tree rings about 1,500 years ago points to a bigger catastrophe—possibly pieces of a giant comet hitting Earth.

Tree rings even help us glimpse events elsewhere in the solar system. When cosmic rays strike nitrogen molecules in Earth's atmosphere, radioactive carbon 14 is formed. High sunspot and solar wind activity means fewer cosmic rays reach the atmosphere, and the creation of carbon 14 falls. By comparing the carbon 14 content of tree rings with other natural objects, scientists have traced sunspot activity back thousands of years.

Tree rings help scientists track climate changes and can even provide glimpses of events that have happened elsewhere in the solar system.

Why does a yo-yo come back to your hand?

Like a turning boomerang, a spinning yo-yo returns to its thrower. Unlike a boomerang, a thin string connects tosser to toy. It's the string that lets a dedicated yo-yoer go on a virtual trick odyssey: Walk the Dog, Hop the Fence, Loop the Loop, Around the World, Reach the Moon.

Even when they can't personally do the tricks, physicists love yo-yos, since they demonstrate so vividly how gravity, momentum, friction, and spin change the motion of an object. Knowing the science behind a yo-yo helps inventors come up with ever more advanced designs—like a $400 yo-yo made of a magnesium alloy, equipped with a sleek system of ball bearings, counterweights, and other devices. The point of high-tech add-ons is to create a yo-yo that can perform even more elaborate tricks. But the simplest wooden or plastic yo-yo is amazingly ingenious already. In fact, people were practicing their yo-yo tricks at least 2,500 years ago.

No one knows when or where the first yo-yo was invented. But we know that the Greeks had yo-yos by 500 B.C.; a painting on a vase shows a kid playing with one. The disc toys in ancient Greece were made of wood, metal, or even terra-cotta (fired clay, like the flower pots). In India, a painted box from 1765 depicts a girl and a yo-yo. Over the centuries, the toy has been known as a disc, an *émigrette*, a bandalore, and a quiz.

All basic yo-yos work pretty much the same way. A string is looped around the axle of the yo-yo; the other end of the string is attached to your finger. When

FAST FACT

The word yo-yo comes from the Philippines, where people have been playing with the spinning spools since at least the 1500s. In the Filipino language Tagalog, yo-yo means "come back."

you drop the yo-yo, gravity pulls it toward the ground. Because the yo-yo is held by the looped string, it spins (rotates) as it drops. As an object falls, it picks up speed. So a falling yo-yo spins fast, faster, and then fastest, when it reaches the end of its string.

A gentle tug on the string will increase the friction between string and axle, so the axle stops slipping. Since the yo-yo is still spinning, its leftover energy starts the string rewinding around the axle. And like magic, the yo-yo starts to climb back up toward

No one knows when or where the first yo-yo was invented. But we know that the Greeks had yo-yos by 500 B.C.: a painting on a vase shows a kid playing with one.

you. As the yo-yo climbs, it loses some of its kinetic energy of rotation—it spins slower, losing momentum. Meanwhile, it gains gravitational potential energy: increasing potential to fall energetically and far once again.

Because of momentum-sapping friction with the string, a yo-yo will tend to stop spinning sooner on each journey up the string, return farther out of reach, and finally stop at the bottom. To keep the yo-yo going, simply apply a small upward pull each time.

Meditations on a yo-yo's return...

Yo-yo has fallen in love with hand, and can't stay away...

Yo-yo is afraid of floor and must escape...

Yo-yo is never happy and must stay on the move!

How come it's still light for an hour after the Sun sets?

Twilight time: a time of purple clouds, deepening shadows, a fading glow in the sky. Still light enough to play outside, but getting harder and harder to read without a lamp. As a song made popular by the Platters in 1958 goes, "Heavenly shades of night are falling; it's twilight time."

Twilight is usually thought of as the time just after the Sun sets in the evening. But the word also refers to the time just before the Sun rises in the morning. During twilight, although the Sun is below the horizon, the sky is still aglow with light, gradually dimming (after sunset) or intensifying (before sunrise).

STAGES OF TWILIGHT TENNIS

CIVIL TWILIGHT
YOU CAN SEE THE NET, THE PERSON YOU'RE PLAYING WITH, BUT NOT THE...

NAUTICAL TWILIGHT
YOU CAN SEE THE HORIZON, NAVIGATE TO THE SNACK BAR, BUT NOT DETECT THE...

ASTRONOMICAL TWILIGHT
YOU CAN SEE THE STARS BUT NOT YOUR TENNIS PARTNER AND HIS LAST...

How come? The light for our evening (or early-morning) activities comes courtesy of the upper atmosphere. Light rays from the hidden Sun are bent (refracted) as they pass from the near-vacuum of space into the gas molecules of the atmosphere. This means that the sky remains lit by sunlight for a time even though the Sun is hidden below the horizon. Since sunlight is also scattered every which way by gas molecules in the air, some of the light even reaches the ground. So it's the still-illuminated sky that creates twilight—in the evening, the afterglow before night sets in.

In fact, there are actually four categories of twilight. During the evening, the first twilight period starts with sunset. Sunset twilight ends when the Sun has dipped a little less than 1 degree below the horizon.

Next comes civil twilight. During civil twilight, it is still light enough to carry on most outdoor activities, like playing tag on the lawn or watering a garden. Big shapes are still visible during this early twilight, even without street lamps or porch lights lit. You may see a few bright stars or planets in the sky. In the continental United States, civil twilight lasts for about 30 to 40 minutes, depending on the time of the year and the location. It ends when the Sun is 6 degrees below the horizon.

Then there's nautical twilight. During nautical twilight, the sky is dark enough that the brighter stars are visible. The horizon is still visible, too, so a sailor at sea could navigate by measuring the altitude of certain beacon stars. By the end of nautical twilight, the Sun has slid 12 degrees below the horizon, and the horizon line is fading into darkness.

Finally, there's astronomical twilight. More and more stars can be seen, but the sky is still too light for an astronomer to do any serious work. When the Sun has sunk to 18 degrees below the horizon, twilight is officially over. Astronomical darkness—real night—has begun.

> Twilight is the time just after the Sun sets in the evening, but it's also the time just before the Sun rises in the morning.

Why are bugs attracted to the porch light at night?

Moths endlessly orbit a porch light on a summer night. June bugs knock on your glass door, lured by the glow of lamps inside your house. Teeny-tiny gnats slip through the holes in the window screen, dazzled by the light over the kitchen sink.

But why? What's in it for the bugs?

Many insects are attracted by lights—but not all. Most female mosquitoes, on the prowl for a blood meal, ignore the porch light and zero in on the human lumbering through the darkness, using the warmth of the person's body as a homing device. However, some adult mosquitoes are attracted to light, and so are many other flying insects.

Insects evolved when moonless nights were truly dark, before artificial lights were invented that outshone the Moon and stars. Scientists say bright lights simply confuse many insects. For example, take moths.

Guiding Light . . .

I'm looking for my house keys.

I'm looking for love!

I'm looking for St. Louis!

Some people argue that certain moths may be genuinely attracted to glowing lightbulbs. Female moths, they say, emit chemicals that give off infrared radiation and attract males. When male moths detect the same radiation coming from a lightbulb, they are irresistibly drawn to it.

Other scientists say that moths aren't attracted to lights at all. Instead, it's all about mistaken navigation. Many moths, flying above the treetops, apparently use the moon as a beacon. They even make adjustments to their flight paths to take into account the moon's ever-changing position in the sky. Scientists say these moths-on-the-move also have biological sensors that can detect Earth's magnetic field lines—especially handy for moonless nights. Pushed by the wind, migrating moths can travel hundreds of miles overnight.

But a lit-up porch light, brighter than the moon, can distract moths flying in the vicinity. And on a Moon-free night, a porch light may be the only game in town. So some scientists think that moths may confusedly lock onto an artificial light as a navigational aid.

Insects evolved before artificial lights were invented that outshone the Moon and stars. Scientists say bright lights simply confuse many insects.

But the Moon is 240,000 miles away, while a porch light is, well, right there. So a moth, navigating to keep the Moon over its right shoulder, can only keep the porch light to its right by continuously flying around it. A sad situation for the moth, which, like a hamster on a wheel, keeps moving but never gets anywhere.

Still, that doesn't explain why some insects fly directly at lights—and bounce off. Theories about bugs and lights are still in their infancy, and there is plenty of room for experiments and more theories. One unproven idea is that some insects are attracted to lightbulbs because of the sound frequencies they emit.

FAST FACT

White lights usually attract more insects than yellow lights do, which is why bug-proof porch lights are golden. And nights crowned by a full Moon may find fewer bugs, especially moths and beetles, tricked into spiraling around the nearest man-made lamp.

Why does the wind whistle, howl, and moan?

Where would a haunted house be without a dark and stormy night—and a high, moaning wind? Likewise, the wind needs the drafty old house—and the tossing trees around it—to create its spooky sound effects.

Why does wind sometimes whistle and moan? According to physicist Jearl Walker of Cleveland State University, the sound effects begin when rushing air encounters an obstacle in its path—say, a tree limb or a telephone wire. As it passes across the wire, the wind becomes unstable. Swirling air patterns (vortices) appear on top of and underneath the wire, creating waves of varying pressure. When the sound waves reach our ears, we hear whistling and sighing. Walker says that while strong winds can make wires vibrate, the wind sounds are actually caused by the swirling air patterns, not the vibration.

The pitch of the sound gets higher as the wind blows faster and the sound waves increase in frequency. Meteorologists say that wind really starts whistling through wires when its speed reaches about 25 miles per hour.

Just like different musical instruments, different trees create different sounds. Pine trees, some say, sound like whispery violins when played by the wind, while the wind in willows may sound like a flute.

And, like someone blowing across the mouth of a jug, wind blowing across the opening of a cavity—say, the chimney of

FAST FACT

Sound waves are back-and-forth vibrations traveling through air or another medium, like water. Air bunches up and spreads out again in waves of varying pressure. A sound wave might get started when a musician claps two cymbals (or an audience member two hands) together, making waves that travel (at about 1,100 feet per second) to your eardrum.

an enclosed fireplace—can create a low-pitched thrum or moan.

Wind can howl, according to Walker, when it blows against sharp edges, such as roof corners. Swirls of air stream off the edge, and some of the waves reflect back into the wind stream. That creates even more whirling vortices in the wind, which also strike and spin off the roof edge. The complex wave pattern, when it reaches our

Pine trees, some say, sound like whispery violins when played by the wind, while the wind in willows may sound like a flute.

ears, makes a howling sound. Winds can also whine at small cracks or holes in a building, such as a window that won't close all the way.

The passage of air from our lungs across our vocal cords, tongue, and lips allows us to whisper, groan, and sing. In the same way, tree branches, overhead wires, building edges, and all the cracks and crevices of the world give the wind its varied voice.

Noises for when the wind is howling your way...

The umbrella eater... The hat grabber... ...The wind sock maker.

How come we see our breath in the winter?

Step outside on a cold January morning, take a deep breath, and then exhale. In winter—or on any cold day, no matter what the season—there is a visible marker of your carbon-dioxide contribution to the world around you. Like a miniature cloud, your breath hangs for a moment in front of your

On frigid, windless mornings in the country, you can sometimes tell where horses in a field stood moments before by the frozen clouds of their breath hanging in the air.

face before it disperses into the air.

But it isn't actually carbon dioxide you're seeing when you see your breath; it's the water that comes out with it. Visible breath is a lot like fog, which is just a cloud hugging the ground. Warm air can hold a lot of water vapor. But as air cools and gas molecules

pack closer together, it reaches its saturation point sooner.

On a warm day or in a warm room, the water vapor you exhale (along with carbon dioxide) simply spreads out as molecules into the air. So no cloud appears.

But when the outside air is cold, it can't hold as much water vapor as the very warm air inside your lungs. Before you exhale, neither the cold air around your face nor the warm air coming from your lungs is completely saturated with water. When the exhaled water molecules hit the cold air, the small parcel of air in front of your face is suddenly supersaturated with water. The water vapor immediately condenses into droplets, forming a tiny cloud. This breath cloud is much like the contrail that can stream out of a high-flying jet. As the droplets disperse and

FAST FACT

A good sign that the wintry scene in that movie you're watching isn't real is a lack of visible breath when the characters speak. Don't see any breath? Check out the snow; it's probably fake, too.

evaporate, your breath disappears, just as a contrail fades into the sky.

There is no set temperature at which you will begin to see your own breath. Whether water vapor condenses into droplets depends on both the temperature and the current air pressure. But you will almost certainly see a small cloud with each exhale when the temperature falls below about 45°F.

Ice Fogs

When the temperature plunges below zero, fogs made of ice can appear. These ice fogs are similar to the icy clouds high in Earth's atmosphere, in which water molecules collect into ice crystals instead of liquid droplets. Likewise, breath fog can freeze. On frigid, windless mornings in the country, you can sometimes tell where horses in a field stood moments before by the frozen clouds of their breath hanging in the air.

Is it true that no two snowflakes are exactly alike?

Ever hear someone say that two brothers or best friends are as "alike as two peas in a pod"? Green peas may not be perfectly identical, though they're featureless enough to fit the bill. But when it comes to being different or unique, most people usually think not of vegetables, but of snowflakes.

What we call snowflakes contain one or many individual snow crystals. Huge flakes dropping swiftly from a winter sky may be clumps of hundreds of crystals. The wetter

Snowflake Pep Talk

Of course you're special! There's not a snowflake like you in the entire universe, or so they say...

and stickier the snow, the bigger the falling flakes.

Even the most dissimilar snow crystals have something in common—six sides or points. Snow crystals are hexagonal because the water molecules they are made from link together into a six-sided lattice as they freeze. As millions and billions of water molecules hook into place, the lattice gets bigger, but stays six-sided, creating a six-sided snow crystal.

Photographs of snow crystals reveal miniature frozen landscapes, often far more elaborate than the most intricate Valentine's Day lace doily. Hidden in snowflakes are inscribed stars and starbursts, flowers and fern fronds, often layered in dizzying kaleidoscope patterns.

A typical tiny snow crystal contains up to one quintillion individual water molecules. The basic form of an ice crystal is a miniature prism with six sides, like a section removed from a hexagonal pencil. The prism can be a short, stubby column or a long, chandelier-prism column. Or the prism can be nearly flat, like a six-sided glass dinner plate.

The crystal's final shape depends mainly

> No one has found two complex snow crystals that look exactly alike, and scientists say that the odds are low that they ever will.

on the temperature in the region of the cloud where it formed. But snow crystals tend to grow into the most intricate star-spoked shapes when the humidity is high. Within the cloud, snow crystals grow facets like those of cut diamonds and branch out like trees on their six points. The icy branches appear because the hexagon's corners jut out and accumulate freezing water molecules faster than the rest of the crystal.

Scientists have found simple crystal columns that look nearly identical. But even human identical twins aren't really identical (for more on this, see page 208), and two identical-looking simple crystals would be different on the molecular level.

However, no one has found two complex snow crystals that look exactly alike, and scientists say that the odds are low that they ever will. Each growing snow crystal follows its own meandering, bouncing path through a cloud. The way crystals were tossed and twirled, the difference in the temperatures and humidity they experienced, and how they fell to Earth all determine their final, unique shapes.

Why is it so quiet after a snowfall?

The snow is falling thick and fast, piling up so quickly that those footprints you recently made have all but disappeared. Also deepening is the sound of silence, as a white blanket is drawn over the landscape.

How come? Some of the quiet is due to fewer sounds to hear: Birds aren't chirping; drivers are avoiding the roads; people are huddled indoors with cups of warm cocoa and hot tea, noses occasionally pressed against the glass to watch the swiftly falling flakes.

But there is more to snowy silence than the absence of activity. A truck lumbers by, but its grinding brakes and rattling cargo are strangely muted. A dog's bark in the distance sounds muffled.

The hush isn't due to the falling flakes absorbing sounds; the quiet lasts for hours after the snow has stopped. In fact, when we

When we wake up on a winter morning, we may know it has snowed even before we look out the window, simply because of the soft silence.

wake up on a winter morning, we may know it has snowed even before we look out the window, simply because of the soft silence.

Scientists say that as new snow piles up on bare ground or old snow, it's the arrangement of the flakes that dampens sounds. Snow crystals come in varied shapes and sizes, from flat plates to pointy stars, and each big flake can be made of dozens of crystals. So as snowflakes land, they don't make a compact, jigsaw-puzzle layer. Instead, they pile up loosely, with plenty of air-filled spaces in between. These spaces or pores in the snow absorb sound like the pores in acoustic ceiling tiles.

Piled-up flakes have two main effects on sound. Sound waves that would normally hit bare ground or concrete and be partially reflected are instead mostly absorbed into the blanket of snow. More important, sound waves traveling parallel to the snow get muffled, too.

How? According to researchers, as sound waves travel across a layer of fluffy snow, the pressure of the passing waves briefly pushes air down into the spaces between flakes. So the waves lose more and more energy due to friction and thermal (heat) effects in their sweep across the pore-filled snow layer. By the time snow-skimming sound waves reach your ears, they are weakened. And you hear a softer, more muffled sound.

In fact, experiments show that what would make a loud bang in summer (like a firecracker or a banging trash can lid) makes a quiet *whoomp* in a winter landscape covered with fresh snow. And the sound will not only be softer, but also more wavery and drawn out.

But a layer of newly fallen snow, piled up in a delicate stack of oddly shaped flakes, is fragile. Blowing wind flattens it. Sunlight melts it. A freezing rain collapses it and adds a coating of solid ice on top. Once the delicate layer caves, its sound-muffling quality (sadly) disappears. The more hard-packed the snow, the more it acts like bare ground or concrete, reflecting and transmitting sound. And noise rises to nearly normal levels.

SOUNDPROOFING BY FRESHLY FALLEN SNOW...

At the Library...
It's quiet, but freezing!

In the Recording Studio...
It's insulated for sound, not temperature.

In your bedroom...
Just the noise of your chattering teeth!

Do flying squirrels really exist?

Bullwinkle the moose would be shocked. If flying squirrels don't exist, who's that character with the leather helmet and goggles that's been his (smarter) sidekick all these years?

Okay, Rocky the flying squirrel doesn't really exist. But real flying squirrels do, and they can make "flights" that carry them hundreds of feet through the air, without an old-fashioned pilot's helmet.

If an ordinary squirrel decided to take a flying leap from the top of a tree, the sun would probably be shining. And he could expect to land in the branches of a nearby tree—or on the roof of your garage.

But if a flying squirrel took the same leap, he would probably do it in the dark. And he could expect to land on the trunk of a not-so-nearby tree—say, 50 feet across the yard—after a graceful sail through the night air.

Flying Squirrel Airlines...

No Delays — Unless I oversleep.

Friendly Service — Unless I'm in a bad mood.

Delicious Snacks — unless I eat them.

Flying squirrels don't really fly; they don't have wings to flap like birds or bats do. But they are expert gliders who can turn, brake, and come in for a soft landing on the hard side of a tree.

There are actually 43 species of flying squirrel gliding around Europe, Asia, and North America. They range in size from the dwarf flying squirrel, about 5 inches long, to the giant woolly flying squirrel, which can measure 4 feet from nose to tail tip. Others include the groove-toothed, hairy-footed, red giant, and smoky flying squirrels.

The two species that swoop around North America are about 8 to 12 inches long. The northern flying squirrel makes its home in Canada and the northern United States. The smaller southern flying squirrel stays mainly in the east and south, from Ontario to Mexico.

Flying squirrels do most of their acrobatics at night. Under the protective cover of darkness, they go looking for dinner: nuts and seeds, fruit and insects, flowers and leaves, sweet maple sap, and birds' eggs and baby birds. Meanwhile, flying squirrels must

There are actually 43 kinds of flying squirrels gliding around Europe, Asia, and North America.

themselves watch out for hungry hawks and owls, raccoons and coyotes, and bored house cats.

For gliding, a flying squirrel has a loose flap of skin like a tarp connected from his wrist to his ankle on each side. Stretching out all four legs and taking the leap, a flying squirrel looks like a mini hang glider floating on a current of air. As he glides along on a gradual downward arc, a flying squirrel pilot turns or changes his angle of descent by using his wrists to tighten or loosen the flaps, and his tail as a handy stabilizer.

To come in for a landing, the squirrel lifts his body, drops his tail, and relaxes his flaps, letting the air act as a brake. Landing on all fours on the tree trunk, the squirrel usually scampers around to the other side (in case something was following). Then, if the journey isn't over, he runs to the top and flings himself into the sky again, making quick progress through the woods. How long each glide lasts depends on the height of the takeoff branch, and the direction and strength of the wind. The longest glides can measure more than 200 feet.

How do icicles form on gutters?

A snow-covered roof on a sunny but frigid day makes a perfect icicle incubator. Sunlight heats the snow, which is also warmed from below by heat radiating through the roof from the attic. As snow melts, water trickles down the shingles to the icy-cold edges and metal gutters. There, it refreezes.

FAST FACT

Icicles can grow more than 3 feet long before their own weight causes them to crash to the ground, sometimes taking gutters (or tree branches) with them.

Water molecules are attracted to other water molecules. So as water continues to run down the roof, pulled by gravity, it collects where its fellow molecules have already frozen. Ice adds to ice, drip by drip. And slowly, an icicle grows toward the ground.

Scientists say that the growth of an icicle is fueled by the interaction between the surrounding air and a thin film of water flowing down an icy surface. The temperature of the liquid water dripping off the roof is higher than that of the freezing air. So a small amount of heat diffuses from the thin film of water coating the icicle's surface into the air around it. The air absorbs heat from the liquid water, causing a mini updraft of cold air around the icicle. Losing its heat, the film of water freezes, adding another layer of ice to the icicle. The effect is amplified because water naturally expands as it freezes (think of ice cubes bulging out of a tray). This process of melting, dripping, and refreezing makes icicles grow into long, glittering spikes.

According to researchers at the University of Arizona, the air surrounding an icicle is the secret to its sharp point. The bulky top is surrounded by a bigger blanket of warm air. The tip grows faster than the base, they say, because the layer of heated air is thinnest at the bottom, and water freezes faster there. The result: a tapering spike.

An icicle's ridges, scientists think, start out as random bulges. These bulges lose heat more quickly than the surrounding areas. Trickling-down water refreezes on the bumps first, making them thicken into ridges. The ridge spacing—about 0.4 inch—is the same on icicles big and small, and scientists in Japan think they know why: As a ridge gets bigger, the water trickling over it is churned more, like a stream flowing over a rock. The churning water doesn't

> The air surrounding an icicle is the secret to its sharp point.

carry heat away as efficiently, slowing down the ridge's freezing. So a regular pattern of ridges forms, rather than one humongous ice bump.

And University of Wisconsin physics professor Thomas Lockhart thinks he knows why hanging icicles themselves are often regularly spaced, like birds on a wire. Drops of melted water grow as big as they can at the edge of the roof before they freeze or fall off. This results in a certain minimum distance between the drops and a rather uniform spacing along the roof for the resulting line of icicles.

The life cycle of an Icicle

A baby is born...   middle age...   The End.

Waa!   Check out my ridges!   Eeeek!

191

Why does bright sunlight make you sneeze?

No one knows when the first human being emerged from a dark cave into bright sunlight . . . and began sneezing uncontrollably. But by the 1600s, English scientist and philosopher Francis Bacon was writing about the phenomenon.

"Looking against the Sunne, doth induce Sneezing," Bacon noted. "The Cause is not the Heating of the Nosthrils [nostrils]; For then the Holding up of the Nosthrils against the Sunne, though one Winke, would doe it."

In other words, the nose can't be the culprit in Sun sneezing, since if you close your eyes, walk out into the Sun, and expose your nose, you probably won't sneeze. What, then, is the cause? Bacon speculated about moisture descending from the brain into the eyes and nose, but had no real answer for the phenomenon. And nearly 400 years later, scientists are still trying to figure it out.

Ophthalmologists note that many patients sneeze during eye exams, when physicians

Bright Lights 'N' Big Sneezes

Trigeminal Tickle — Hey, I'm going to...

Solar Sneeze — AH-AH-AH

Triple Ah-choo! — Gesundheit! — choo!

shine very bright light into their eyes in a darkened room. So ye olde Sunne doesn't need to be out for the sneezing fits to commence.

When scientists look into an unexplained phenomenon, it usually gets a formal-sounding name. So sneezing in bright light has been dubbed the photic sneeze reflex (since light is made of particles called photons), solar sneezing, and even ACHOO (for **a**utosomal dominant **c**ompelling **h**elio-**o**phthalmic **o**utburst), which is a cute way of saying that when you sneeze in the Sun, your genes made you do it.

Photic sneezing does seem to run in families, and scientists think that we inherit the tendency to sneeze in the Sun from our parents. No one knows exactly how it works, but the stimulus seems to start in the eye's optic nerve. The optic nerve runs near the face's trigeminal nerve and into the same nerve hub in the brain. (And in photic sneezers, these wires may be, in some sense, crossed.) Part of the trigeminal nerve branches into the nose. So when the optic nerve reacts to very bright light after a period of darkness, neurons in the nerves

> Photic sneezing—sneezing in sunlight—seems to run in families, and scientists think that we inherit the tendency from our parents.

leading into the nose may fire off, too. Presto: a volley of sneezes.

According to one study, the majority of photic sneezers sneeze three times in a row. Scientists say that the number of sneezes—2, 3, or even 40—may be genetically determined, too. One mystery: Why photic sneezers don't sneeze every time they encounter bright light after a period of darkness. Scientists speculate that there may be a certain brightness threshold required to trigger the response.

While Sun sneezing is usually annoying, it can actually be hazardous for drivers emerging from long tunnels or pilots in dim cockpits turning their planes into the Sun's glare. But sunlight isn't the only odd sneeze-promoter. Some people sneeze each time they pluck their eyebrows.

FAST FACT

Up to 35 percent of us occasionally sneeze when we emerge from a dark or dim place (like a movie theater) into brilliant sunlight.

How come my dog can hear so well?

Your dog is frantically barking at the front door; you look out and don't see a thing, not even a meandering squirrel. Has Fido finally lost his mind? Or—as the UPS man pulls into the driveway a minute later—does your dog know something you don't?

Being dog-eared may be a bad thing for a book, but it's a very good thing when it comes to hearing. The average dog is a lean, mean hearing machine, picking up on the softest sounds from hundreds of feet away, and perceiving sounds (like a tooting dog whistle) where we hear only silence.

The higher-pitched the sound, the more sound waves reach the ear each second. Humans hear sounds ranging from about 20 to 20,000 Hertz (cycles per second). But dogs hear sounds in a wider frequency range of about 40 to 60,000 Hertz.

So low, rumbling sounds may seem about the same to you and your dog. But above 20,000 Hertz, most human beings hear only the sounds of silence. Which is why, when we

Can You Hear What Dogs Hear?

Dogs can hear a can being opened within 50 miles...

Make that 60 miles away!

Dogs can hear the mailman 60 blocks away...

make that 70 blocks away!

Dogs can hear you "think" it's time to take them out.

From anywhere in the universe!

get a sonogram exam at the doctor's office, we aren't bothered by the very high-pitched sound (2 to 13 million cycles a second) emitted by the ultrasound machine.

But dogs can perceive all the hidden-to-us sounds between 20,000 and 60,000 Hertz. So when a 24,000-Hertz whistle is blown, the average dog will hear it (even if the pooch chooses to ignore the call).

High-frequency noises sound louder to dogs and are sometimes downright painful. Your dog can also hear sounds at lower volumes (and at up to four times the distance) as you. So Max the puppy hears that quiet hybrid car coming up the road long before you do, making his preemptive barking look just the slightest bit crazy.

A dog can also pinpoint where a sound is coming from, simply by orienting its ears. Some 20 separate muscles around a dog's ear can tilt, raise, lower, and swivel the ear in the direction of a sound, enabling dogs to zero in on the source in a fraction of a second. Plus, each ear can move on its own. So a dog can keep one ear turned toward a passing squirrel and the other cocked at the back door, awaiting the call in to dinner. Dogs that sport the pointy, upright ears of their wolf and fox relatives generally hear better than dogs whose ears are floppy or flappy.

> **Dogs can hear sounds in a much wider frequency range than people can.**

Sharp-Eared Ancestors

Why do dogs have such good hearing, especially at high frequencies? Scientists say canine hearing has been passed down from the ancestors of domestic dogs, such as wolves. The ability to hear very high-pitched sounds allows wolves to hear the soft, squealing sounds of small prey like voles, mice, and rabbits, even when they are underground. Hearing sounds at long distances also allows wolves to connect with other members of their pack, since they can detect familiar howls from miles away.

At School

Have you ever wondered why fingernails on a blackboard make that horrible sound? Why your face turns red when you read a report to the class—or when someone points out the rip in your pants? Or whether it's true that 90 percent of your brain is actually (annoyingly) idle when you are trying to solve a math problem? Sometimes, the real puzzles to solve in school aren't on the test . . .

What are chalk and chalkboards made from?

Once upon a time, every schoolroom had a black chalkboard stretching across the room—usually behind the teacher's desk. Teacher and students used the board to solve math problems, diagram sentences, practice penmanship, and draw pictures. Some students even used the board to write—over and over again—"I will not___" (fight at recess, talk during fire drills, eat paste).

Chalk sticks were fun to write with, although they occasionally made that shivery *scritch* across the board. Some students were picked to erase the board at the end of the day and take the big, charcoal-gray felt erasers outside to clap together and watch the chalk dust be carried off by the wind.

The first chalkboards were made from dark slate rock, framed in wood. These individual slates were used by students like paper notebooks. Students wrote on the boards with small pieces of slate, scratching out addition problems and practicing

spelling. Later, slivers of chalk were used for writing, making the slates easily erasable.

By the mid-1800s, manufacturers began constructing huge slate chalkboards for the front of classrooms, with handy ledges to hold chalk and erasers. Big chalkboards allowed teachers to demonstrate problems to a whole classroom of students.

Chalk is made from the fossilized skeletons, shells, and armor of zillions of long-dead sea organisms, from algae to bivalves.

Chalk is actually a kind of soft limestone that is mined from the ground. About 50 to 98 percent of chalk is calcium carbonate, the main ingredient in antacids like Tums. Chalk is made from the fossilized skeletons, shells, and armor of zillions of long-dead sea organisms, from algae to bivalves, which piled up on the ocean floor in a chalky mud. Chalk deposits are found in land formerly covered by the ocean, and formed about 70 to 135 million years ago.

Chalk can be white, yellowish, or gray. A deposit of chalk may contain steely hard flint, fragments of glittering quartz, clay, and rust-red iron. Scientists estimate that chalk deposits like the towering cliffs of Dover in England grew at the glacial rate of about 0.02 inch a year.

(Already famous, the Dover chalk was made even more popular by a World War II song—"The White Cliffs of Dover"—that hoped this fortress against invaders would someday be a symbol of peace.)

In the 1960s, schools began replacing slate chalkboards with black or green boards made of porcelain-coated steel. And chalk made of chalk was mostly replaced by chalk made of gypsum, a harder, less dusty mineral also used to make Sheetrock for walls. Today, more and more schools are installing shiny whiteboards, trading chalky sticks for colored felt-tip markers. No more chalk dust to get in our hair, make us sneeze or wheeze, or cover the teacher's sleeves. And, alas, no more *scritching* sound.

FAST FACT

Besides making a fine chalkboard, slate was used to make roof tiles so durable that the 100-year-old originals still top many Victorian houses and barns.

Why do fingernails (and sometimes chalk) sound so awful on a blackboard?

There's an official name for the horrible sounds that emanate from a blackboard: chalk squeal. Scientists say that the explanation for squeaking chalk involves both friction and resonance.

Chalk squeal and—shudder—fingernail screech occur when frictional forces aren't constant as chalk meets board. Friction is the force that puts on the brakes on an object in motion. Scientists define friction as "the force between two solid surfaces that resists sliding." The main cause of friction is an overly friendly relationship between the atoms of two surfaces—like the bottom of a bookcase and the floor. At the spots where two such objects make

10TH ANNUAL NAME THAT AWFUL SOUND CONTEST !

200

contact—called junctions—their atoms have formed bonds.

When we drag chalk across a blackboard at certain angles and with enough pressure, it sticks to the board, slips, jumps to a new spot, and then sticks again. Scientists call it the stick-slip phenomenon. Since each jump covers such a tiny distance, we don't see gaps in the letters written on the board.

But each time the chalk sticks, it emits a burst of noise, which gets louder if the chalk is pressed harder. Researchers say the screech occurs because the natural resonances of the chalk are excited by the stick-slip forces where chalk meets board. The chalk's vibrations are reinforced (they resonate), becoming stronger. So as the chalk stutters across the blackboard, it makes a squealing sound. The slipping and sticking also occurs when you drag your fingernails down a blackboard, which usually tops the list of sounds that make us flinch.

The Worst Sounds

A 2006 survey in the United Kingdom rated fingernails on a blackboard second among Britain's least favorite sounds. Number one: children screaming. Also found irritating were car alarms, dentists' drills, ring tones, and dripping faucets.

Interestingly, many of the 20 most irritating noises involve the stick-slip phenomenon, including a knife on a plate, a squeaky door, a chair scraping the floor, and someone (excruciatingly) learning to play the violin.

What is it about the noises generated by sticking and slipping objects that is so loathsome? A 1980s experiment at Northwestern University had volunteers rate different sounds, including a metal drawer being opened and Styrofoam rubbing on Styrofoam. The sounds were wince-worthy even when high-pitched tones were filtered out. It turns out that it's the middle-to-low tones of stick-slipping that make us shudder most.

Using sound modeling, the Northwestern researchers found that the most detested noises had a sound profile similar to the alarm cries of macaques. Perhaps, they speculate, such sounds may trigger some deep-seated reaction that helped us survive, once upon a time. So if the screech of a subway train's brakes makes you cringe, you may have a lot of ancestral company.

Do we really use only 10 percent of our brains?

Imagine a small wedge, just 10 percent of your brain, struggling to take care of everything you need to know and do, while the other 90 percent of your brain's gray matter just sits there humming, like an idling car engine. Not going anywhere, not doing anything. All that brainpower, just twiddling its thumbs. You could find a cure for the common cold, invent a car that gets 200 miles a gallon, and write the next

100% Brain Workouts!

Learn to read and sing Chinese folk songs...

classic of world literature—if you could only flip the switch and turn on that lazybones part of your brain.

Practice your balance beam routine...

But if you do come up with a world-changing creation, it won't be because you found the magic recipe—the right nutritional supplements, concentrating very, very hard, repeating "I will use 100 percent of my brain" 100 times—to turn on your whole brain. Because the fact of the matter is, the other 90 percent has been working all along.

Scientists who study the brain say that the 10 percent theory is a myth. Like the urban legend about human-eating alligators in the sewers, it's been repeated so often that we think it must be true. And the 10 percent legend continues to pass around because it speaks to our dreams and desires. If only we could find the formula to unlock that sleeping 90 percent, then any one of us could paint like Van Gogh, compose like Bach, write like Shakespeare, think like Einstein.

Neuroscientists point out that both common sense and modern technology show why the 10 percent story is wrong. Losing just a little brain tissue in an accident can have drastic consequences, they say, and injury to even small areas of the brain in a stroke can affect the ability to speak and move. In fact, scientists say, there doesn't seem to be any brain part where damage, if it happens, doesn't show up as some loss of function. And electrical stimulation of the brain during brain

> While everyone uses his whole brain, the brain can be exercised, like a muscle, and become smarter.

surgery, according to the late Barry Beyerstein, a Canadian scientist, reveals no unused areas: No matter where the probe touches, it mines a storehouse of emotions and memories, or stimulates body movements.

Further, PET scans, which use a radioactive element to visualize the activity of the working brain, have found no part that is dormant. Our big human brain uses so much energy and costs the body so much to support, scientists say, that it wouldn't have evolved if most of it were not ordinarily used.

The good news: While everyone uses his whole brain, the brain can be exercised, like a muscle, and become smarter. When you learn something new—how to speak French, how to throw a curveball, how to solve a quadratic equation—you actually grow new connections between brain neurons. (Their size, shape, and function may change, too.) Recent studies show that vigorous physical exercise, like running, can also create richer neural connections. The brain thrives on stimulation and challenge, giving you the brainpower to achieve whatever you want to do most.

Paint your toenails in a crossword puzzle chat room, while finishing your homework.

How come my face turns red when I have to give a presentation to my class?

Does your face turn beet red when you trip and fall in front of your friends? When you discover an unzipped zipper during a big party? Or even when you're singled out for praise from a teacher—in front of the whole class?

If so, you're not alone. A majority of human beings blush when they are uncomfortable or embarrassed. Blushing is just another way—like grinning and grimacing—the body communicates our inner feelings without using words.

Your dog may sometimes appear guilty and embarrassed about something it has done. But as far as anyone knows, human beings are the only animals that blush when they get flustered. (The pharaoh hound breed of dog does blush. When these dogs

COLOR ME...

Yikes

Eeegads!

oh, NO!

get happy and excited, their noses, the rims of their eyes, and the insides of their ears turn rosy pink.)

Why are humans such champion blushers? First, there are our complex brains, trained from an early age to consider moral and social issues. Then there's our mostly fur-free (and definitely feather-free) facial skin, perfect for displaying every fleeting emotion— whether we want our feelings revealed or not. Being human, it's all too easy to wear your heart on your sleeve—or, actually, on your face.

Most people get occasionally red-faced when embarrassed around others. But many also blush when they are all alone, just thinking about some mortifying situation. Women seem to blush more than men. We also seem to blush more when we're young than when we're older and feel we have "seen it all." As we age, we may also feel more sympathetic toward our own mistakes.

Blushing is involuntary; like sneezing, it just happens. Redness quickly spreads across face, neck, and ears (and sometimes down chest and arms). Blushing or flushing occurs when small blood vessels suddenly expand.

Blushing is just another way— like grinning and grimacing—the body communicates our inner feelings without using words.

Extra blood rushes in, and we get that boiled-lobster look. We also may feel hot and tingly, perhaps even light-headed.

It all starts with the body's autonomic nervous system (ANS), which automatically regulates body functions like heart rate, pupil size, and the swelling and shrinking of blood vessels. Blushing is controlled by a part of the ANS called the sympathetic nervous system, which prepares us for "fight or flight" in stressful situations. While you're not likely to be chased by an enraged bear in everyday life, your heart may beat faster on a plunging roller coaster. Likewise, blood may rush to your face when a plate of ravioli slides into your lap in the school cafeteria.

Most facial flushing is perfectly normal, a sign that we are thoughtful, sensitive people. But sometimes, a red face can be the sign of something amiss.

If you are always turning bright red and sweaty, it may mean an overactive sympathetic nervous system. Excessive blushing can also be due to rosacea, a facial condition that can cause red bumps, visible blood vessels, and irritated, bloodshot eyes.

Why do some kids have curly hair and others have straight hair?

Whether it grows in cascading waves, wiry curls, dangling ringlets—or is waterfall-straight—all hair is made of a protein called keratin. And inside keratin is one of the keys to curly versus straight hair.

All proteins are made of smaller units called amino acids. Two of keratin's amino acids, methionine and cysteine, contain sulfur atoms. (Sulfur gives rotten eggs their distinctive odor, and this smelly mineral is the "top note" in the scent of singed hair.)

Picture a sticky strand of spaghetti, kinked and curled because it's stuck to itself in several spots. Curly hair is hair with many sulfur atoms bonded to other sulfur atoms in the amino acid chains. The more disulfide bonds or links, the curlier the hair.

You inherit your hair type—curly, wavy, or straight—from your ancestors. Scientists

Tell It Like It Is Salon

You have ze loveliest pile of deceased protein I've ever seen!

206

say that one or two genes control how many sulfur bonds will form in your hair. The shape of the hair follicle, likewise determined by genes, also plays a part. Like dough pushed through a cookie press, hairs emerging from round follicles will have round shafts. Very round hairs tend to be straight and resistant to bending, like plastic drinking straws.

Oval-shaped follicles will sprout oval-shaped, flatter hairs, which are naturally more bendable and prone to wave and curl. (Just as it's easier to bend a flattened Coke can than an unflattened one.) The very curliest hair

> You inherit your hair type—curly, wavy, or straight—from your ancestors.

strands may be nearly as flat as ribbons.

No one seems to like the hair they have, which is why curls get straightened and poker-straight strands get permed. Chemical straighteners and permanents work by breaking the disulfide bonds in each strand. Relaxed hair can be styled straight; straight hair wound into curls. A second chemical forces sulfur atoms in hair strands to rebond in their new positions while hair is setting.

The downside? About 10 percent of the disulfide bonds don't re-form, leaving hair weak and vulnerable to breaking.

Bad-Hair Days

For many natural curlyheads in the Northern Hemisphere, July is a bad-hair month. They complain that their blown-out/slicked-down/ironed-flat/chemically straightened hair simply frizzes out into an unruly mass on hot, humid days. How come? Hair protein is held together by hydrogen bonds as well as disulfide bonds. (Hydrogen bonds also bind two atoms of hydrogen to one atom of oxygen in a water molecule.)

Humid air is saturated with H_2O, and hair absorbs water molecules from the air. The incoming water molecules disrupt the hair's hydrogen bonds—weaker than sulfur bonds—as atoms shift around and rebond. The hair's hydrogen bonds relax a bit, allowing the stronger disulfide bonds to pull hair into tighter curls. Meanwhile, the added water swells each strand, making hair frizzy.

How come identical twins are sometimes different heights?

Identical twins result when an egg, already fertilized by a sperm, splits in half. Each half contains the same gene lineup as the original embryo. And so each baby is born with the same DNA. Identical twins are the same sex, have the same blood type, and often look almost exactly alike. But, although identical twins have duplicate DNA, they don't grow up to be carbon copies.

We're exactly alike in every way!

Same-sex twins presumed to be identical may actually be half-identical (one egg split in two, then fertilized by different sperm). Or they may be fraternal (two different eggs, two different sperm). Mary-Kate and Ashley, the acting Olsen twins, look very much alike, but are actually fraternal twins—sharing no more DNA than any two sisters. The only way to know for sure whether two babies are identical is by DNA test.

Even in true identicals, one twin's DNA may undergo a chance mutation. For example, one twin of a pair was born

Twins, the oh-so-subtle difference...

No one could tell us apart... right?

with a cleft palate (a split in the upper lip and mouth). Comparing the twins' DNA, researchers discovered a variation in one tiny bit of DNA out of billions of bits in a cell.

When an identical twin develops Type 1 diabetes, the other's chance of developing the disease is only 50 percent. The reason may lie in a mutated gene, or, perhaps, in the environment.

The first environment is the mother's womb. Identical twins often share one placenta from which they receive nutrients from their mother's blood. But in about 10 percent of single-placenta twins, one gets more nutrients than the other. In one-third of identicals, each twin has its own placenta, another possibility for unequal nourishment. Or one twin may occupy a not-so-good position in the uterus, with less room to grow.

FAST FACT

About 23 percent of identicals are mirror twins, offspring of a fertilized egg that splits a few days late, after it's already developed right and left sides. In mirror twins, moles, hair patterns, and other features are reversed (including, sometimes, the positions of internal organs).

Other variables: One twin may be injured or deprived of oxygen at birth. Some twins are separated and adopted by vastly different families. Twins growing up together can have different friends, opportunities, and experiences. Genetics accounts for most of how twins turn out but can't account for everything.

As soon as I learn to wiggle my ears, we'll be completely identical...

For example, identical twins develop similar but distinct eye patterns and fingerprints during their months in the womb. (Besides genes, fingerprints are affected by factors like nutrition and blood pressure. Higher blood pressure swells finger pads, influencing forming patterns.)

As twins grow up, scientists say, it's not unheard of for one to be a full 4 inches taller, wear a different shoe size, have a different IQ, be fatter or leaner. (Identical-twin studies indicate that weight is determined 70 percent by genes and 30 percent by environmental factors like diet and exercise.)

In gym class, I got a charley horse. What caused that, and where did it get its name?

It can wake you up in your dark bedroom like a shot, and you may even yell out loud. But it's not a nightmare, it's a knot in your leg muscle. It's a charley horse, a cute name for an excruciatingly painful cramp.

Charley horses usually visit legs (calves or thighs) or feet (arches), but they may also strike the hands. They are most likely to occur when we are in bed resting or when we are overusing a particular muscle.

A muscle cramp means a muscle is locked into a spasm that won't relax. Muscle cramps have a laundry list of causes. Exercising harder or longer than usual can fatigue muscles and cause a buildup of lactic acid, causing cramps. But not exercising at all can diminish blood circulation to the legs—also causing cramps.

> Charley horses usually visit legs (calves or thighs) or feet (arches), but they may also strike the hands.

Dieting, taking diuretics to reduce bloating, or sweating buckets on a hot day can cause the body's minerals (electrolytes) to become unbalanced. A loss of potassium, for example, can cause muscle cramps in legs, feet, and hands. Eating a banana or drinking orange juice can help restore potassium.

More cramp triggers: Wearing high heels, pointing the toes, repetitive or prolonged motion (like gripping a pencil for the three hours of a placement test), not drinking enough water. To keep cramps away, stretch

GIVE YOURSELF A MASSIVE CHARLEY HORSE!

lift weights for ten hours...

...point your hooves really hard for an hour...

...then put on your high heels and go dancing.

muscles frequently, especially before and after exercise.

To stop the pain of a charley horse, some advise stretching the clenching muscle. But others say stretching may just make the pain worse. They suggest shortening the muscle: If you are awakened by a charley horse in your calf, pull your foot up to your backside to ease the stretch on the muscle. Then gently rub your calf lengthwise (rather than across). Heat may help relax the muscle; ice may ease the pain.

Even after the cramp fades, the spot may be sore for days. Just as if you'd been kicked by a not-so-friendly horse named Charley.

Etymologists (people who study word origins) say that the term *charley horse* may have come from the world of baseball.

Charley horse was first seen in print in the late 1880s. One story guesses that it came from a horse named Charley used by the grounds crew at a Chicago stadium in the 1800s. The idea being that injured baseball players were compared to the lame old horse.

But word-origin experts say that a more plausible explanation involves famous baseball players named Charley or Charlie. One example: Charley Radbourne, a Boston player in the 1880s, was nicknamed Old Hoss. Running the bases in a game, Radbourne's leg muscle seized up, making him fall to the ground. A player rushing to help supposedly asked, "What's the matter with you, Charley Hoss?" And so may have started the tradition of calling an especially painful cramp a charley horse.

Why does the height of a basketball's bounce gradually decrease?

No matter how bouncy the ball, the first bounce is always the best. Even a small rubber SuperBall will high-bounce only so many times before it peters out. And each bounce is a little less high than the last. It's almost as if the ball were becoming tired from all the effort of springing into the air. Until at last, utterly exhausted, it stops dead-still on the ground.

Left to its own devices, a bouncing ball gradually loses energy to its surroundings. Imagine holding a ball over a wooden floor, say, 5 feet up. The poised-to-fall ball has potential energy—gravitational potential

FOLLOW the BOUNCING BALL...

The first bounce hurts the most, see...

Ouph!

On the second bounce there's less pain!

By the third or fourth bounce, you're ready for it to be over.

OOh! or to start again!

ooh!

energy. Let the ball go, and gravity will cause it to accelerate toward Earth.

When the ball begins falling, its potential energy is transforming into kinetic energy, energy of motion. A tiny bit of energy is lost through friction with the air, changing into heat energy. Just before the ball hits the floor, nearly all of its potential energy has turned into kinetic energy—the ball simply has no farther to fall.

When the ball lands, it presses down on the floor—and the floor presses back. A bit of energy is transferred to the floor, which vibrates from the impact. This vibration spreads into the air, and we hear the *thud*. The very fact that we hear a *thud* means that the ball has lost—to the wood and to the room—some of the energy it started with. The ball and floor are also heated a little by the impact, the heat energy radiating into the air.

Squishing from the impact, the ball is actually motionless for a split second. The flattening or dent has absorbed and is holding most of the energy the ball had. At this instant, the ball has elastic potential energy, as it had gravitational potential

Left to its own devices, a bouncing ball gradually loses energy to its surroundings.

energy when suspended overhead.

As the ball unsquishes, its molecules returning to their former positions, the energy is released as kinetic energy, and our round friend springs into the air. However, the ball doesn't make it all the way up to the 5-foot height from which it was dropped. An average ball will rebound 60 percent—3 feet, in this case—on the first bounce. A basketball may rebound 80 percent. An extremely bouncy SuperBall may rebound to 90 percent of its original height.

The amount a ball rebounds, according to University of Virginia physicist Louis Bloomfield, is equal to the amount of energy the ball has held onto. So a ball that rebounds to 60 percent of its former height has retained 60 percent of its original energy—and has lost 40 percent to its surroundings.

Each time the ball falls back to the floor, it loses more energy. So each bounce is a little lower than the last. Until finally, its energy spent, the ball rolls to a rest. To keep a ball bouncing, you need to expend some energy yourself—which is why dribbling a basketball can get tiring.

Why do we get dizzy from spinning around?

t's like having an all-day amusement park ticket, every day: Simply twirl in the yard, faster and faster. Then drop to the ground, watch the sky turn, and feel the ground fall underneath you.

These cheap thrills are provided courtesy of the inner ear. Although we associate the ear with hearing all the sounds of the world, it's also in charge of our sense of balance. Tightrope walkers have perfected their balance; for the rest of us, a sense of balance keeps us walking a straight line across the room, instead of wobbling to one side and toppling over.

The inner-ear sensors tell the body whether it is upright or lying down, moving or standing still. How? Since gravity is always tugging us to Earth, the inner-ear mechanism evolved to sense how the body is oriented in relation to the pull.

This mechanism is called the vestibular balance system, and it's hidden away in the upper ear. The otolithic organs (utricule and saccule) are covered in the gelatinlike

PUTTING THE TWIRL INSIDE YOUR WHIRL!

oh! He's turning around...

...and around...

...and around!

otolithic membrane. Embedded in the jelly are some of the ear's hairlike cells, along with tiny stony bits called otoconia, made of protein and calcium carbonate (the main ingredient in Tums and in schoolroom chalk).

Here's how it works: When your head tilts or your body shifts in relation to gravity, the calcium crystals, which are attached to the hair cells, shift, too. This causes the hair cells to bend, firing off signals through the nervous system to the brain. The brain interprets the signals and recognizes your new position.

Meanwhile, in its three semicircular canals, the ear is sensing motion in three

Dizziness comes courtesy of the inner ear. Although we associate the ear with hearing, it's also in charge of our sense of balance.

dimensions. The canals contain a fluid called endolymph and more of those handy hair cells. As your head moves, so does the fluid (although due to inertia, it lags a bit). The moving endolymph stimulates the hair cells, sending more signals to the brain.

When you spin around, your endolymph fluid spins with you. That, in turn, signals the brain that you're spinning. But when you suddenly stop, the fluid's inertia keeps it spinning for moments more. The message from hair cells to brain? "Still spinning!" So while you're now still, your brain perceives that you're continuing to turn—making for that dizzy feeling.

Out for a Spin

Why do we also see the world turning when we're dizzy? When the head tilts or turns, the eyes move in the opposite direction to compensate, so that we see a stable image. This is called the vestibular-ocular reflex, and it's a case of our eyes being cued by our ears. If you've been spinning and suddenly stop, the lag time for your ears results in a lag time for your eyes, too, which continue sliding from one side to the other.

When the ears' endolymph fluid finally stops sloshing, your brain registers that you've stopped, too. And that spinning, falling feeling—the dizziness—fades away.

We used dry ice in our school play to make fog. How does it do that?

When you pour a carbonated soft drink into a glass, tiny bubbles rise from the surface into the air (and go right up your nose). Now imagine those bubbles changing into snow. That's how dry ice works.

The bubbles are carbon dioxide gas, trapped in the can or bottle. When you open the soda, the bubbles rush up and out, escaping into the air. Once in the air, they're as invisible as the rest of the gases we're always breathing in—nitrogen, oxygen, argon, and dozens more.

At ordinary temperatures and air pressure, carbon dioxide (CO_2) is a gas. But like other

You're on Thin Ice...

I can't see!

BLAM!

I'll sublimate you next!

If you're skating on dry ice... If it's in your thermos... Or if you decide to have a snowball fight with it.

substances, carbon dioxide can also be a liquid or a solid. Take water, for example. A sloshy, drinkable liquid at room temperature, water turns into a gas (steam) when heated to 212°F (100°C), and into a solid (ice) when its temperature drops to 32°F (0°C).

Carbon dioxide can also take liquid or solid form. But carbon dioxide has a special property. Instead of transforming from gas to liquid to solid, like water, carbon dioxide goes straight from gas to frozen solid (and back again) at ordinary pressures. To turn carbon dioxide into a liquid requires a big squeeze—at room temperature, a pressure of 30 atmospheres. Many fire extinguishers contain liquid carbon dioxide, held under just such high pressure.

Carbon dioxide freezes into a snowy mass at –109.3°F. We call a block of frozen carbon dioxide dry ice because it doesn't melt into a liquid. Instead, a cloud of gas continuously rises from the shrinking block, vanishing into the air. (The scientific term for this process is sublimation.)

To make dry ice, manufacturers first lower the temperature of CO_2 to –71°F or lower, and compress the carbon dioxide into liquid in a containment vessel. Then they release the liquid CO_2. The rapid expansion and speedy evaporation of the liquid chills the rest of the carbon dioxide in the container, turning it to snow. (Which is also what happens when carbon dioxide snow forms on the nozzle of a spraying fire extinguisher.)

The CO_2 snow is pressed into blocks of dry ice. The ice is sold as a refrigerant to keep frozen items solidly frozen during shipping. (Dry ice must be handled with tongs and insulating gloves, since skin will freeze to it on contact.)

Since dry ice goes straight from solid to gas as its temperature rises, it can't be kept in an ordinary sealed container. Otherwise, gas will build up inside, and then *boom*—a deafening explosion.

Which brings us to an old party trick (and science experiment): Put dry ice into a balloon, tie it shut, and throw it into a swimming pool. The weight of the ice will cause the balloon to sink and disappear. But as the ice warms and turns to gas, the balloon swiftly rises back to the surface and bursts, making a startling explosion in the water.

Imagine the tiny bubbles from your soda changing into snow. That's what dry ice is.

How does salt melt ice on the school steps and sidewalk in winter?

When salt is sprinkled on an icy sidewalk or road, holes are punched through the snow and ice. It's a mystery: How can a cold bag of salt act like hot gravel?

Here's how it works. In liquid water, molecules slip-slide past one another. The molecules' chemical bonds hold the liquid together. But molecules are always separating and reattaching to other molecules across the way, like dancers at a square dance.

The liquid dance of molecules happens when they are at the right temperature (and pressure). Apply enough heat, and—like dancers escaping an overheated auditorium—the water molecules will gain so much thermal energy that they fly apart

Sidewalk Condiments...

The oregano didn't melt anything, the dill didn't melt anything, let's try basil.

into a gas. At ordinary air pressure, water turns to steam at 212°F and up.

Take too much heat away—chill the water to 32°F and below—and the molecules gradually lose energy. Unable to continue their do-si-do, they will cling stiffly together, turning to ice.

But even when water turns to ice, there is still movement. Individual molecules vibrate slightly in their lattice of crystal. And freezing isn't a smooth process. Some molecules, still in the liquid phase, bump into the forming ice and stick. Others break free from the icy patch and return to being liquid. At 32°F, a parcel of water is balanced between freezing and melting.

And this brings us to salt. Salt molecules are made of linked-up sodium and chlorine atoms. Water molecules are made of two hydrogen atoms and one oxygen atom. Because of how its atoms are arranged, a water molecule generates a tiny electric field.

When salt is dumped onto ice, there is an immediate reaction. Salt molecules come into contact with the electric field of water molecules. This electric field tugs the salt molecules apart. The separated atoms are called ions, because they have

Adding salt short-circuits the freezing process and, in effect, lowers the freezing point of water.

an electrical charge. Sodium ions are positive, chloride ions negative. Water molecules, feeling an electrical attraction, cluster around the ions.

The molecules hanging around the dissolved salt don't glom onto the forming ice. Meanwhile, remember, other water molecules naturally are breaking free from the ice. The result? Since more water is turning from ice to liquid than from liquid to ice, the ice melts. Adding salt short-circuits the freezing process. So salt, in effect, lowers the freezing point of water.

(In fact, dissolving *any* substance in water—from sugar to alcohol—will do the same thing. Salt is simply cheap and available. And on just one mile of pavement, it takes 500 pounds of salt to form a brine of saltwater to keep ice from re-forming.)

However, as the temperature plummets, more water molecules freeze onto ice than escape into liquid, requiring extra salt. Below about 25°F, road crews use salt with added calcium chloride, increasing its melting effect. As the temperature drops near 0°F and below, workers spread grit to give tires more traction, since salt mixtures can't keep up with the freezing.

When you're riding on a school bus, why do you fall forward when the bus driver suddenly brakes?

It happens on the bus, but also on the subway, in cars, on a bike. You're riding along. Suddenly, there's a dog crossing the road, or someone's pulled the emergency cord, and bang—the brakes are on, and you are thrown forward. If you're unlucky (or un-seatbelted), your tender forehead may hit a windshield, or you may go flying over the handlebars.

The question is, why don't *you* stop when the vehicle does? The answer is inertia, which has been with us for the entire

INERTIA RULES!...UNLESS THE FORCE IS WITH YOU!

Just try to get Darth to stop mowing the lawn!

Or attempt to make lazy Princess Leia clean up her room!

But save the elbow grease for Luke Skywalker, battling inertia on the planet Hoth!

He's evil 'N' FAST!

Mañana!

Ride yourself to school!

13-billion-year history of the universe, and is still mysterious after all these years.

Inertia means that whatever you're doing, you'll tend to continue doing it unless some force intervenes. So you may sit like a zombie in front of Saturday morning cartoons until your mother makes you go outside. Or you'll stay on a team you're tired of just because you played that sport last year. Whether you're sitting still, or just continuing to move in the same old direction, it's all inertia.

Inertia can also be very useful. It helps us finish a task, once started: picking up stick after stick in the yard, pedaling mile after mile on a bike, getting up day after day to go to school.

So much for psychological inertia; what throws you forward on a bus is real, physical inertia. Isaac Newton put it this way, some 300 years ago: Every body continues in its state of rest, or of uniform motion in a straight line, unless it is compelled to change that state by force impressed thereon.

When you're riding on a bus, the bus and your body are traveling forward in space. When the brakes are put on, frictional forces stop the wheels. But because of inertia, your

You don't stop when the vehicle does because of something called inertia.

body goes on blithely traveling forward (at least until it hits the seat in front of you).

More massive things have more inertia. That makes them harder to move when they're stopped—or harder to stop when they're moving. Like a boulder. Or a big guy on that suddenly braked bus; he'll be harder to stop if he runs into *you* as he hurtles to the front.

And in the real world, there's always something to slow things down. For example, friction. Despite inertia, a ball won't roll endlessly, once it's started, because even a very smooth surface—even an endless expanse of ice—will rub against the surface of the ball, gradually slowing and stopping it. In this universe, perpetual motion machines aren't allowed.

FAST FACT

The Moon would keep right on going, too—flying off on a straight-line tangent into space—if Earth's gravitational force didn't keep pulling on it, compelling it to circle in place.

Why do songs get stuck in your head?

It could be the pop song they played on the radio from morning until evening ("I'm gonna soak up the sun . . ."). It could be the jingle from a commercial you saw last night ("Break me off a piece of that Kit Kat bar . . ."). Or it could be from the boat ride you went on at Disney World ("It's a small world after all . . ."). Whatever the trigger, you've got a snippet of music playing over and over in your mind. And it's driving you a little crazy.

Like yawning, catchy tunes—especially those with words—seem to be contagious. Just mention a song like "Dancing Queen" (or nearly any ABBA tune, for that matter), and someone within hearing distance will get it stuck in their head. Others can't hear the words "My Sharona" without enduring hours of relentless repetition, thanks to The Knack.

So why does the brain act like a broken jukebox, the same piece of music clicking on again and again? The last several years have

ESCAPE FROM AN EARWORM?

REPEAT YOUR NAME BACKWARD...

NOJ Etihw, NOJ Etihw.

PLAY THE RADIO LOUD!!!

SING A SONG YOU HATE MORE THAN THE EARWORM!

It's a small small world!

seen a small flurry of research into the viral brain tunes known as earworms. Like the earworms wielded by a diabolical Ricardo Montalban in *Star Trek II: The Wrath of Khan,* musical worms enter our ears and burrow straight into our brains. The reason seems to involve the human brain's love of patterns, and its dogged compulsion to fill in musical blanks.

A survey of college students by marketing professor James Kellaris of the University of Cincinnati found that nearly everyone experiences stuck songs. While certain songs turn up again and again on earworm lists, Kellaris says that each of us tends to be bedeviled by our own do-over ditties.

Researchers say that the music most likely to get lodged in the brain has a simple, catchy, repeating tune and/or lyrics (or even an unexpected musical twist), and has been heard frequently on radio or TV. The brain seems to dip into its repeating repertoire most often when we're tired or anxious.

Dartmouth University researchers used MRIs to image the brains of volunteers as they listened to music, including the earworm-worthy theme from *The Pink Panther.* The catch: Bits and pieces of the tunes were missing. Researchers found that

Tunes that get stuck in your head are known as earworms.

the auditory cortex in the listeners' brains remained active during the gaps in familiar tunes, automatically filling in the musical blanks. In effect, people couldn't stop their brains from continuing a well-known tune.

It's in the auditory cortex, researchers think, where songs become memories.

In our music-heavy environment, with tunes playing in stores, restaurants, elevators, and in every earphoned ear, stuck songs are a fact of life. How to switch off the inner music? If it's July but your brain is playing endless loops of "The Little Drummer Boy," try turning on the radio for a musical change. But if "The Lion Sleeps Tonight" comes on, it's time for a new strategy. Getting involved in an attention-grabbing activity, from reading to playing a sport, may, at least temporarily, reset your compulsive brain.

FAST FACT

The stickiest songs are usually pop songs played hair-tearingly often on the radio. Even if we frantically change stations, hearing the first few bars may be all it takes for an earworm to crawl in.

What causes the popping sound when you crack your knuckles?

Human beings have probably been lacing their fingers together, stretching out their arms, and cracking their knuckles after a tedious session of toolmaking (or homework writing) for many thousands of years. Yet it wasn't until the 1970s that scientists figured out what makes that satisfying popping sound.

The knuckles are the joints linking hand bones (metacarpals) to finger bones (phalanges). The knuckle, or metacarpophalangeal joint, allows us to grip things (like a pencil) between our fingers, using a system of ligaments and tendons.

All of the body's joints, from knuckles to knees, are cushioned by a thick liquid called

It ain't just at breakfast anymore...

SNAP! *Oooh*

CracKle! *feels good!*

PoP! *Yeah*

synovial fluid. Synovial fluid, which has the feel of egg whites, contains dissolved gases like carbon dioxide and oxygen (think egg-white soda pop).

The slippery fluid fills a fibrous capsule surrounding the joint. When you crack your knuckles by pulling your fingers back, you temporarily widen the space between the joints, stretching the capsule and increasing its size.

With its container expanding like a balloon, the synovial fluid is suddenly under less pressure. And with the fluid's pressure swiftly dropping, its trapped gases begin forming bubbles, small pockets of vapor, in the liquid. As the joint stretches to the max, the pressure drops so low that the bubbles burst, sending small shockwaves through the synovial fluid. And like a mini sonic boom, we hear a crack or pop. (Scientists say that a second sound peak may be caused by the fluid-filled capsule stretching to its limit.)

Although the bubbles burst, the gas doesn't immediately redissolve in the joint fluid. In fact, X rays show that it takes about 15 to 30 minutes for the tiniest bubbles to completely disappear. Lingering bubbles keep the capsule expanded. As the gas dissolves, the capsule shrinks back to its normal size.

All of this explains why you can't crack a knuckle over and over again in rapid succession: The capsule can't form big, pop-worthy bubbles if it's still stretched out. But once the gas has redissolved, the stage is set for another satisfying *snap-crackle-pop* of the knuckle variety.

Old Wives' Tales?

While knuckle-cracking can be annoying, can it really cause arthritis? Scientists say no. Arthritis causes pain, swelling, and stiffness in joints. The kind of arthritis that usually affects knuckles is rheumatoid arthritis, a disease caused by an overactive immune system that attacks the body's own joints. Osteoarthritis, the more common kind, occurs when cartilage around joints wears away over time. According to one 1990 study, knuckle crackers had no more arthritis than the abstainers. However, the study also found that a knuckle-cracking habit may injure the soft tissue around the joint, causing the hand to swell and reducing grip strength (making it harder, for example, to open stuck jar lids).

While doing math in school, I wondered: What is the last number in the world?

A song says that "one is the loneliest number," but it would be even lonelier to be the last number. Hanging out there at the end of the line—right at the edge of the abyss—it would be cold comfort to have an incredibly long list of numerals in your name.

But while there may be a zillion good reasons for not having finished a homework assignment, even a gazillion doesn't come close to being the last number, since a bazillion (or more) is always just over the horizon.

From the beginning, human beings have been preoccupied with counting things and making up names for big numbers. For example, the largest named number in ancient Greece was 10,000; they called it a myriad. (Today, *myriad* just means "many.")

> A googolplex is the highest number that English has a name for, but it isn't the end of the line for numbers.

But Greek scientist Archimedes recognized that the world contains numbers of objects far greater than a myriad. In his work *Sand Reckoning*, Archimedes estimated that it would take about 10^{64} grains of sand (the number 1 followed by 64 zeroes) to fill the universe.

While scientists like to write numbers using powers of ten (10^3 is 10 × 10 × 10, or 1,000), they have also named many large numbers. The number 1,000,000,000 is a billion in American English and is sometimes called a milliard in British English. And while a zillion isn't a real number, an octillion is: It's the number 1 followed by 27 zeroes. An octovigintillion is 1,000 followed by 28 groups of three zeroes.

One very big number was named by nine-year-old Milton Sirotta, in 1938.

Milton's mathematician uncle, Edward Kasner, asked his nephew what he would call the number one followed by a hundred zeroes. Milton decided it was a "googol."

Beyond the googol, there's the googolplex, the number 1 followed by a googol zeroes. A googolplex is so enormous, astronomer Carl Sagan noted, that if it could be written out on a strip of paper, the paper couldn't be stuffed into the known universe.

And the universe is vast: 78 sextillion miles separate us from the most distant quasar. To appreciate such numbers, Kasner, like Archimedes, suggested thinking about grains of sand. A thimble, he said, can hold many more atoms than there are grains of sand on Coney Island beach—about an octillion atoms, in fact.

A googolplex is the highest number that English has a name for, but it isn't the end of the line for numbers. To any imaginable number, we can always add 1 (or 1 million). Even if we tire of naming numbers, there's no end to the counting, even when the universe has run out of objects to be counted. There is no last number; numbers can mount up forever.

Scientists have proposed different rules for naming large numbers, resulting in tongue twisters like septenquadragintillion (1,000 followed by 47 groups of three zeroes.) But the biggest numbers you can think of are up for grabs, so feel free to make up your own name for your favorite gigantic number.

Suggested Big Number Names...

Huge-a-gabillion — The number of hot dogs I can eat?

Mega-Quin-tuple-zillion — The number of times I like to watch a movie?

Grande-Sexocto-bazillion — The number of minutes I talk on the phone each month?

On Vacation

Wherever you go, there you are—wondering. Even (or maybe especially) when you're on vacation, trying to get away from it all. Where does all that sand on beaches come from? What makes the ocean taste so salty? How do enormous, heavy cruise ships stay afloat? And why, oh why, do our eyes look red in so many of our vacation photos? Take a little trip through some holiday conundrums.

Why is the longest day of the year in summer not also the hottest?

As spring slips into summer, the days get longer, the nights shorter. Days lengthen from a bit more than 12 hours in late March to about 15 hours in early June in the northern continental United States.

How come days and nights aren't always 12 hours each? Blame it on (or thank) Earth's tilt. Imagine a spinning top, whirling around an imaginary vertical axis. Now imagine the top still spinning,

FAST FACT

Summer solstice day is the longest of the year, but only by seconds. On June 20, 2008, the day length in hours and minutes (15 hours 6 minutes in New York City) is the same as on June 18, 19, 21, 22, and 23.

but tilted a bit to one side. Like the top, our spinning blue planet is tipped at a 23.5 degree angle from the straight-up-and-down. So we travel around the Sun at a slant.

One trip around our star equals one year. As the year unfolds, Earth's fixed tilt means that the top half of the planet is leaning toward the Sun for half the year, away the other half. When the Northern Hemisphere is tipped toward our fiery star, it's summer vacation time. Meanwhile, in the Southern Hemisphere, the tip-away means winter cold and long nights.

As the Northern Hemisphere leans toward the Sun, days lengthen. We receive more sunlight. And the Sun's rays hit the hemisphere more directly than in winter, as the Sun climbs higher and higher in the sky. All of this means a gradual heating of the atmosphere, soil, and oceans.

The summer solstice is not actually a day,

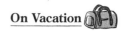

Diary: Planet Earth

Vernal Equinox

Must change tilt for a total tan.

but a single moment in time. In the Northern Hemisphere, it marks the point at which the Sun is highest and farthest to the north in the sky for the year.

According to the U.S. Naval Observatory, the official summer solstice for 2008 is June 20 at 23:59 Universal Time (11:59 P.M.). Universal Time is five hours ahead of U.S. Eastern Standard Time, four hours ahead of Eastern Daylight Time. So on the U.S. East Coast, the summer solstice is at 7:59 P.M. on Friday, June 20.

After the solstice—which means "sun stands still"—things begin to go backward. Earth's orbit begins to shift the Northern Hemisphere away from the Sun. The Sun

appears a bit lower in the sky each day and more southerly. And days gradually get shorter, losing minutes each week.

But summer temperatures don't reach their peak until a month after the longest days. Why? The ground heats more slowly than the air, the oceans more slowly still. So the atmosphere loses some of its late spring/

Summer Solstice

Out all day and night — things are heating up.

Autumn Equinox

Whew! Time to cool down.

early summer heat to the cooler oceans and land. While the air receives less heat from the Sun in the post-solstice weeks, it keeps more as soil and oceans warm up. (Meanwhile, the slower-to-heat ocean holds on to its heat longest of all.) So heat is still accumulating after the solstice, and temperatures hit their average maximum in July and August.

How does a compass work?

Before there was a Global Positioning System receiver in every high-end car (or in the backpacks of wayward hikers), there was the magnetic compass. In fact, before there were cars and nylon backpacks, explorers and sailors and pirates used their trusty compasses to find their way around the big, featureless ocean. Even on a cloudy night, with no stars to guide you, a small piece of magnetized metal, mounted so that it could swing freely, told you which way was north.

> Compasses work because we live on a magnet—one that's 25,000 miles around.

What's so special about north? If you know where north is, you know it all. Face north, and south will be behind you, east on your right, and west on your left.

A compass seems to have a mind of its own. Its tiny floating metal pointer experiences an invisible pull, even through walls

MAN WITH MAGNETIC PERSONALITY POINTS NORTH...

and mountains. Turn the compass, and the pointer doesn't turn with it: It stays stubbornly pointed north, feeling a deep attraction that we are unaware of.

Compasses work because we live on a magnet—one that's 25,000 miles around. Earth acts like a bar magnet, with opposite poles at the north and south. Scientists think the magnetism comes from rotating currents in the liquid iron in Earth's core.

But Earth's imaginary bar magnet does not line up exactly with its real north-south axis. And the pole in the north is slowly drifting west. So follow a magnetic compass needle pointed at N, and you will actually end up traveling a bit northwest.

Scientists measure magnetic field strength in teslas, and Earth's field registers at about .0001 of a tesla. By comparison, the field around a refrigerator magnet may be 20,000 times stronger. Although Earth's magnetism isn't strong enough to pull piles of paper clips to the north and south poles, it can influence a swinging compass needle. (A magnetic compass can make a mistake, however, if there is a nearby magnetic field or chunk of iron to distract it. The fields around a wire carrying an electric current, for example, can give a little tug to an unsuspecting compass needle.)

The first compasses may have been

FAST FACT

Earth's magnetic poles drift over time, and the entire field can reverse itself. About 800,000 years ago, compass needles would have pointed south.

made more than 2,000 years ago. They were simple: a bit of lodestone (magnetic iron ore) attached to a piece of wood, floated on liquid. The piece of wood, pulled by the lodestone, aligned itself with Earth's magnetic field.

People found they could magnetize slivers of metal by rubbing them on a lodestone. On ocean voyages, sailors carried a lodestone so the onboard compass could be reactivated when its magnetism wore off.

In the early 1900s, scientists unveiled the gyroscopic compass. A gyroscope is a kind of spinning wheel, mounted in such a way that its axis is free to orient itself in any direction. Once spinning, a gyroscope steadily points in one direction. Gyrocompasses are set to point north, even as earth rotates under them. Since a gyro compass isn't affected by Earth's magnetic field, it can be adjusted to point to *true* north—along the direction of Earth's axis— doing the magnetic compass one better.

Can you really figure out where you're going by using the pole star?

What if there were one star that seemed fixed in the sky, standing above the North Pole like a glowing directional beacon? A star to steer by: That's Polaris, a.k.a. the North Star. It's helped human beings (and perhaps even migrating birds) find their way in the dark for many hundreds of years.

The star's full Latin name is Stella Polaris—the pole star. Polaris has also been called the Lodestar, since, like a compass or lodestone, it helps us locate north. The ancient Romans also called the star Navigatoria.

Polaris is not the brightest star in the night sky. But you can easily find it on a

Miss Pole Star Pageant
Polaris reigns supreme...

...For now honey!

...Then it's my time to shine

In about 13,000 years!

So cool your jets!

clear night in the Northern Hemisphere. Follow an imaginary line from the outermost stars in the Big Dipper's bowl, to the tip of the Little Dipper's handle. That's Polaris.

If you stood near the North Pole and looked up, here's what you would see: Polaris, almost directly overhead. And, if you took a time-lapse picture, all the other stars would appear to slowly circle it as the night wore on.

But Polaris's exalted status is just a coincidence. The North Pole traces a small circle over 24 hours as Earth turns. Since the pole happens to be pointed at Polaris, the star is centered overhead, with the others seeming to circle it as Earth rotates on its axis. (There is no South Star, since the South Pole doesn't happen to be pointing toward one.)

Polaris wasn't the first pole star, nor will it be the last. Everything in space is in constant motion relative to everything else. And Earth wobbles on its axis, so the North Pole points toward different stars over thousands of years. So while Polaris wears the pole star crown for now, a star called Thuban held the

> **While Polaris wears the pole star crown for now, a star called Vega will wear it in about 13,000 years.**

honor 5,000 years ago. By 13,000 years from now, the bright star Vega will reign as pole star, to be replaced again by Thuban (Alpha Draconis) by the year 17,000. And then good old Polaris will come around again.

As Earth has changed position relative to the stars, there have been centuries in which there is no pole star to guide us—and there will be again, as the North Pole gradually points away from Polaris in coming centuries. We're lucky to be living in a time in which we each have our own personal OnStar navigation system—a real star.

Know Your Pole Star

Polaris is located about 430 light years (about 2.6 quadrillion miles) from Earth. If you could travel to its solar system, you'd find that Polaris is a massive yellow star some 2,000 times brighter than our Sun. Polaris is a kind of star called a Cepheid variable; it slowly brightens and dims a bit over the course of days.

Driving through the country, we saw vultures circling above a field. Why do they circle dead animals?

Vultures have gotten a bad rap. We see a pack lazily circling above a field and imagine they are waiting for some unfortunate creature to die, after which they will swoop in to pick at the remains. Actually, however, vultures first become interested in an animal carcass about 24 hours after the animal's death, when they are able to pick up its scent on the air.

When you think about it, vultures have something in common with a shopper cruising the supermarket meat cases. Nature's meat cases are the fields and roads where animals

Leftovers for Lunch Bunch...

It smelled ok, but it didn't taste good.

often die from old age, illness, or accidents.

The vulture seen most often in the United States, the turkey vulture, has a bright red turkeylike head, perched on a body covered in black-brown feathers. (Others found in the United States are black vultures and California condors).

Compared to most other birds, a turkey vulture's brain has a much bigger smell (olfactory) center. Couple that with large, wide-open nostrils and turkey vultures are champion smellers, able to detect a few wafting scent molecules (mmmm, dead squirrel) in a trillion molecules of air. In one experiment, turkey vultures found two chicken carcasses hidden in the tropical rain forest—and completely invisible from the treetops—by the second day, simply by sniffing them in the air far above.

While vultures prefer fresh meat, the birds' cast-iron digestive systems allow them to dine on dead animals well past their prime. The problem with putrid meat (besides the foul taste and smell) is the dangerous microorganisms it can harbor. A vulture's digestive tract neatly destroys incoming bacteria and viruses, and even the deadly botulism toxin.

> When threatened, a vulture may projectile-vomit an acidic stream of digested food, right at the attacker's eyes.

A vulture may eat 25 percent of its 3- to 4-pound weight in dead raccoon, possum, or cow at one sitting. When threatened (say, by a bear or coyote), a vulture may projectile-vomit an acidic stream of digested food, aimed right at the attacker's eyes. Besides repulsing the predator, vomiting lightens the vulture's heavy load, allowing it to lift off in a quick getaway.

Vultures hang out in the air above a carcass only for a short time as they decide whether it's still fresh enough to eat. To remain on top of a thermal (a column of rising, heated air), birds fly in circles. As the air lifts them, the vultures travel in a spiral pattern. Once they decide it's really dinner—and that no menacing animals are nearby—they descend gracefully to the ground.

FAST FACT

A turkey vulture's wing span can extend 6 feet. Vultures soar through the air, following updrafts and thermals in a seemingly effortless glide, little or no flapping required.

Why do raindrops seem to fall at a slant when you are riding in a car?

R ain slanting against the windshield as a car drives down a dark country road—can a spooky old house *not* be just around the bend? It's a familiar scene in the movies. But it also rains sideways when you're riding the school bus home—with nary a haunted house in sight.

Wind can blow raindrops sideways, making umbrellas useless as rain pelts your legs. But even when there's no wind, rain

FRAMES OF REFERENCE...

A dog is driving the car...

That fire hydrant looks like a good place to stop.

The rain is falling sideways...

will appear to fall slantwise when you see it through the windows of a moving car.

How come? It all depends on your frame of reference. A reference frame could be the inside of your house, the cabin of an airplane, a moving elevator, the back of a merry-go-round horse, the front seat of your car, the surface of a planet— the list is endless.

Depending on your reference point, an object in motion can be seen as moving in different directions. When you drop a penny inside a rising high-speed elevator car, the penny is falling from your reference point. But from the building's reference point, the penny is rising along with the elevator.

Which brings us to the moving auto. If you were standing on the sidewalk watching a car go by in the rain—on a windless day—the raindrops would appear to fall straight down, the car passing under the perpendicular curtain of water.

But to a passenger inside, it's a different movie. The car is driving forward through the rain at a certain speed. Everything outside the car

> **When you drop a penny inside a rising elevator car, the penny is falling from your reference point. But from the building's reference point, the penny is rising.**

appears to be moving at an equal speed *backward*. And that includes the raindrops. But the raindrops have a velocity downward, too. So from the passenger point of view, raindrops appear to fall at an angle between the two directions (down and back)—at a slant.

Moving reference frames affect everything—including where we see distant stars. The planet on which we stand is moving: rotating, and circling the Sun. Meanwhile, our whole solar system— the Sun and its tag-along planets—is traveling along the rotating rim of the Milky Way Galaxy. So when we look at other stars from Earth, we are not standing still—and neither are they.

To figure out where stars should be in the sky at a particular time of year, the most important motion to take into account is Earth's around the Sun. Rather like a car speeding through raindrops, Earth speeding through starlight on its journey around the Sun makes starlight appear to shift sideways to observers on the ground.

Likewise, it's such apparent shifts in the stars that let us deduce that Earth is, in fact, moving.

Why do wheels appear to spin backward when a vehicle speeds up?

We've all seen it in movies or old TV westerns—as the stagecoach (or train) picks up speed, its fast-moving wheels appear to switch direction, slowly turning backward. We also occasionally see the phenomenon in real life, with both spinning car tires and whirling ceiling fans.

What causes the backward effect? The answer, it turns out, depends on whether the effect you see is on film, in a fluorescent-lit room, on the freeway at night, or in daylight.

There's no argument about what's happening when we're watching, say, a stagecoach on film. A motion picture camera takes many snapshots a second of the scene unfolding in front of it, adding up to thousands of individual images on a long strip of film. Because the pictures are taken in quick succession, there's little motion lost between each one.

When you view the finished movie, snapshots of the action flash by on the screen. As they do, your brain keeps the previous image in mind as you see the next one. The action appears continuous—just as it was in real life.

But when a filmed wagon wheel rotates at just the right speed, the backward effect occurs. How? If one snapshot is taken with a spoke in the six o'clock position, the same spoke may have sped around to 5:59 when the next snapshot is taken. And the next shot may be of the spoke frozen at the 5:58 position. When your eyes and brain put the motion together, the wheel seems to slowly turn backward. The illusion is a kind of camera strobing—as in a dance club, when flashing strobe lights freeze dancers in a series of positions.

A similar illusion can occur in real life, in a room lit by fluorescent lights at night.

Mikey the movie...

Mikey reaches warp speed entering kitchen...

According to University of Texas neuroscientist David Eagleman, fluorescent lights actually go on and off 60 times a second, and the strobe-light effect can make a ceiling fan appear to turn backward. The flickering sodium-vapor lights on the freeway at night can have the same effect, he says, on our perception of spinning car wheels.

What about the backward effect in broad daylight? Some scientists think that the brain/eye system may process visual information in individual units—like a movie camera's individual snapshots of motion.

However, Eagleman believes that this snapshotting view of the brain is wrong. He has done experiments showing that the daylight backward effect is real, but can be explained by the way the brain interprets motion from the right and left.

When the brain sees a pattern moving from the right to the left, Eagleman says, more of its leftward than rightward motion detectors are activated. But in a kind of brain neuron rivalry, the rightward detectors win out now and then, and a moving pattern appears to reverse itself.

To see the real-world effect for yourself, Eagleman suggests staring at your home ceiling fan. During the daytime, with all artificial lighting off, turn the fan on at a slow speed. Then make yourself comfy—say, on the couch—because seeing the illusion can take 8 minutes or more. With patience, Eagleman says, you should eventually see the fan running backward for a few seconds.

Mom appears in doorway...

...the spokes of Mikey's wheels appear to go backward...

Why does the wood in a petrified forest feel like rock?

In a scary movie, when a character seems rooted in place with fear—even when he should be turning and running the other way, as fast as he can—it's because he is petrified. To be petrified with fear is to be frozen like a statue.

Likewise, petrified wood is wood that has literally turned to stone. Unlike a living tree, channeling food and water up through

THE PETRIFIED LUNCH BOX ...

Unearthed in North Dakota...

It weighs 87 pounds!

Filled with permineralized potato chips that would make awesome paperweights...

I think they were barbecue

its bark and branches, a petrified tree is a "frozen" statue of its former self. What sounds like a mad-scientist plot is just a way nature accidentally preserves once-living things, giving us, as a side benefit, a window into the past.

A petrified log may look like a wooden log, complete with growth rings and bark. But touch it, and you'll realize that the log is really a reincarnation of the original, cast in solid rock. The colors may be very different, too—how often does an ordinary log have patches of orange and red, or glitter like rhinestones? And just try lifting a petrified log—even a smallish log has the weight of a concrete garden ornament.

A chunk of petrified, or permineralized, wood is a fossil, like a dinosaur bone or the imprint of an ancient fern leaf in rock. Most wood ends up decaying and disintegrating over time, gets burned up, or is digested by insects, bacteria, or larger animals. Wood that becomes petrified escapes this fate by being quickly buried—say, in a catastrophic mud slide, or in volcanic lava or ash flow—which preserves it in an oxygen-free environment. Then, when some mineral-rich water percolates through the muck, the statue-making process begins.

And a calcified bologna sandwich fit for museum display

Somebody's locker must have smelled really bad!

Oh, yuck!

FAST FACT

Because wood is sometimes set in stone, bearing many of its original markings and rings, we get glimpses of what the landscape and climate were like millions of years ago. The many petrified logs found in South Dakota include several species of palm tree, revealing a semitropical past for this now temperate state.

Over time, the buried log's cellulose cells lose their fluids, while water from outside seeps into cracks, between cells, and into empty cells. As the water evaporates over time, it leaves minerals like silica or calcite or marcasite behind. Gradually, the tree's structure fills with minerals. And as the minerals harden over the centuries, the original log is replaced, cell by cell, by a stone replica.

Petrified wood's rainbow of colors reflects the minerals that made it. So a calcified log will be white (unless it's exposed to the browning effects of sunlight). Impurities in the invading minerals affect the color, making no logs exactly alike. Iron adds reds and yellows; manganese and copper create blue or green patches. Crystals of quartz and other minerals make petrified wood glitter.

Why and how do snakes shed their skin?

Human skin cells, once dry and dead, flake or peel off bit by bit. White dandruff sprinkles down on our shoulders. A sunburned arm peels. But what if we woke up one morning to find our skin dull, loose, and gray—and we had to work our way out of our skin suit? Even after shedding the old skin, we might be inclined to call in sick to work or school, and spend the day on the couch.

Snakes really do shed their skin in one whole piece, slithering out of their scaly skin suit as if it were old clothing. Stumble across the left-behind skin and you might think, for a moment, that it is a snake. Look closer and you'll see a pale, almost transparent casting of a snake, with two holes where alert eyes once looked out.

Young snakes outgrow their skin, shedding (molting) their too-tight suits up to four or more times a year. And skin wears out, so even full-grown adult snakes shed theirs once or twice a year, usually in spring and summer.

The skin shed is the thin outer layer, the epidermis. Under the old skin, a shiny new epidermis has been growing. Just before shedding, the snake's body secretes an oily substance into the space between the skins, to help the old skin slip off.

A snake about to molt looks dull from head to tail. Even its eyes are cloudy, pupils obscured by about-to-be-shed skin scales. Imagine being a snake—skin loosening all

FAST FACT

Rattlesnakes keep part of the skin on their tails, which is modified into a new rattle each time they molt. So by counting the number of rattles on a rattlesnake's tail, you'll know how often it has shed its skin.

over your body, eyesight dimmed—and you'll understand why snakes hide out and stop eating for a few days during molting time.

When, finally, skin becomes uncomfortably baggy, a snake will sometimes rub its face against a tree, fallen branch, or rock. But some snakes simply slither across the forest floor, peeling as they go. The skin around the lips comes loose first, and a snake must force the skin back over its head like someone removing a knit cap. By sliding against rough surfaces and through narrow crevices, a snake pulls the loose skin back over its neck and body, sliding out of the

> Young snakes outgrow their skin, shedding (molting) their too-tight suits up to four or more times a year.

skin as if it were a snug sleeping bag.

As the snake emerges through the old mouth-hole, the used skin has turned inside out, like a peeled-back sausage casing. The snake that slithers away from its worn-out skin looks like a brand-new reptile, its new skin supple, bright, and colorful, its eyes once again clear.

While a tossed-off, stretched-out skin may make a good souvenir for a hiker, it's also a handy (and decorative) building material. Birds like the great crested flycatcher collect snakeskins to outfit their new nests.

NO MATTER WHAT SHAPE YOUR SKIN IS IN...

If we were like snakes, we could trade it in...

Hey, I'm 10 years old again!

Be young forever and...

Whaddya mean I can't play the part of a newborn?

have a thousand-year career in Hollywood.

Thank you for this, my 400th Oscar.

How do snakes move without legs?

Human beings and deer run, dogs and horses trot, and fish and otters swim. And there's a unique word to describe how snakes move: slither.

Slithering looks a lot like sliding. Except that while we might slide across a frozen pond, or down a slippery water slide at a theme park, a snake slides across a gravelly driveway or a pile of firewood. Snakes can even glide *up* the trunk of a tree.

But snakes only look like they're slip-sliding away. The snake method of locomotion depends on friction, just like ours. With no legs, arms, wings, or fins, snakes have evolved a "Look, Ma—no hands!" way of getting where they want to go.

Scientists think snakes evolved from random mutations among lizards that lived on the ground or in underground burrows. The new reptiles evolved long, cylinder-shaped bodies (and extra-long internal organs), while abandoning pesky eyelids,

FAMOUS SLITHERING SNAKE MOVES

In the Garden of Eden... In your basic Western... And in action movies.

The slow crawl was effective—I didn't want to frighten Eve.

The Serpentine method gives me the speed I need to chase cowboys.

Doing the Concertina makes climbing ice walls a snap. Indiana Jones, eat your heart out!

outside ears, and legs. (Some snakes, like pythons and boas, have tiny, underdeveloped hind legs, hints of the true legs of their lizard ancestors.)

Snakes do just fine without legs, catching prey, escaping predators, tunneling into sand, slithering through trees, and swimming like pros. Snakes move themselves along a surface mostly by squeezing and releasing muscles around their ribs. These muscles are attached to sets of belly scales that grip the ground like tire treads.

Rather like horses walk, trot, canter, and gallop, snakes use four basic motions to get from here to there. (Unlike horses, not all snakes can use all four movements.)

All snakes do the slither, the undulating crawl also known as the serpentine method. This familiar snaky movement is S-shaped, familiar from movie westerns featuring a threatening rattler. Muscular waves move the snake forward as it pushes sideways against objects or raised areas on the ground (or against the resistance of water in a pond). It's the speediest of snake movements. The fastest known snake speed is about 12 miles per hour.

Heavier snakes also use rectilinear motion—the caterpillar crawl. Pythons often move this way. The snake creeps forward in a straight line, pushing some belly scales down to grip the ground while sliding other scales forward.

Sidewinding is practiced by snakes that live on desert sand. Miss Snake tosses her head and front section to one side. While the rest of her body is catching up, she throws her head to the other side, provoking another mad dash by her hindquarters.

Finally, there's the concertina, in which a snake alternately stretches and shortens his body like an accordion. Concertina motion is especially useful in tight places, or for creeping across a slippery surface.

Snake Stats

There are more than 2,700 species alive on Earth. Snakes are members of the reptile class. While reptiles have been around for about 300 million years, snakes only evolved about 95 million years ago. The largest reptiles, the dinosaurs, roamed Earth for about 130 million years before snakes arrived to be stepped on.

Why does poison ivy make us itch?

Ever walk through the woods and casually brush against a vine—say, wending its way up a tree trunk? And wake up the next morning wearing a bright red, unbearably itchy rash . . . complete with chicken-pox-like blisters? If so, you've had a close encounter with one of nature's most unpleasant plants: poison ivy.

Poison ivy is just one of the irritating members of the cashew family (scientific name Anacardiaceae). Other plants in the family include poison oak, poison sumac, pistachio, mango, ginkgo trees, and, of course, the cashew. All contain allergens similar to those in poison ivy. Workers on cashew farms in places like India actually develop itchy rashes on their hands from touching the resinous oil of cashew shells. (See page 32 for more on cashews.) And if you are sensitive to poison ivy, you may even get a little itchy from handling the rind of a mango.

While cashews, pistachios, and mangoes are fine to eat (except for those who are allergic to them), the whole poison ivy plant is a menace, from the bottom of its roots to the tip of its stems.

The culprit is urushiol, an oily substance that spreads on your skin when you touch any part of the plant. Urushiol can remain active on a surface for years. As little as one nanogram (.000000001 of a gram) can cause a rash in a sensitive person. According to some estimates, 1½ teaspoons of urushiol would be enough to make everyone on Earth itchy.

Between 60 and 80 percent of us are sensitive to poison ivy. The body's own immune system causes the problem, reacting to urushiol as it might to ragweed pollen—as an attacking foreign body. (Birds and many other animals, on the other hand,

> According to some estimates, 1½ teaspoons of urushiol would be enough to make everyone on Earth itchy.

find poison ivy berries both harmless and delicious.)

People sensitive to poison ivy get an itchy, blistering rash if they brush against a plant that has been broken or bruised, releasing its oil. Just because you didn't react to poison ivy in the past doesn't mean you won't in the future—sensitivity can change over time. If you think you've come into contact with poison ivy, wash your skin with cool or warm (not hot) soapy water right away, to remove oil before it bonds to skin proteins.

Poison ivy is considered a shrub or a vine. Its leaves come in groups of three leaflets (which turn beautiful shades of red and yellow in the fall). The plant also sports tiny flowers and green or white-yellow berries. Some varieties creep up trees and over rocks. Poison ivy resembles other harmless plants, like Virginia creeper (which has five, or sometimes four, leaflets). Wild raspberry (blackberry) also looks a little like poison ivy, but you can tell them apart: Raspberry plants have easily seen (and felt) thorns.

Swallowing poison ivy is extremely dangerous, since the result could be a swollen-shut throat, preventing breathing. Never throw poison ivy into a fire; breathing the burning oil can cause a fatal reaction in some people. All of which explains why poison ivy is the plant with its own warning rhyme: "Leaves of three? Let them be."

249

When you drop a stone into a lake, why does it make ripples on the surface?

When you watch watery circles spread out from the spot where a stone has sunk and disappeared, you are witnessing one of the basic mechanisms of the universe—waves. It's a very wavy world.

Imagine you are at the beach. As you play in the ocean, waves push against you and wash over you, as wind makes water build up and then subside. Meanwhile, breezy waves pass through the grasses on a nearby sand dune, and ripples appear in the sand itself.

You hear the shrieks and laughter of the other beachgoers as sound waves travel through the air and hit your eardrums. The

MAKING WAVES

summer sun beats down on your back, in waves of electromagnetic radiation. Some of these waves, the ordinary visible light waves, simply bounce off. Those that reach your friend's eyes enable her to see you.

The higher-energy light waves—the ultraviolet—actually push into your skin, causing it to make more protective melanin. Your skin gets darker and may burn. Every so often, a very high-energy wave—a gamma or cosmic ray from the depths of space—penetrates the atmosphere, and passes straight through your body.

Human society runs in waves, too. History repeats itself in a series of waves, war alternating with peace, long skirts alternating with short, yo-yo sales going up, down, and up again. Emotionally, we are also up and down and up again. Meanwhile, continents slam together and then drift apart, again and again, nature's cyclical solving of Earth's jigsaw puzzle.

Of course, just thinking about all these waves is generating electrical waves inside your brain.

A wave coursing through water or other matter—a mechanical wave—isn't a thing

A wave coursing through water or other matter—a mechanical wave—isn't a thing itself, but a passing disturbance.

itself, but a passing disturbance. When wind causes a wave to pass through a wheat field and reach the edge, the wheat doesn't go running across the road. The wave is an undulation passing from row to row, like a rumor passed from person to person.

Likewise, when you drop a rock into a pond, the water doesn't speed away from the stone. Instead, a disturbance travels though the water, causing it to rhythmically rise and fall in place. (A duck, ripple-riding, will bob up and down.)

Here's how it works: The stone pushes a circular volume of water down into a trough as it falls in. Around the hole, a ring of water crests in reaction. That causes an even larger ring of water to sink, and so on. Presto: spreading concentric circles.

Throw a second stone in nearby, and two sets of circles will overlap. In some places, the crests or troughs of the waves may coincide, making bigger waves. In other places, a crest will coincide with a trough, canceling both waves out. There, the water will be still.

Without a source of energy, waves lose energy and fade away. So be prepared with a pile of rocks to keep a pond in ripples.

Looking at our campfire, I wondered: What exactly is fire?

The ancient Greeks thought fire was one of four basic elements: earth, water, air, and fire. Philosopher Heraclitus thought that fire was, in fact, the primary element. The world, he said, "was ever, is now, and ever shall be an ever-living fire." The philosopher Anaximander believed Earth was surrounded by misty spheres; beyond was an enormous fire. The Sun and stars were just glimpses of the fire through the mist, like the light of a lightbulb glimpsed through cutouts in a lampshade.

Many believed that the Big Fire was the source of both creation and destruction. Which is understandable, because even a small fire is constantly in motion, like energy dancing in place—and capable of devouring everything in its path.

According to scientists, an object can be on fire without producing a flame—for example, a red-hot coal.

Fire was so dazzling, terrifying, and mysterious to people for all of human history that trying to solve its riddle helped develop a whole branch of science: chemistry. In trying to figure out fire, human beings discovered something even more fundamental: oxygen.

Artist and inventor Leonardo da Vinci was among the first to note that a flame goes out without air, like a living being suffocates. Others noted the odd fact that when metals were heated by a flame, the leftover powder weighed more than the original metal—as if something had been added.

By the 1700s, French chemist Antoine-Laurent Lavoisier realized that air is made up of gases. It was one of these gases—oxygen—that was sucked into all burning materials, and that added weight to heated metals.

Soon, scientists had figured out that oxygen atoms combine, over time, with carbon and hydrogen atoms in a hydrocarbon like wood. From the fast burning of a wood fire's leaping flames, to the much slower, more controlled burning of food inside the body, oxidation goes on continuously all around us. It's why a newspaper yellows as it ages.

Fire is oxidation sped up by heat. If a fuel (like wood) is heated while exposed to oxygen, the oxygen will bond much more quickly to the fuel's hydrogen and carbon atoms. The process can accelerate to the ignition point, when heat can be felt and seen (as light). The first flames may appear, and instead of a yellowing newspaper, you have a burning torch.

Fuel burned in a fire can be solid (a chunk of wood or lump of coal); liquid (gasoline or kerosene); or gas (natural gas or propane). According to scientists, an object can even be on fire without producing a flame (like a red-hot coal).

The flame itself, however, is a gas—a collection of hot gases, including carbon dioxide and steam—rising from a burning material. When you look at flames, such as those dancing on a burning log, you may also see solid particles of soot—glowing embers—rising into the air.

The Fire Inside...

You've started the oxidation process, deep down inside of me.

Is there enough air down there?

How does high altitude, like in the mountains, affect cooking?

Do your cakes rise like soufflés—only to collapse with a plop? Do you make a cup of tea using boiling water—and then find it tepid rather than piping hot a minute later? Do your Tollhouse cookies emerge from the oven with the texture of chocolate-studded hockey pucks?

If so, you might be a New Yorker vacationing in Colorado Springs, or a Miami resident on a trip to Salt Lake City.

Why is cooking in the mountains different from cooking near sea level? If you've ever climbed a high mountain, you know that the higher you trudge, the thinner

High-Altitude Cooking ...

The coffee is cold...

The chicken's not cooked...

Let's order out!

254

the air gets. At sea level, Earth's atmosphere weighs on each square inch of us (and of everything else) with about 14.7 pounds of pressure. But as air thins out high up, it exerts less and less pressure.

As the pressure on water drops, it takes less energy for water molecules to break the bonds they share in a liquid. So the higher the altitude, the less heat it requires for water to boil, changing from a liquid to a gas (steam).

At sea level, water boils at the old familiar 212°F. But with every 500 feet in elevation, the boiling point drops by about 1 degree. At 14,000 feet up, on Pike's Peak in Colorado, water boils at a not-so-hot 187°F, making for a rather pale and tepid cup of tea.

So at elevations above 3,000 feet, foods cooked in liquids, such as rice, beans, or braised meats, must be cooked longer before they are done. Baked goods require trickier adjustments. Leavening gases like those released by yeast expand more as air pressure drops, making breads and cakes rise too quickly. Moisture evaporates faster during cooking, since water boils away at lower temperatures. And because the

At 14,000 feet up, on Pike's Peak in Colorado, water boils at a not-so-hot 187°F, making for a rather pale and tepid cup of tea.

climate is usually arid higher up, even dry ingredients like flour may be drier than usual. The result can be rock-hard cookies and desiccated brownies.

So to make pie in the sky—or cookies and cake—you must get creative with old-favorite recipes. High-altitude cooking experts advise reducing leavening like baking powder ⅛ teaspoon for each teaspoon in a recipe. Likewise, reduce sugar by about 1 tablespoon a cup, and add 1 to 2 tablespoons of liquid to each cup of liquid. Don't overbeat eggs. And make sure pans are well greased, since cakes will stick more. Oven temperatures must be adjusted, too—sometimes up, sometimes down.

Of course, it could be worse: You could be cooking on Mars. The air pressure on the Martian flatlands is only about 1 percent that of Earth's sea-level pressure. So according to scientists, a cup of fresh water would begin to boil at or about 34°F. If the thought of dipping your teabag into a cup of icy-cold boiling water doesn't seem like fun, just imagine trying to bake red velvet cake on the red planet.

We went to California on vacation and saw no fireflies. How come?

Surprise: Kids (and adults) who've never traveled outside of California may have seen fireflies only in picture books, movies, TV commercials—and at the Pirates of the Caribbean ride at Disneyland. Lightning bugs are noticeably absent from California lawns and fields.

But in much of the United States, fireflies are the first sign of summer, winking on and off as they rise from the lawn like flying lanterns. We call them lightning bugs or fireflies, but they are actually beetles.

Baby fireflies (larvae) hatch out of eggs hidden in the soil. Unlike adults, little fireflies glow around the clock, tiny lights in the grass. The glow is probably protective, warning off hungry creatures that associate the light with a firefly's bitter taste.

Splendor in the not-so-California grass...

You're cute. How about a date?

You're a dork... With an antenna problem!

Will you kiss it and make it better?

But when adult fireflies flash their taillights, the show is usually about mating. Males fly back and forth in the night air, sending out flashes of light in a pattern. Females rest on leaves and twigs, watching the display. If a female is interested in a particular male, she will flash back.

Firefly light is made in cells called photocytes. By letting oxygen into its abdomen, a firefly sets off a reaction between light-making chemicals luciferin and luciferase, plus energy compound ATP. The released energy excites the atoms in luciferin, which give off photons of light.

There are nearly 2,000 different kinds, or species, of fireflies on Earth, living on every continent but Antarctica. In the United States alone, there are more than 170 different species. Some prefer open fields, others swamps, and still others like living in the woods. Some flash mainly at dusk, while others wait for the darkest hours of the night. Some flash with a green light, others with a yellow or even amber light.

In the United States, most lightning bugs live east of the Mississippi River. According to Tom Turpin, an entomologist (scientist who studies bugs) at Purdue

> **When adult fireflies flash their taillights, the show is usually about mating.**

University, there are other kinds of fireflies in California and other western states. They come in two main varieties: The so-called "dark fireflies," in which the adults don't fly and only the larvae glow. Or the glowworm fireflies, in which the babies and wingless adult females glow.

The firefly species in which adults flash *and* fly—the lightning bugs—stay east of the Rocky Mountains, Turpin said. They prefer warm, moist places and have never crossed the dry, geographical barrier of the eastern Rocky Mountains or the deserts of the southwest. So flying lanterns won't be seen at night in California, Washington, Oregon, Nevada, Wyoming, Idaho, New Mexico, Arizona, Colorado, or western Texas.

FAST FACT

Even in places where lightning bugs are abundant, they prefer the country and suburbs to the inside of big cities. Which is why you probably won't see any fireflies competing with the neon lights in New York's Times Square.

Where does the sand on beaches come from?

It's a familiar summer whine: "Can we go to the strip of sediment today? *Please?*"

Okay, maybe it isn't so familiar. But the beach really is a strip of sediment, the stuff you find at the bottom of rivers and streams. Sediment is always being moved around by water, and beaches are no exception—built of shifting sands, they change size and shape from season to season.

Just how much sand is on a beach? Too much, according to the Walrus and the Carpenter in Lewis Carroll's *Through the Looking-Glass,* who "wept like anything" at a beach full of sand. " 'If seven maids with seven mops / Swept it for half a year, / Do you suppose,' the Walrus said, / 'That they would get it clear?' / 'I doubt it,' said the Carpenter, / And shed a bitter tear."

In just 1 cubic foot of sand, there are about a million grains.

The Carpenter was right. In just 1 cubic foot of sand, there are about a million grains. Mathematicians at the University of (beach-heavy) Hawaii used sophisticated math programs to figure out how many grains of sand lie on all the world's beaches. Their estimate: 7,500,000,000,000,000,000 (seven quintillion five quadrillion).

Where does all that sand come from? Most of the sand and pebbles on ocean beaches actually comes from inland mountains. Mountain rock erodes in wind and rain, washes into rivers, and is carried to the sea. Sand also sifts down from eroding rocks and cliffs behind a beach.

Rivers are slower and less powerful than they once were, and carry mostly silt, the tiniest particles. But in the past, especially after the ice age 10,000 years ago, melting ice swelled rivers to torrents. Roaring rivers hauled boulders to the ocean, along with pebbles and coarse sand.

After particles pour into the ocean, they are carried along the shore by currents and tossed up onto the beach by waves. When a wave breaks on the shore, rivulets of sand-laden water run up the beach. Some of the water sinks down through the beach; some backwashes into the ocean. If the wave isn't too strong, more sand is deposited on the beach than flows away. And so beaches are built.

Waves tend to be gentler in summer than in winter. Fierce winter storms whip up big, powerful waves, which tend to pull sand from the beach. Meanwhile, sand is also picked up by high winds and blown inland. People who live at the shore may find the winter beach narrowed, the ocean dangerously close to their houses.

But in summer, when the ocean is calmer, the beach is rebuilt by the sea. The "sand budget" isn't always balanced, however, which is why some shore communities have taken to hauling in sand to replenish the supply. Over the long run, the biggest enemy of beaches may be global warming. If polar ice continues to melt and the oceans continue to rise, many beaches will exist only on old postcards.

STILL SWEEPING AFTER ALL THESE YEARS...

Why is the ocean so salty?

Ever get splashed by a wave and taste a mouthful of ocean? Seawater is about as salty as a glass of water with a teaspoon of salt stirred in.

The sea contains an almost unimaginable amount of salt.

Compare your glass of salty water to the oceans. Oceans cover about 70 percent of Earth's surface. The ocean basins are filled with about 3,496,000,000,000,000,000,000 gallons of water, or about 3.5 sextillion gallons. Dissolved in that vast volume of water are about 50 quadrillion tons of solids. And about 85 percent of those solids are sodium and chloride—the minerals that make table salt.

Pour 1 cubic foot of seawater into a container and let it evaporate in the sun, and you'll return to find a salt mound weighing about 2.2 pounds. According to the U.S. Geological Survey, if we could remove the oceans' salt and sprinkle it over Earth's surface, it would pile up 500 feet high everywhere. In New York City, salt would

Salt Water Taste Test

Crisp and lightly salted, tastes like... the Adriatic?

Full bodied and firmly salty, from... the Dead sea?

Fruity yet delightfully salty, could it be... my bath water?

fill the streets up to the windows on the 40th floor of buildings.

Compared to the oceans, the average river or lake is decidedly unsalty. (Evaporate a cubic foot of water from a typical lake, and you'll be left with about 1/6 ounce of salt.) Fresh water from rivers flows into the oceans day and night, year after year. And yet the oceans stay salty. How did the salt get there—and why hasn't it gotten diluted over time?

Most of the salt in the oceans was carried down from the land. Pelting rain, blowing wind, and flowing rivers wash salts out of rocks and soil on land, eventually carrying it into the sea. In addition, salts seep in from volcanic vents on the ocean floor. Salts also sift into the sea from volcanic eruptions on land.

If we could remove the oceans' salt and sprinkle it over Earth's surface, it would pile up 500 feet high everywhere.

Over hundreds of millions of years, salt carried into the oceans has built up to its current staggering level. And rivers carry some 4 billion more tons of dissolved solids into the oceans yearly.

Once in the ocean, salt tends to stay put. When the heat of the Sun evaporates water from the ocean's surface, it acts like a distiller. Water vapor rises from the ocean; nearly all of its salt stays behind. According to oceanographers, a sodium atom that washes into the ocean from a river will, on average, remain for 237 million years.

Mystery of the Missing Calcium

Rivers carry more calcium than chloride into the oceans, but the oceans contain 46 times more chloride than calcium. How come? Shellfish like clams, mussels, and oysters extract calcium from seawater to build their shells; shrimp, crabs, and lobsters use the calcium to form their carapaces. When seawater becomes saturated with calcium, it can be deposited on the seafloor as calcium carbonate (limestone)—also the main building material of coral reefs.

How come salt water makes it easier to float?

If you've ever compared floating in the ocean to floating in a backyard swimming pool, you know there's a difference. It's easier to float lazily around in the ocean, with no pesky sinking knees. In the even saltier Great Salt Lake in Utah, you'll bob like a buoy.

Objects sink through water for the same reason they fall through the air: gravity. Gravity is the attraction matter feels for other matter. The more matter packed densely together in one place, the greater its gravitational pull. An enormous chunk of matter like Earth has enough gravitational pull to make a baseball fall down through the air and a stone sink in a pond of liquid water.

So an object that floats rather than sinks is floating because the liquid is pushing it up, exerting a force opposite to the force of gravity. A scientist from ancient Greece named Archimedes summed up what

262

happens: An object in a fluid is buoyed up by a force equal to the weight of the fluid it displaces.

But whether an object floats or sinks depends on whether it displaces enough water to hold its own weight. So when it comes to floating, what counts most is density—how much mass is packed into a given volume.

If a solid object is denser than the water it took the place of, it will sink. An iron frying pan is denser and weightier than a skillet-size volume of water. So tossed into a lake, it will sink straight to the bottom, tugged down by gravity.

But if an object is less dense than water, like an inflated beach ball, it will float. A beach ball is a thin elastic sheet surrounding a big bunch of thin air. But a beach ball–size parcel of water is much more densely packed and heavy than an actual beach ball. A beach ball not only floats, it actually takes about 9 pounds of force to press a gallon-size beach ball into water.

But even objects whose average density is greater than water (and end up sinking) also experience its buoyant force. A rock sinks, but some of its weight is buoyed up, making the rock lighter underwater than on land.

The denser the liquid, the more weight it will hold up. A solid chunk of steel, for example, would bob around nicely in even-denser liquid mercury.

Which brings us to salt. When you take a certain volume of water and add salt, you are making a denser liquid. A cubic foot of fresh water weighs about 62.4 pounds, but an equal volume of salty ocean water weighs about 64 pounds. So an object that sinks in fresh water may float in salt water. (Utah's Great Salt Lake is 12 to 25 times as salty as the sea, and most people float effortlessly on its surface. The tricky part is staying submerged.)

See for yourself how salt water makes objects more buoyant: Fill a glass about halfway with tap water. Gently slide an egg into the glass—and watch it sink, since it's denser than water. Now stir in some salt. Keep adding salt, about a tablespoon at a time, until your egg rises off the bottom and begins to float.

> It takes about 9 pounds of force to press a gallon-size beach ball into water.

How Your Cruise Ship Stays Afloat

If you've ever dropped a cell phone over the side of a cruise ship, only to watch it sink slowly beneath the waves (while your ship packed with people floats on), you may have wondered: What floats my boat?

We know how beach balls stay afloat (see page 263), but cruise ships and ocean liners are made of thousands of tons of heavy steel. Steel is certainly denser than water. Why doesn't it sink? Here's the trick: The metal is in the form of a shell, not a solid block. And much of the matter in the enormous volume of a ship is actually trapped air (think of a ship-shaped beach ball, framed of steel). So the ship as a whole is actually less dense than the (huge) parcel of water it would displace if it were submerged.

The biggest ocean liners displace more than 80,000 tons of water. According to Archimedes, an object floating in water is pushed up by a force equal to the weight of the water it displaces. Since a ton is 2,000 pounds, that means the largest passenger ships are buoyed up by more than 160 million pounds of force.

How does an oyster make a pearl?

Even though a pearl hasn't been cut into facets like a diamond, it's as if you can see below its surface. There is an iridescent depth, a soft glow, as if the pearl were lit from inside. When people first found pearls hidden in the sand-encrusted shells of rather slimy little creatures, they must have been astonished.

It's hard to believe such a perfect object could be made—not even on purpose!—by an irritated mollusk. Many mollusks make pearls—mussels, oysters, some clams and abalone. But it's the saltwater pearl oyster that does it best; oyster pearls have a special glow.

Here's a surprise: Pearls grow because of how mollusks eat dinner. Oysters are filter feeders; water flows through their slightly open shells, and they strain the tasty algae out.

But the current that pushes algae water through an oyster's shell can also carry in unwanted debris. Like sand. A tiny piece of broken shell or coral. Or even a parasite worm.

Wouldn't you be an irritated oyster if bits of junk washed up against you, ruining your

ONE MAN'S JEWELRY IS ANOTHER MAN'S BACKACHE

He's making a necklace for me, although he'd never admit it!

Ow!

comfortable little home? Well, even without hands, oysters have a way of bagging up the trash so that it doesn't annoy them.

Here's how it works. Between the shell and the oyster's soft body is a layer of living tissue called the mantle. The mantle makes nacre, that iridescent, slick substance coating the inside of some shells. Nacre is also called mother-of-pearl. It's made from a translucent mineral (aragonite) and a gluey substance (conchiolin). Layers of nacre look lustrous.

When a bit of debris lodges in an oyster shell, the mantle tissue swings into action, churning out nacre to cover it.

Month by month, layer by layer, the debris becomes coated in mother-of-pearl. If nacre surrounds the debris completely and evenly, a round pearl is gradually built inside the shell.

Pearls are rare, round pearls are rarer, and big, round pearls are rarest of all. Most pearls are tiny, irregularly shaped, and rather dull. After all, the oyster didn't set out to make a bead for a necklace—it just wanted a little relief from the gravel in its side.

> **Most pearls are tiny, irregularly shaped, and rather dull—after all, the oyster didn't set out to make a jewel.**

Down on the Farm: Pearls with Culture

Because perfect natural pearls are so rare—and because it's so dangerous to dive down to search for them—gem dealers developed pearl farms. Pearl farmers insert a tiny bead made of mother-of-pearl and a snippet of living mantle tissue into a baby oyster. Then they patiently wait for a pearl to grow. Nearly all pearls in jewelry nowadays are cultured pearls.

But cultured pearls with great inner glow or "orient" are nearly as rare as good natural pearls. Finding pearls that match in size, shape, and color for just one necklace strand can take years of opening oysters and sorting pearls. That's why a single necklace can sell for $350,000 or more.

In the future, scientists say, oyster tissue (without the oyster) may be cultured in a lab and then allowed to secrete nacre around beads. Presto: test-tube-baby pearls!

On a trip to Mexico, my grandmother bought us jumping beans. How can beans jump around?

Jumping beans aren't jumpy from too much caffeine, but they do have a secret that makes them very jittery.

It all begins with a flowering shrub that grows only in the deserts of Mexico, Central America, and the southwestern U.S. Next, add a special jumping bean moth, which is attracted to the flowers.

The shrub *Sebastiania pavoniana* blooms in the summer. Gray moths, smaller than dimes, lay their eggs among the tiny flowers, right on the seed capsules. Now, the fun starts.

Each capsule has three sections or carpels, a seed lurking in each one. When the moth eggs hatch, tiny larvae emerge and

Larvae seem to move their beans more when it's hot, perhaps angling for a shadier spot.

worm their way inside the carpels. Warm and safe, they begin nibbling away at the tasty seed.

Late in the summer, the carpels split up and drop to the ground. Not every carpel was visited by a moth, so some spill out healthy seeds to grow more shrubs. Others shelter wriggling larvae.

Here comes the jumping part. Propelled by their wormy tenants, the carpels jerk and roll around on the ground, like brown beans come alive (despite their name, they don't really leap into the air). But what's amazing is that the "beans" move at all, since each weighs as much as the larva propelling it.

267

How do the larva budge their beans? The answer, surprisingly, lies in home renovation. Once a larva has gobbled up its seed-food, the inside of its carpel is empty. So the larva gets busy decorating, spinning comfy silk to line the walls of its brown house.

When it wants to move, a larva grabs the silk webbing with tiny legs, snapping its body (and even slamming its head into the wall). This sends the bean house skidding across the ground, where it may roll for some distance. Larvae seem to move their beans more when it's hot, perhaps angling for a shadier spot. As a fringe benefit, the jumping may spook hungry birds. But mostly, the idea seems to be to maneuver the beans into a safe, secure location, such as a crack beneath a rock. There, a larva can spend the winter transforming into an unimaginable future version of itself.

As the weather turns chilly, the larva wraps itself in a thick cocoon. Its bean lies still now, as the larva changes into a mummylike pupa. But just before it enters pupadom, the larva does one last bit of remodeling: It etches the outline of a perfect, circular trapdoor into the wall of its house, slicing through most (but not all) of the circle.

As summer comes around again, pupa has become moth. With the rains that make desert shrubs bloom thrumming on its carpel, the moth takes the wake-up call and pushes against the escape hatch cut months before. The door swings open; the moth flies out into the warm air.

After mating, a female moth looks for the shrubs where it all started—and creates a brand-new crop of jumping beans.

INSIDE A PRE-MOTH MOSH PIT

Meet the jumping bean larva in his silky digs!

Watch him smash his head on the wall!

See the head bangers get all worked up and jump around!

While on vacation in the Caribbean, I saw a ring totally surrounding the Sun. What was it?

Even in the heat of summer—or in the Caribbean tropics—the highest clouds are made of glittering ice rather than liquid droplets of water. Haloes around the Sun can appear when sunlight passes through the ice crystals of these frigid clouds.

Droplets of water are round (spherical). But ice crystals can freeze into many different shapes, all of them six-sided (hexagonal). (Think of the endless variety of snowflakes, all hexagonal, but each one uniquely beautiful.)

The cloud crystals that bend sunlight into a halo are much like the six-sided glass prisms that hang from a chandelier. Except that cloud prisms are made of frozen water,

and they hang in the sky, illuminated by the Sun rather than by lightbulbs.

Millions and millions of such ice crystals make up the wispy white clouds known as cirriform clouds. Not only do ice crystals hang in the air; they continuously fall within their clouds, tending to line up with the airstream they fall through. These ever-sinking, not-quite-aligned ice crystals—struck to brilliance by sunlight—are responsible for the ring we sometimes see around the sun.

Here's how it works: As sunlight enters through a side of one of those tiny ice prisms, it bends (refracts). When it exits the other side of the crystal, the light

> The Sun halo is a pale, rainbowish ring, with red on the inside and blue on the outside.

Almost a Rainbow

Except the colors are paler.

It only comes in two sizes.

— small

← medium

It's round instead of an arc.

bends again as it passes into the open air. A bright halo appears because the bent light emerging from millions and millions of crystals combines to form a cone shape.

The size of the halo in the sky depends on just how much the incoming sunlight is bent by the ice crystals. Most of the sunlight enters through the sides of the crystals and is bent at an angle of about 22 degrees. When you stretch your hand to arm's length and spread your fingers—placing your thumb on the Sun—your little pinky finger should just reach the 22-degree halo.

(Even larger, 46-degree haloes are possible, but don't occur as frequently. These bigger haloes are formed by light that passes through the bases and sharply bent points of the ice crystals.)

The Sun halo is a pale, rainbowish ring, with red on the inside and blue on the outside. You may glance up and see a Sun halo after you notice that the quality of light has changed—that the light around you appears an iridescent, pearly white, as if it were filtered through a crystal curtain.

Big, pale Moon haloes can also form at night, when moonlight sifts through high, icy clouds. And in the daytime, so-called sun dogs—brightly colored, changing patches of light in clouds flanking the Sun—can be caused by sunlight refracting from drifting crystals in the wispiest cirrus clouds.

When we were feeding ducks on our vacation, I wondered: Is it true that a quack doesn't echo?

If a duck waddled into a cave and quacked, would the result be a reverberating silence? If you think the answer is a resounding "yes," then the sounds issuing from a duck's bill must be very different from all the other sounds around us.

Why a duck? Why not a barking dog, or a bleating sheep? Is quacking really that unusual, defying the laws of physics and the acoustics of the average cave? Scientists say nope. It turns out that, just like train announcements in a subway station, quacks echo nicely when a duck finds itself in an

Rarely Heard Duck Quack Echoes ...

Spelunking duck quack echoes...

Showering fool duck quack echoes...

Bouncing off buildings duck quack echoes...

271

echo-y place. But how many of us have ever spent time in a cave (or an empty train station) with a very vocal duck?

To settle the duck question, British scientists recruited a white duck named Daisy to waddle into the fray (and into a reverberation chamber) to see if quacks really echo.

Echoes are sound waves that bounce back at us from a smooth, hard surface. When you shout into a cave, the hard stone walls bounce much of the sound waves back at you, like light from a mirror. Instead of seeing yourself, as in a mirror, you hear yourself. So an echo chamber is a kind of ear mirror.

To make the best echoes, a surface should be relatively flat, smooth, and at a 90-degree angle to the ground. Sound travels through air at about 1,100 feet per second at sea level. To hear an echo, you must be standing far enough away from a sound-reflective surface. Otherwise, the sound will shoot back too quickly and overlap your original words.

To amplify the echo, it helps if there are walls angled from the main reflecting wall, as in a cave, to bounce stray sound waves back. Reverberation chambers, such as the one used by University of Salford researchers in the United Kingdom, are designed to maximize echoes, behaving acoustically like mini cathedrals.

Salford professor and echo expert Trevor Cox recorded Daisy the duck's voice first in a room designed to dampen echoes. (Result: soft quacks). Then Daisy moved into the reverberation chamber, where her quacks bounced and, yes, echoed.

But echoing quacks just aren't that impressive. Quacks tend to start out soft and trail off, with the end of the quack blending into its echo. So even if you met a duck in an echo-y spot, you'd have a hard time telling echoes from quacks.

Ducks with Accents

Ever-vigilant British researchers have also discovered that ducks have regional accents, quacking one way in Cornwall, another in London. Cockney ducks, living in the din of the city, are loud and excitable, with quacks like shouts and laughs. Rural Cornish ducks, roaming quiet country fields, are more laid-back, their quacks soft and giggly.

We saw kangaroos at the zoo—what other animals are marsupials?

As a group, marsupials have been around for at least 85 million years. They are mammals, which means they nurse their babies with milk like cats, cows, and people. The word *marsupial* comes from ancient Greek and Latin words meaning "pouch" or "purse." While humans struggle with strollers and baby carriers, most female marsupials have handy baby-size pouches built right in.

Although they are known as the pouched mammals, what makes a marsupial a marsupial is more than a furry pocket. Teeny-tiny babies are the real marsupial specialty. A newborn kitten or human baby looks like a smaller version of its parents.

Marsupial babies are so tiny, undeveloped, and featureless that they don't resemble their mom or dad at all. A newborn kangaroo, for example, is the size of a honeybee.

Marsupial newborns are so small because they haven't been in their mothers' bodies long enough to grow very much. The average pregnancy for a marsupial mom lasts only 12 to 37 days. Compare that to a cat pregnancy, which lasts about 63 days, or a human pregnancy of 9 months. Unlike other mammals, marsupials don't have real placentas to nurture a baby for weeks on end.

Marsupial babies finish their development outside the womb. Once born, a teensy marsupial crawls, hand over hand, to its mom's nipples. (If mom has a pouch, the nipples are found inside.) Clamping its mouth over a nipple (which expands to "lock" baby in place), it drinks milk and continues to develop for months—until it looks like a real animal baby.

Kangaroos are the most famous marsupials, but there are many others.

Did you ever play possum—pretend to be asleep so you could get out of doing some chore? Real opossums play possum by falling over in what appears to be a dead faint, confusing animals (like dogs) that are chasing them. Opossums, who live in the woods all over North America, are

FAST FACT

Marsupials tend to have smaller, less complex brains and many more teeth than other mammals.

the continent's only marsupials.

There are big-bruiser marsupials like the 6-foot-tall, 200-pound gray-and-red kangaroo and dollhouse-size marsupials (the 2-inch-long, 0.1-ounce mouselike ninguai). There are cuddly-looking marsupials (koalas) and scary-looking marsupials (Tasmanian devils, ferocious doglike creatures). And then there are bandicoots (small, long-nosed hoppers), numbats (not bats, but striped anteaters), and wombats (also not bats, but shuffling, snouty animals). All together, there are about 280 living species of marsupials.

In effect, marsupials went their separate evolutionary way as mammals, developing their own brands of mice, moles, wolves, cats, and anteaters (in addition to unique animals like kangaroos). Some speculate that if marsupial evolution had continued with no competition, there might today be the equivalent of marsupial primates, such as marsupial chimps. Or even, some say, a strange variety of marsupial human.

What's the difference between frogs and toads?

The words *frog* and *toad* have very different associations. Toads have been associated with cauldron-stirring witches (powdered toad, anyone?) and are seen as poisonous. One of the dictionary meanings of *toad* is "a contemptible person or thing."

By contrast, frogs have a kindlier, gentler image: kids catching frogs at the pond in summer; old-fashioned frog-jumping contests. And—far from being poisonous—frogs' legs are often found on the menu at French restaurants. A frog can also be a clasp on clothing, that "frog in your throat" when you feel hoarse, or the little crosshatched holder put in a vase to hold flowers upright.

So frogs are associated with nostalgia and things sweet (or at least not scary), while

275

toads are considered rather unsavory. And yet, even though most frogs are harmless, some of the world's most poisonous animals are poison dart *frogs*.

In fact, scientists say, there's about as much difference between a frog and a toad as between jelly and jam.

Frogs and toads are both amphibians, the group of animals that has the enviable power to live happily both on land and in water. (Amphibian comes from the Greek words *bios* and *amphi,* meaning "life on both sides.") Together, frogs and toads make up an order called Anura, which makes them anurans. There are almost 3,000 separate species, or kinds, of frogs and toads.

While some toady anurans are classified into their own toad family—Bufonidae—others aren't. In fact, biologists say that there isn't a precise definition of frog versus toad—so it's perfectly acceptable to call all anurans frogs.

> **Frogs and toads are both amphibians, the group of animals that has the enviable power to live happily both on land and in water.**

However, here are some things you may observe that help you tell animals called toads from those called frogs:

- Frogs are usually moist and smooth; toads tend to have dry, bumpy skin.
- Frogs have long, powerful hind legs and move in startling jumps; toads are less active, have short hind legs, and tend to walk rather than hop.
- Frogs are more often found living in or near water; toads are happy in your garden.
- Frog feet are usually webbed; toads' feet have separated toes.
- Most frogs have teeth; most toads are toothless.
- Frogs lay their eggs in mounds in still water; toads lay eggs in long strings.

If you're still wondering whether the jumpy little animal you're looking at is frog or toad, you can simply announce that it's an anuran and be perfectly correct.

Looking at our vacation photos, I wondered: Why do our eyes turn red in flash photos?

When an animal's eyes glow green or yellow in the headlights, it's a sign of good night vision. A special layer of cells in the back of the eye reflects light back like a mirror. Some of that light is reabsorbed by the eye, letting a deer, raccoon, or opossum see better in the dark. (For more on this, see page 150.)

But human eye-glow doesn't lead to anything but weird-looking birthday photos—Mom, Dad, and little Billy leaning over the candle-studded cake, all with gleaming red eyes. If a camera steals your soul, perhaps a flashbulb replaces it with something demonic.

Actually, the creepy red-eye effect is due to something a lot more benign—those

277

pesky blood vessels in the back of the eye.

The ingredients for the red-eye effect are simple: a dark night or dim room, a camera with a flash, and a person willing to look straight into the lens (or better yet, at the flash itself).

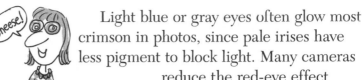

When the flash goes off, light streams through the pupil, the eye's adjustable porthole. The eye's lens focuses the light on the light-collecting retina in the rear, which is fed by a crisscrossing network of blood vessels. When the burst of white light hits the vessels, they absorb light from the blue-green end of the spectrum and reflect back red. Ruby-red light shoots back out through the eye and into the camera lens. Presto: the possessed effect.

In a dim room, our pupils are already open wide. And because of the way our eyes' iris muscles must bunch up to close the pupils, they don't shut very fast. So when the flashbulb goes off, the pupil doesn't have time to close down—and the bright, focused light shoots straight through. Outdoors in the daytime, pupils are already at their most constricted, so a flash photo won't show red eyes.

> **The ingredients for the red-eye effect are simple: a dim room, a camera with a flash, and a person looking straight into the lens.**

Light blue or gray eyes often glow most crimson in photos, since pale irises have less pigment to block light. Many cameras reduce the red-eye effect by setting off several quick flashes before actually taking the picture. That way, the pupils have time to constrict before the final flash.

To avoid red-eye, try taking pictures with more room light and no flash. In a camera with an adjustable flash, point the bulb at a white ceiling or wall rather than at the people you're photographing. You can also use photo-processing software to reduce the red in the final photograph.

FAST FACT

In an ordinary flash photo, a lack of red can sometimes indicate eye problems. When one eye glows red and the other looks normal, it can mean that eyes are pointing in slightly different directions. No red in one or both eyes could be a sign of cataracts, a clouding of the eye's lens. And a white spot instead of a red pupil can be a telltale mark of an eye tumor called retinoblastoma.

Find Out Even More!

Check out these websites for more information on many of the topics in this book.
For links, go to www.workman.com/products/9780761144298.

Around the House

View a picture of a candle burning in microgravity at www.nasaexplores .com/show_58b_teacher_sh.php?id= 02122494157. And read Faraday's scientific ode to candles at http://www.fordham.edu/ halsall/mod/1860Faraday-candle.html.

Glass music underwent a revival in the 1980s, with new instruments and modern materials. To hear samples of this "angel music," visit www.glasharfe.de/glasharfe/ texte/samples.htm and http://www.ilio.com/vienna/ instruments/elements/index.html#demos.

To see how gene mutations change how fruit flies look (one fly sports curly wings), visit www.exploratorium .edu/exhibits/mutant_flies/mutant_flies.html. To browse the entire fruit fly genome, go to http://flybase.bio .indiana.edu.

For fast facts on fungi, visit www.herbarium.usu.edu/fungi/ funfacts/factindx1.htm and http://www.microbeworld.org/ microbes/fungi/.

To see cashew apples and nuts on the tree, and learn more about their processing, visit www.uga.edu/fruit/cashew.html.

To find the calorie counts of thousands of everyday foods, visit www.nal.usda.gov/fnic/foodcomp/ search. To search for the calories in favorite restaurant foods, try www.calorieking.com/foods.

For more about copper, visit www.copper.org/education. To try some experiments with copper pennies, see www .exploratorium.edu/science_explorer/copper_caper.html.

For more on melting ice cream, visit www.foodsci .uoguelph.ca/dairyedu/icstructure.html.

Read more about how thorny ice cubes form at www.its.caltech.edu/~atomic/ snowcrystals/icespikes/icespikes.htm. To view a short movie of a spike growing on a cube, visit www.physics.utoronto.ca/%7Esmorris/ edl/icespikes/icespikes.html.

For more on freezing hot versus cold water, along with links to more sources, see www.weburbia.com/physics/ hot_water.html.

For an animated demonstration of how polar and nonpolar molecules (like those in oil and vinegar) avoid each other, visit http://bioweb.wku .edu/courses/BIOL115/Wyatt/wku/ Biochem/polar.html.

Don't be chicken: See a red jungle fowl

in all its scarlet glory at www.centralpets.com/animals/birds/wild_birds/wbd4315.html.

For more on the chemistry of cow's milk, visit www.foodsci.uoguelph.ca/dairyedu/chem.html.

To see the meniscus effect that makes Cheerios form a ring, and for more about surface tension, visit www.chem.purdue.edu/gchelp/liquids/tension.html.

For more on the Leidenfrost effect, which makes water dance across a hot pan, see www.wiley.com/college/phy/halliday320005/pdf/leidenfrost_essay.pdf.

For more teakettle tales, including the sound of the noise water makes as it heats to a boil, visit www.rain.org/~mkummel/stumpers/28sep01a.html.

Shower curtain annoying you? See an animated demonstration of Bernoulli's principle at http://home.earthlink.net/~mmc1919/venturi.html.

For more on the electric Life Savers phenomenon, visit http://pages.towson.edu/ladon/wg/candywww.htm.

Me, Myself, I
To view microscopic close-ups of damaged and knotted hair, visit http://www.hair-science.com/_int/_en/index.aspx. Click on "So Sturdy Yet So Fragile," and then "Revisiting a Hostile World." Images of severely matted hair can be found at www.pg.com/science/haircare//hair_twh_99.htm.

To see the eyebrow flash in action, visit http://evolution.anthro.univie.ac.at/institutes/urbanethology/brows.html.

Compare the hands of different primates at http://instruct1.cit.cornell.edu/courses/biog105/pages/demos/106/unit08/8a.primates.html. See a chimpanzee's hand close up at www.acclaimimages.com/_gallery/_pages/0028-0401-1106-5058.html.

For more on the stuff in our ears, including close-up photos of ear wax in all its yucky glory, visit www.tchain.com/otoneurology/disorders/hearing/wax2.html and http://medweb.uwcm.ac.uk/otoscopy/newpage6.htm.

Out in the Yard
For more about skunks, including pictures of domesticated skunks in many colors, visit www.skunk-info.org/colrmark/marks.htm. To watch a movie of a skunk spraying an intruder (caution: gross), see www.terrierman.com/skunk.htm.

For everything you ever wanted to know about chlorophyll, visit http://scifun.chem.wisc.edu/chemweek/CHLRPHYL/Chlrphyl.html.

To see what a bird's legs, toes, and tendons really look like, visit www.enaturalist.org/topic.htm?topic_ID=60.

See a brown-eyed puppy whose tapeta reflect bright blue at http://members.aol.com/alikacoton/christie/Christie_pups_6.html. See a wolf spider's eyes gleam like white beacons at www.amonline.net.au/spiders/toolkit/hairy/see.htm.

To see a photo of planet Venus in the afternoon sky, and to learn how to find the planet for yourself even when the Sun is shining, visit www.fourmilab.ch/images/ venus_daytime.

To see how perceived distance makes an object like the Moon look bigger or smaller, visit www.howstuffworks .com/question491.htm.

To see star-nosed moles up close, and to watch a short film of one snatching a snack at lightning speed, visit http://vanderbilt.edu/exploration/stories/starnosedmole .html.

For more on tree-ring mapping, visit www.nps.gov/seki/ fire/pdf/firehistory.pdf.

To learn how to use a yo-yo, make it "sleep," and do basic and advanced tricks, visit www .begin2spin.com.

To figure out when twilight periods begin and end in your area, visit www.cmpsolv.com/los/sunset.html. Listen to the song "Twilight Time" at www .celebritydirect.org/platters/listen.htm.

To hear six different wind sounds, visit www.word-detective.com/howcome/. To read naturalist John Muir's account of the sound and fury of a forest windstorm, visit http://pweb.jps.net/~prichins/w-storm.htm.

For more about how snow crystals form, including a gallery of stunning crystals, visit www.its.caltech.edu/~atomic/ snowcrystals/. Create your own virtual paper snowflake at http://snowflakes .barkleyus.com.

At School

To see the chalky towering cliffs of Dover, visit www.bbc.co.uk/england/sevenwonders/southeast/ white_cliffs/.

Listen to both squealing chalk and scraping fingernails at www.sounddogs.com/results.asp?Type=&CategoryID =1036&SubcategoryID=11.

For more about rosacea, visit www.rosacea.org. To view the American Sign Language signs for embarrassed, visit www.lifeprint.com.

On Vacation

To watch an animated film on Earth's tilt and seasons, visit www.astro.uiuc.edu/ projects/data/Seasons/index .html.

Vernal Equinox

Must change tilt for a total tan.

For more on petrified wood, including a photo gallery, see www.yourgemologist.com/Kids/ petrifiedwood/petrifiedwood.html. Make an online visit to Arizona's otherworldly Petrified Forest at www.petrified.forest.national-park.com/ info.htm.

To make your next trip into the backyard itch-free, view pictures of poison ivy at http://poisonivy.aesir.com.

For more on ripples and waves, visit http://earthguide.ucsd.edu/wav/.

For more about jumping beans, visit http://waynesword.palomar.edu/ plaug97.htm.

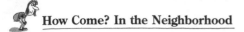

View moon rings online at http://antwrp.gsfc.nasa.gov/ apod/ap000515.html and www.astropix.com/HTML/ SHOW_DIG/009.HTM.

Hear 12 different frogs and toads (speaking frog and toad) at www.naturesound.com/frogs/frogs.html.

For a close-up of the red-eye effect, see http://en.wikipedia.org/wiki/ Image:Redeyephotoimage.jpg. For more on retinoblastoma, see http://www.lovejoey.com/ redeye.htm.

Special Thanks

Since in the world there are no complete or permanent answers, science is most truly about knowing what questions to ask. Thanks to the curious people of all ages who provided the wonderful questions in this book:

Jai Aiken
Natasha Akins
V. V. Anand
Rahul B.
B. M. Vignesh Babu
T. R. Balakrishnan
Timothy Bausch
Kaitlyn Behnke
Kimberly Belkin
V. Bhuvaneswaraj
Victoria Bindert
M. Blake
Jessica Bolz
Elizabeth Bourguet
David Brannan
Brenese
Nico Capetola
Jessica Cardosa
Nina Carin
Fahima Choudhury
Ben Clark

Bob Clark
Tara Cohen
Grace Connolly
Lauren Corley
Jensen Daniel
Susan Davniero
C. DeCoste
Ashleigh DeLuca
Brittany Deniz
Dennis Dioud
Samantha DiSalva
Kathryn Durkin
R. Ezilaraci
Natalie Feingold's class
Aileen E. Fitzgerald
Frank Fodera
Kari Freling
Joe Genduso
Jackie Graebe
Gareth Graff
Robert Hamilton
Mary Ellen Hay's
    science class
Jaquann Holley
Katie Hooper-Weiss
Jerry Hostetler
Lauren Ippolito
Rodney Jackson

Jason
Ryan Jerome
Alma Jimenez
John Knapp's
    fifth-grade class
Patricia Jones
Russell Judge
Kayla
Tom Kelley
Kenneth Kim
Robert Kneeter
Jennifer Koenig
Zan Kostoulas
M. Arun Kumar
Mel Kutzin
T. Lakshminarayanan
Shanti Lanning
Will Letzler
O. Lliguicota
Evan Malloy
Jorge Marca
Courtney Markes

Marvel
Zain McIntire
The Miller family
Marshall Miller
P. Ramana Mohan
David Montes
Meaghan Moran
Deonta Muhammad
Anne Murphy
J. Krishna Murthy
Kimberly Napolitano
Jerry Nutter
Cathy O'Regan

Katie Olander-Beach
Ronald Orson
Oscar
Eli Pace
Shiju P. Paul
Michael Payne
Alec Pemara
Karen Perez

Samantha Persaud
Remanu Phillips
Robert Pigott
Bijoy Prakash
Kim Price
Vinisha Purohit
Melanie Redfearn

Tom Rofrano
Jim Rossi
Stephanie Ryba
Jonathan Sanchez

Paul Sanderson
K. Sathyanarayan
Jenna Schott
Valene Schultheis's
    fifth-grade science
    classes
Pat Schwab
Alex Schweitzer
Jerry Segal
Jeff Shermer
E. V. Sindhura
Janet K. Smith
Brian Sohs
John Spain
Kevin Spellman
Edward Sprague IV
C. J. Srinivasan
Courtney Stiles

Nicky Stiles
Christian Surmanek
Jonathan Tam
Jeff Tanner
Leslie Taylor
Tony Taylor
Katie Travers
Kacy Tromblay-Cox
Kevin Tung
Cherie Wangenstein
Annleigh Wallace

Olivia Waters
Robin Weinstein
Sammy Weinstein
Donald Weisse
Buz Whelan
Kristen Wihouski
Bob Williamson
Christopher Willig
John D. Wilson
Yer Yang
Felicia Yen
Claire Ziffer

Index

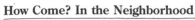